CORRUPTION
Expanding the focus

CORRUPTION
Expanding the focus

Edited by Manuhuia Barcham,
Barry Hindess and Peter Larmour

Australian
National
University

E PRESS

Published by ANU E Press
The Australian National University
Canberra ACT 0200, Australia
Email: anuepress@anu.edu.au
This title is also available online at http://epress.anu.edu.au

---

National Library of Australia Cataloguing-in-Publication entry

Title: Corruption : expanding the focus / edited by Manuhuia Barcham,
              Barry Hindess and Peter Larmour.

ISBN: 9781921862816 (pbk.) 9781921862991 (ebook)

Notes: Includes bibliographical references.

Subjects: Corruption.

Other Authors/Contributors:
              Barcham, Manuhuia.
              Hindess, Barry.
              Larmour, Peter.

Dewey Number: 364.1323

Cover design and layout by ANU E Press

Cover image: www.CartoonStock.com

ACADEMY OF THE SOCIAL SCIENCES IN AUSTRALIA

Contents

Contributors

Manuhuia Barcham is Managing Director of Synexe.

Peter Larmour is Professor of Public Administration and Policy at the University of the South Pacific. He holds an adjunct position at The Australian National University.

Barry Hindess is Emeritus Professor in the School of Politics and International Relations at The Australian National University.

John Uhr is Professor of Political Science in the School of Politics and International Relations at The Australian National University.

Richard Mulgan is Emeritus Professor in the Crawford School of Public Policy at The Australian National University.

Lisa Hill is Professor of Politics in the School of History and Politics at the University of Adelaide.

Bruce Buchan is Senior Lecturer in the School of Humanities at Griffith University.

John Clammer is a Visiting Professor at the United Nations University, Tokyo.

Arlene W. Saxonhouse is Caroline Robbins Collegiate Professor of Political Science and Women's Studies at the University of Michigan.

Acknowledgements

The chapters in this book are based on papers presented some years ago at a workshop in Canberra. We are extremely grateful to the College of Social Sciences and Law, the Crawford School of Public Policy and the Research School of Social Sciences, all of The Australian National University, and to the Workshop Program of the Academy of Social Sciences in Australia, without whose assistance the workshop would not have been possible. As often happens with edited volumes based on workshops, versions of some of our contributions have appeared elsewhere and this is acknowledged in the chapters concerned. As often happens also many participants contributed far more to this collection than our table of contents suggests. We are particularly grateful for the energetic participation of David Armitage, J. Peter Euben, Mark Findlay, Seamus Miller and Tim Lindsey, whose contributions to this collection are not otherwise registered within it. We are grateful also for the invaluable guidance of two anonymous readers, the editorial assistance of Carolina Caliaba Crespo and Helen Moore, and the advice of Marian Sawer.

1. Introduction: How should we think about corruption?

Barry Hindess

Like Caesar's Gaul, the contemporary literature on corruption can be divided into three parts,[1] with very little overlap between them. One part, by no means the largest or most influential, is, like this book, largely produced by professional academics. It is analytic and historical in character, focusing on how corruption has been or should be defined. The other two, while not uninterested in questions of definition, are more directly related to policy issues. They are produced by a shifting population of academics, policy professionals and activists who focus largely on the public sector and view corruption as improper conduct of a kind that, in the one case, has damaging economic effects and/or, in the other, deviates from the formal duties of public office. Few of those who write on corruption contribute to more than one of these literatures (notable exceptions are Euben, 1997; Johnston, 2006; Philp, 2007), although two of our contributors—Mulgan and Saxonhouse—make a point of relating their discussions of corruption in Western classical antiquity to the contemporary public policy treatment of corruption.

Much of the literature that focuses on the damaging economic effects of corruption is sponsored by the Organisation for Economic Cooperation and Development (OECD), the Word Bank and international development agencies, and the international anti-corruption non-governmental organisation (NGO) Transparency International (TI). This literature is concerned with the impact of corruption on economic growth and, accordingly, tends to see corruption as a particularly serious problem for non-Western countries. Not surprisingly, this perspective also suggests that an important part of the corruption on which it focuses is likely to involve the conduct of Western businesses operating in these countries. Susan Rose-Ackerman, who has worked closely with the World Bank in her studies of corruption, presents a clear example of this approach in her *Corruption and government* (1999). She begins by asking why so many poor countries have low or negative rates of economic growth even when well endowed with natural resources or a highly educated labour force, as some of them are. An important part of her answer is corruption, which, she argues, is likely to be particularly severe in countries with 'dysfunctional public and

---

1 Caesar's remarkably self-serving account of the Roman subjugation of the Gauls between 58 and 50 BC divides Gaul into regions inhabited by the Belgae, Aquitanians and Celts (whom the Romans call Gauls). Regions closer to Rome that were inhabited by Gauls, most of which had been brought under Roman control before Caesar began his campaigns, are not covered by his classification.

private institutions'. In her view, such institutional problems mean these countries will be characterised by 'a pervasive failure to tap self-interest for productive purposes' (pp. 1–2).

Rose-Ackerman takes as her benchmark for the identification of dysfunctional institutions 'the archetypical competitive market', which works to channel self-interest 'into productive activities that lead to efficient resource use'. She contrasts the workings of competitive markets with less desirable conditions in which people use resources not only for productive purposes, but also to obtain an advantage for themselves 'in dividing up the benefits of economic activity—called "rent-seeking" by economists' (p. 2). Since rent-seeking behaviour diverts resources from productive activities, it serves to restrain economic growth. *Corruption and government* suggests that, other things being equal, countries with high levels of public sector corruption will be poorer overall. The remedy lies in major institutional reforms of the kind promoted by the 'good governance' programs of the World Bank and other international agencies.

This developmental perspective commonly focuses on what it sees as the limitations of non-Western cultures, and especially on cases in which conduct that was once acceptable 'no longer fits modern conditions' (p. 6)—a focus questioned by Peter Larmour's chapter in this collection. In contrast, the problems that concern public regulatory agencies are largely within their own jurisdictions, so these agencies also tend to focus on the practical problems involved in their attempts to regulate the conduct of public servants and politicians. As part of this focus, such agencies clearly require a workable definition of corruption. For example, Section 8 of the Act that established the NSW Independent Commission Against Corruption (ICAC), which is itself modelled on the Hong Kong ICAC, identifies 'corruption' as the type of conduct that adversely affects the honest or impartial performance of official functions, involves a breach of public trust or the misuse of information acquired by officials in the course of their public functions.

As for the academic literature on how corruption has been or should be identified, we can hardly do better than refer to important papers by Peter Euben (1989) and Mark Philp (1997). First, Euben points out that the original—and still very common—use of the idea of corruption is to identify some damaging impurity, intrusion or distortion that prevented something from developing as it should. A foreign element in a chemical compound, stones in a packet of rice or seeds or decay in meat or vegetables are all examples of corruption. He notes that the *Oxford English Dictionary* gives several related meanings of corruption, most of them 'having to do with decay, degeneration, disintegration, and debasement. Corruption implies decay, where the original or natural condition of something becomes infected' (Euben, 1989, p. 221). The image of corruption as an infection or damaging impurity of the body politic appears throughout the history of political thought, as the contributions to this volume show.

Second, a seminal paper by Mark Philp (1997) offers a closely related argument. After noting that several competing definitions of corruption are in play in contemporary debate (corruption is defined, for example, as conduct that damages the public interest, as deviating from the formal duties of office, as flouting legal norms or as an abuse of authority designed to maximise an official's income), Philp argues that definitional disputes have obscured the fact that the basic meaning of corruption is not in dispute: 'it is rooted in the sense of a thing being changed from its naturally sound condition, into something unsound, impure, debased, infected' (p. 29). If there is a problem with the definition of political corruption, he argues, it does not lie in any disagreement about the meaning of corruption itself but, rather, in the practical application of this understanding to politics. This is the result of a lack of general agreement about the 'naturally sound' political condition and thus about what should count as a deviation from that condition. To address this issue would be to enter a field of intractable debate that most students of corruption have preferred to avoid. I should add that Philp's point about 'the basic meaning of corruption' applies equally well in areas other than politics. Arlene W. Saxonhouse's contribution to this volume is a case in point; she discusses the uses of the concept of corruption in relation to literary genres.

Leaving this last issue to one side for the moment, we can say that two assumptions, which this book aims to question, dominate contemporary discussion of corruption: *first*, that corruption is primarily an economic issue, both in its content (the exchange of money for favours) and in its most important effects (on economic growth, development, and so on); *second*, that corruption involves a blurring of the distinction between public and private. These assumptions are often joined by a *third*, which we also dispute: that, while corruption is universal, its most significant impact is likely to be found in developing countries. Corruption is thus presented as if it were a matter of misconduct on the part of public officials who are seen, especially in poor countries, as pursuing their own private interests and likely to act corruptly in return for money and other favours, thereby undermining economic development.

Our subtitle, 'Expanding the focus', suggests two closely related responses to this conventional understanding of corruption. One is that it is far too narrow and the other is that there is much to be gained from rejecting the view that the most important issues around corruption concern its impact on economic activity[2] and, consequently, from taking a broader view of the significance of corruption. The essays in this book show that viewing corruption as a matter of public officials pursuing their private economic interests is considerably narrower than the view of corruption to be found in earlier periods of Western thought.

Before considering these chapters directly, however, it is worth noting a few of the ways in which corruption has been understood in the history of the West. We begin with the monumental *History of Rome* (*Ab Urbe Condita Libri*), written by the Roman historian Titus Livius (Livy) (59 BC – AD 17). After noting how the Romans had acquired their empire, Livy's preface invites his imagined Roman reader to consider the Romans' 'morals, at first as slightly giving way…how they sunk more and more, then began to fall headlong until he reaches the present times, when we can neither endure our vices nor their remedies' (2006, p. 3). Livy's image of moral decay following the accumulation of wealth and power is significant for our purposes, not because it offers a new or interesting account of corruption, but because it re-emerges, many centuries later, in *The history of Florence* (1979 [1525]b, pp. 548–74), by Niccolò Machiavelli (1469–1527). Machiavelli had already written his own commentary on Livy (1979 [1525]a, pp. 167–418).[3] Machiavelli's views on corruption are examined more systematically in Chapters 4 and 5 of this collection. For the moment the thing to say is that *The history of Florence* turns Livy's story of the move from success to moral decay into an account of societal corruption—a dangerous infection of the political community that appears and reappears in a cyclical pattern. Echoing arguments developed earlier by the Arab historian Ibn Khaldun (1332–1406 CE/732–808 AH),[4] Machiavelli stresses that states 'always descend from good to bad and rise from bad to good':

> For ability brings about tranquillity, and tranquillity laziness, and laziness chaos, and chaos ruin; and, in like manner, from ruin is born order, from order ability, and from this quality glory and good fortune. And so, prudent men have observed that literature develops after arms, and that in nations and city-states generals are born before philosophers. For after an effective and well-organized militia has produced victories, and these victories have ensured tranquillity, the strength of such brave

---

2   The economist Jeffrey D. Sachs (2006) argues that the impact of corruption on economic development has been much overrated.

3   It is easy to read Machiavelli's *History of Florence* as if it were structured by his interpretation of Livy, but this, in turn, may have been structured by his reading of Book 6 of Polybius's *The histories* (Hexter, 1956), written some 200 years before Livy's work (2006).

4   See Ibn Khaldun (Kalpakian, 2008; Katsiaficas, 1997), especially Chapters 18 (headed 'Sedentary culture is the goal of civilization. It means the end of its life span and brings about its corruption') and 30 ('A refutation of philosophy. The corruption of the students of philosophy'). The parallels between Machiavelli's and Khaldun's cyclical accounts of the history of states are undeniable, but it is not clear whether Machiavelli knew of or was influenced by Khaldun.

minds cannot be corrupted with a more honorable laziness than that of literature, nor can this laziness enter into well-organized cities with a greater and more dangerous deception than with that of literature. Cato was well aware of this when Diogenes and Carneades, both philosophers, came to Rome as ambassadors to the senate; when he saw that the Roman youth began to admire these men, aware of the evil that could enter his native city as a result of the honorable laziness, he made it a law that no philosopher could be received in Rome. Nations have come to ruin because of this. (Khaldun, 2004, pp. 557–8)

Machiavelli and Kahldun see corruption as a product of the luxury that follows success. It would be easy to identify the corruption in this case with elite misconduct, as Syed Alatas's (1990) rendering of Ibn Khaldun's discussion suggests. Yet both Kahldun and Machiavelli treat elite misconduct as an important symptom of broader societal corruption, not as its cause. Corruption in this last sense—as a destructive societal condition—has what we would now regard as an obvious economic aspect in the form of luxurious consumption, but it is fundamentally a political problem, a weakness of the polity that manifests itself in various forms, including a militarily incompetent elite. Machiavelli offers a powerful view of corruption as a societal condition seen as neither an economic phenomenon nor a matter of blurring the division between public and private. Richard Mulgan's and Arlene W. Saxenhouse's contributions to this volume reinforce the point that corruption does not have to be understood as a matter of public versus private. Both authors show that, in the political thought of Western classical antiquity, the corruption of the body politic was not always seen in these terms. Instead, Plato and Aristotle viewed corruption in terms of a dualistic world view that contrasted an ideal realm of truth and goodness with the empirical realm of change and decay. To the extent that the ideal provided a standard with which to judge the empirical, any existing government could be seen as inescapably corrupt.

These examples show that, in the political thought of Western classical antiquity and late medieval Europe, corruption was commonly understood, as we believe it should be understood, as a condition of the body politic. Since the late eighteenth century this has not been the prevalent view held in the West and amongst the international agencies that the West dominates. In the past two centuries the term 'corruption' has been increasingly used to designate problematic behaviour on the part of one or more individuals, or behaviour that is often seen as a matter of using one's public office for the purposes of illicit private gain. Some commentators (for example, Euben, 1989, 1997) have deplored this development, seeing it as resulting from the triumph of liberal individualism and as leading to an individualistic and economistic view of corruption and a corresponding loss of concern with the public good.

Yet we do not have to return to the classics or to Machiavelli's Italy to find influential alternatives to the view that corruption is primarily an economic phenomenon. Lisa Hill's discussion of Adam Ferguson in Chapter 6 reminds us that, in his analysis of the problems facing the commercial societies of his time, Ferguson drew on the same patrician story that Machiavelli had used of the moral decay of the Roman people with the rise of the Empire. Hill presents Ferguson as arguing that prosperous empires gave rise to specialisation, overextension and hedonism, which eroded the civic spirit. Although progress and commercialism were inevitable and natural, their effects should be countered by enhancing civic competence and awareness, including political activism. He saw conflict and factional divisions as providing citizens with the lessons that would underpin ongoing reform and promote the development of 'liberty and just government'.

I should add that about the time that Ferguson was speculating about the fate of commercial societies, we find David Hume (1711–76) worrying about the impact of political parties on the conduct of government but without using the term 'corruption'. His essay 'Of parties in general' (1987 [1777]) maintains that:

> As much as legislators and founders of states ought to be honoured and respected among men, as much ought the founders of sects and factions to be detested and hated; because the influence of faction is directly contrary to that of laws. Factions subvert government, render laws impotent, and beget the fiercest animosities among men of the same nation, who ought to give mutual assistance and protection to each other. And what should render the founders of parties more odious is, the difficulty of extirpating these weeds, when once they have taken root in any state…They are, besides, plants which grow most plentifully in the richest soil and though absolute governments be not wholly free from them, it must be confessed, that they rise more easily, and propagate themselves faster in free governments, where they always infect the legislature itself, which alone could be able, by the steady application of rewards and punishments, to eradicate them. (p. 55)

Contemporary readers are likely to find that the most striking feature of this passage is its treatment of partisan politics as a kind of infection. Far from focusing on the economic impact of sects and factions, Hume is concerned with what he sees as their destructive political effects. The American Federalist James Madison (1751–1836) takes a related view in his discussion of the problem of faction:

> By a faction I understand a number of citizens, whether amounting to a majority or minority of the whole, who are united and actuated by some

common impulse of passion, or of interest, adverse to the rights of other citizens, or to the permanent and aggregate interests of the community. (Madison, et al., 1987 [1788], p. 10)

It is worth noting that a faction in Madison's sense might well consist of a majority of the population. In contemporary terms, we might think of a faction as a pressure group, or simply as a person or organisation that is represented by one or more lobbyists. Madison's concern seems to be less with the overall effects of factions than with the possibility that a single faction might come to dominate legislation or other government action. Yet, as Hacker and Pierson (2011) argue with particular reference to the United States, there are grounds for concern, on the one hand, that the real business of government may be conducted less in cabinet offices and representative assemblies than in private negotiations between the government of the day and assorted lobbyists and, on the other hand, that electoral politics and factional disputes within and between parties may be little more than theatrical distraction. We might regard this condition as a kind of corruption, and one that is not attributable to the machinations of any single faction or interest.

If we were to accept Madison's view of the problem of faction, we would have to say that democracy itself is a significant source of governmental corruption, primarily because it secures conditions in which 'faction'—the partisan interests of a popular majority, or even of a powerful and well-organised minority—may be able to divert government from its pursuit of the interests of the community.

On the other hand, those who put their trust in democracy would have to say that the Madisonian distrust of faction is itself a likely source of corruption because elected officials and public servants who shared this view of the danger posed by popular majorities might be tempted both to ignore the issues raised by Hacker and Pierson and to subvert the machinery of democratic government.

Democracy was originally understood as one of three basic forms of government. Aristotle defined a state as 'a body of citizens sufficing for the purposes of life' (1988, pp. 21–2) and he went on to say that the state may be governed by the one, the few or the many. Democracy was the last of these cases: government by the many. Our contemporary idea of democracy, of government by the people, carries a similar sense. It is not a matter of government by the one, a king or a dictator, or by the few, an unelected ruling party or a military junta.

Aristotle was far from being an unequivocal supporter of democracy. Like other Greek philosophers, he regarded democracy as a source of a particular kind of political corruption (Farrar, 1988). The basic idea here is not very different from Madison's: that government by the people is in danger of being dominated by the poor—and poorly educated—majority, who might act collectively to form a faction in Madison's sense. Whenever this happened, the conduct of government could be expected to reflect the ignorance and prejudices of this faction and it would be open to manipulation by unscrupulous demagogues. In fact, Roberts (1994, p. 11) argues that this negative perception of the majority dominated Western discussion of democracy until well into the nineteenth century.

When representative government began to develop about the end of the eighteenth century, it was not usually seen as a kind of democracy (in Federalist Paper No. 10, Madison called it a 'republic', arguing that a republic of this kind was superior to democracy) but rather as a defence against the dangers of popular rule. To be sure, it did give the people as a whole a limited role in government, and it was seen for this reason as a way of avoiding the kinds of corruption that had been associated with rule by a king or aristocracy (government by the one or the few). Yet, because it restricted the people to the election of those who would govern them, leaving the actual work of government in the hands of a minority of elected politicians and public servants, it was also seen as a way of avoiding the dangers that had traditionally been associated with democracy. The contemporary identification of democracy with representative government is a result of nineteenth and twentieth-century developments, and it involved a radical transformation of democracy's earlier meaning (Dahl, 1989, 1998).

I have argued that the view of corruption as a matter of public officials pursuing private interests is narrower than the view of corruption to be found in earlier periods of Western thought. Yet there is no reason to believe that the changing meaning of the term 'corruption' necessarily reflects any lessening of public concern with the condition of the body politic. While public-choice theorists may not draw explicitly on the older meaning of corruption, for example, it is clear that this group of economists and political scientists (Brennan & Lomarsky, 1993; Buchanan, 1978; Buchanan & Wagner, 1977) is very much concerned with what would once have been called corruption of the body politic; the same is true of the 'classical' liberalism of Friedrich Hayek (Gray, 1982). Or again, as I have argued elsewhere (Hindess, 2000), the early arguments in favour of representative government clearly present it as a means of keeping in check the corruption of government by any kind of factional politics that drew on the short-term interests of the poor and poorly educated majority. Much of the history of Western political thought since the emergence of this new form of government can be seen as focusing on the new sources of corruption created by the institutions it required—most especially, of course, on the opportunities it appears to create for politicians, public servants and business interests to pursue their own private advantage—or their factional view of 'the permanent and aggregate interests of the community'.

If these claims seem contentious, I would say only that many of the concerns that were once associated with the idea of corruption still play an important part in public life. My discussion here focuses on the issues of impurity (or contamination) and faction. Before proceeding with this discussion, it is worth noting that, while there is a sense in which democracy can be seen as a source of corruption, there is another in which corruption is a threat to democracy. Popular control over government and political equality are central to modern understandings of democracy (International Institute for Democracy and Electoral Assistance, 2008), although both are clearly open to interpretation. Yet on almost any understanding of these terms, popular control and equality will both be subverted by corruption in the public sector. If the decisions of public servants are influenced by bribes or improper inducements offered by their political masters, there is no sense, however indirect, in which they are subject to popular control. Nor does the influence of bribery augur well for political equality between citizens.

Turning now to the issue of impurity, the political life of many contemporary states is organised, at least in part, around concerns about the presence of unassimilated alien groups within the community—Indians in Fiji, Muslims in Australia and the member states of the European Union, Christians and Muslims in India. The sense of impurity invoked in these cases suggests an obvious set of political solutions in the form of stricter immigration controls, citizenship tests or 'ethnic cleansing'. This last term is a recent invention but the practices it refers to have played an important part in the history of most contemporary states (Mann, 1999). Impurity is at issue in another way in the anti-elitist appeals of populist politics. The underlying message of these appeals is that political and other elites—educational, cultural, economic—pretend to speak for the public interest but in fact represent only themselves (Sawer & Hindess, 2004). Populism is often regarded as a kind of extremism but it is a pervasive feature of modern states whose rulers generally claim to act in the interests of the people (Schedler, 1997).

While the word 'corruption' is not often used in relation to these issues, the concerns over alien intrusion and elitism both appeal to an underlying idea of impurity or distortion—in fact, to something like the original sense of corruption discussed by Euben and Philp. Using the example of New York City, Frank Anechiarico (Anechiarico & Jacobs, 1996) has argued that attempts to limit corruption amongst public officials may have destructive effects on the efficiency and effectiveness of the public service. The examples noted here suggest that there are dangers in taking the concern for purity too seriously. It is not obvious that corruption, in the sense of impurity, is something to be avoided.

I noted earlier that the problem of faction was a significant concern in the political thought of Hume and Madison. It has since been a major issue in liberal thinking about government. Indeed, if representative government can be seen as avoiding one possible source of governmental corruption—the misguided enthusiasms of the people—it clearly opens the way for the corruption of government by professional politicians and public servants. This last has been the concern of populist politics on the one side and of public-choice theory and other forms of neo-liberalism on the other.

In fact, the history of representative government could be written as a story of attempts to limit the effects of the new sources of governmental corruption that it creates (Hindess, 2000). Populism addresses the issue by offering to replace conventional politicians with politicians of a different kind—that is, with political professionals who pretend not to be professional politicians. Inheriting the older tradition of distrusting the people, liberalism addresses the issue rather differently, through institutional design that aims to deal with the problem of faction: checks and balances, rational, bureaucratic administration and codes of conduct for public officials (Goodin, 1996). Where, as often happens, these devices are seen to be unsuccessful, it proposes a different approach: reducing the temptations of, or the opportunities for, corrupt conduct. Rose-Ackerman's influential study quoted above is an excellent case in point. Another approach is to reduce the amount of government responsibility—for example, by privatising government utilities and public services or by limiting the areas in which governments attempt to regulate economic activity. Rose-Ackerman's discussion focuses on the benefits of such changes. In effect, they promise to reduce the opportunities for corrupt conduct by reducing the scope for administrative discretion on the part of public officials, if necessary by privatising areas of government activity. Yet such reforms also have disadvantages, and it is far from clear that the positive effects always outweigh the negative. There are well-known problems with the process of privatisation itself—developments in Russia since the end of communist rule provide a host of flagrant examples (Krastev, 2004). There are equally familiar problems of a decline in standards— safety, security of employment, service provision—as a result of privatisation or a reduction in administrative regulation. My point here is not that privatisation is always bad or that state regulation and public provision of services are always good. It is simply that minimising the scope for certain kinds of corruption need not always be the most important concern.

Another of Rose-Ackerman's recommendations is that professional politicians and senior public servants should receive salaries that are competitive with those in private business. The assumption here seems to be that those who are well paid will be less susceptible to bribery than those who are not well paid. Yet, even if this were the case, this remedy would have the effect of creating a significant income gap between a cadre of professional politicians, senior public servants and business figures on the one hand and the rest of the population on the other. It is likely to lead, in other words, to a version of the problem of faction.

This last point brings us back to the original, and still the most general, view of corruption as an infection of the body politic. In contrast with this view, the economistic understanding seems both too narrow and too narrowly technical. It is too narrow because its focus on minimising economic corruption can obscure, and can even extend, more general problems in the workings of government. It is too narrowly technical because the identification of these more general problems depends on how we understand the common interest—a notion that is notoriously open to dispute. In this respect, to treat the problem of corruption as if it were amenable to technical solution is also to ignore the contentiousness of political life.

These then are the issues that underpin the collection of chapters that makes up this book. In exploring the multiple ways in which corruption has been conceptualised, these chapters collectively challenge the narrowness of conventional understandings of corruption. In addition, explicitly or implicitly, they suggest that there is much to be gained from taking a broader view of the significance of corruption, and, in particular, from refusing to accept that the most important issues concern the impact of corruption on economic activity.

Outline of the book

Our principal concern in this book is to show that there is nothing natural or inevitable about a view of corruption either as an economic phenomenon or as blurring the distinction between public and private. Accordingly, five of our eight substantial chapters focus on conceptions of corruption that have been influential in the history of Western political thought, most of which view corruption not so much as an individual failure but as a societal phenomenon. Our three remaining chapters focus on contemporary issues.

We begin with two chapters on the Greeks of Western classical antiquity, especially Aristotle, Plato and Thucydides. I noted earlier that Richard Mulgan and Arlene W. Saxonhouse locate their contributions in relation to contemporary debates. First, Richard Mulgan presents Aristotle, and to a lesser extent Plato, to undermine what he sees as the moral absolutism of much discussion of corruption by contemporary political theorists. Aristotle uses the Platonic distinction between ideal forms and mundane realities to argue that existing polities are inevitably corrupt, whereas in modern thought 'corruption is seen as remediable, at least at the systemic level'. The Greeks recognised that existing regimes were always less than perfect. They did not use the ideal of a polity without corruption to set an impossible standard or model of constitutional 'best practice' to which all states are expected to aspire—for example, as a condition of receiving loans from richer countries.

Aristotle sees the rule of law not as marking the difference between corrupt and non-corrupt government, but as a practical, if imperfect, means of restraining corrupt conduct, inhibiting rulers from making ad-hoc decisions to suit themselves. In many respects, Arlene W. Saxonhouse's chapter reinforces Mulgan's negative view of absolute standards while offering a rather different perspective on the Greek view of corruption itself. Using the 'basic' understanding of corruption identified above—as undermining the pure or natural condition of the thing corrupted—she shows that Plato and Thucydides corrupted existing literary forms to establish what they saw as a new grounding for knowledge, a knowledge that would be 'a possession for ever'. For both Plato and Thucydides, the incorruptible is not to be found in worldly politics but in 'the intellectual access to the truths to which their novel literary products lead us'.

Saxonhouse adds a twist of her own to Mulgan's distinction between the Greek view of corruption as inevitable and modern thought in which it is seen as avoidable, at least in principle. She describes Plato and Thucydides as 'political pessimists' and contrasts them with Hobbes—a political 'optimist' who believed that the science of politics as he taught it could lead to 'an incorruptible polity'. All three saw knowledge as rising above 'the corruptible world' but viewed this relationship in radically different ways. Hobbes's 'legacy to the modern world' was a dream of unity between knowledge and politics, whereas these ancient Greeks offered 'tools to understand and assess' the corruptible, political world but made few claims about the capacity of knowledge to transform it.

Before proceeding, let me make two further points about these two chapters. First, it is tempting to see Saxonhouse's distinction between optimists and pessimists as an example of the moral absolutism that Mulgan warns against. To say that corruption is inescapable is not to say that all forms of corruption are equally bad or that nothing can be done about any case of corruption that one encounters. In fact, far from suggesting that there is nothing to be done, Mulgan's Aristotle offers sound advice on how a community might avoid the most extreme varieties of corruption. In this respect, he is far from pessimistic. Second, I will have something to say later about the use of the word 'modern' in these and a few of the later chapters.

The next two chapters move us on from the world of Western antiquity to the medieval West. In Chapter 4, Manuhuia Barcham identifies two European perspectives on corruption that were influential in the years between the fall of the Western Roman Empire and the Renaissance. First, Augustine viewed politics as a form of restraint on humanity's earthly life necessitated by the Fall, and thus saw no intrinsic value in political life. From this perspective, it made little sense to think of politics as something that might or might not become corrupted. Second, the European rediscovery of a number of classical texts about the beginning of the second millennium CE resulted in a renewed interest in classical understandings of both political life and its corruption. In effect, the medieval Christian focus on the importance of moral values was brought together with the classical emphasis on the value of reason with the result that political and moral reason were readily seen as indistinguishable.

If, as Philp (1997) maintains, political corruption means a departure from the naturally sound condition of political life, we should expect the emergence of this novel view of political life to be accompanied by a correspondingly novel perception of corruption. Political corruption was thus perceived largely in terms of the adverse consequences of conduct that were contrary to natural reason: the exercise of power for other than moral ends and especially the rule of tyrants who pursued their own interest rather than the common good. Barcham shows, in conclusion, how this model of politics and its corruption eventually collapsed in response to the emergent late-medieval belief that different aspects of human life possessed their own intrinsic form of reason—a belief that effectively negated the possibility of appealing to an overarching natural reason as a guide for human action.

Bruce Buchan's Chapter 5 traces a different path through the same historical period, beginning with a view of corruption as both a personal vice and a failing of the polity, and then guiding us through the interplay between contrasting notions, for example, of private, individual morality and collective, social morality, 'the body politic' and 'the political community', and the loss of virtue and the decay of physical bodies. He brings his story through to parts of seventeenth-century Europe, and England in particular, where the appearance of 'commerce and trade as new and influential political forces bedevilled late-seventeenth-century British political thought'. In this period, he detects 'expansive understandings of corruption alongside narrower modern understandings'. The metaphor of the 'body politic' became increasingly anachronistic, while the political community came to be defined in terms of 'the requirements for a flourishing market and solvent state'.

We might quibble with Buchan's use of the term 'modern' in this context—just as we might with Mulgan's, Saxonhouse's and Hill's uses of the term in Chapters 2, 3 and 6 respectively. I turn to this issue below. We might also wonder whether commentators in seventeenth-century England understood the market and 'solvent state' in terms that would be familiar to us today (Walter, 2008).

These points aside, the conclusion to Buchan's narrative leads us directly into Lisa Hill's careful examination of the contributions of the Scottish Enlightenment's two Adams, Ferguson and Smith, whose work, she argues, marks 'a transitional moment' in late-eighteenth-century understandings of the term 'corruption'. Both saw a danger of corruption in the rise of commercialism and its accompanying changes. The differences between them lay in their aetiologies of 'progress and the commercial age'. Ferguson was 'deeply ambivalent about progress', which he saw as inducing corruption. In his analysis of the problems of his own time and in proposing remedies for them, Ferguson draws on the patrician account of the decline of Republican Rome, which we noted above in Livy and again in Machiavelli. This leads him to the familiar conclusion that prosperous empires give rise to specialisation, overextension and hedonism, all of which erode the civic spirit. Although progress and commercialism were inevitable and natural, their effects should be countered by enhancing civic competence and awareness, including political activism. He saw conflict and factional divisions as providing citizens with lessons that could promote ongoing reform and the development of liberty and just government.

In contrast, Smith was essentially 'optimistic about the effects of commercialism'. Hill describes his ideas as 'eccentric' in his own time, but as nevertheless working towards a 'modern' conception of corruption in defending the now conventional liberal values of impartiality, universalism, neutrality, formal equality of opportunity and rule of law. She describes Smith's approach as 'classical' in its conception of corruption as encompassing not only the conduct of public officials, but also features of whole societies, and in adopting the old dichotomy of the 'healthy' or 'corrupt' republic. Yet, in contrast with the classical view, what he actually saw as health and virtue related to commercial rather than civic values: 'the good polity is the natural market economy of self-regarding, lawful and mutually forbearing agents.' Rather than imagining an ideal polity as a standard against which corruption could be judged, Smith envisaged the natural, spontaneous order of the system of natural liberty and the market: 'agents must be permitted the freest possible use of their bodies, minds and properties provided there are no violations of either the public interest or the system of natural liberty.' Both individuals and societies could be corrupted by relics of the pre-commercial age: laws and regulations, slavery, dependency, religious fanaticism and political factionalism—all of which obstruct progress.

The division of labour, in Smith's view, was one of the few corrupting features of the new economic order but, weighing this against the wealth it produced, it yielded more rather than less human happiness all round. His remedy for all forms of corruption was more progress, including education to inculcate patterns of civility suitable for people who participate in market society. Thus, while Ferguson identified hedonism (Epicureanism), privatisation, civic quiescence and the breakdown of exclusivist social categories as corrupting elements that inhere in progress and modernity, Smith saw these elements as possible solutions to the potentially corrupt state. Conversely, the elements that Ferguson sought to recover—national identity, social intimacy and civic virtue—were those that Smith saw as remnants of a pre-commercial age that ought to be purged in order to prevent corruption and promote the flowering of a natural (broadly liberal) free state.

I noted earlier that one could quibble with Bruce Buchan's use of the word 'modern' in his chapter. The same might be said of Richard Mulgan's and Lisa Hill's chapters. Christine Helliwell and I have argued elsewhere that 'modern' and related terms—'modernity', 'modernising', 'pre-modern' or 'postmodern', and so on—are problematic, not least because, unless their use is very carefully qualified, they invoke a Eurocentric ideology of progress, suggesting that inhabitants of Western Europe, along perhaps with America, Japan and a few other places, are more rational than and, in other respects, some distance ahead of the rest of humanity (Helliwell & Hindess, 2011; Hindess, 2008). As a result, it is difficult to use these terms without implying the disparaging judgment that, while much of the contemporary world and many of our contemporaries are indeed rational and modern like us, the remainder have yet to reach this exalted condition. Similarly, when the modern or 'modernity' is said to be found at some period in the past, the suggestion is that a small part of the world shared some of the characteristics that we now regard as modern and that the rest of the world in that period did not.

Of course, 'modern' is often used without any disparaging intent, as it is, for example, in the chapters noted here. In most of the instances where it appears, 'modern' could be replaced with a term that is less obviously loaded—'recent', 'contemporary', 'post-reformation', and so on—without any serious loss of meaning. Yet, even when there is no disparaging intent, the progressivist connotations of 'modern' are hard to escape.

Along with the progressivist connotations of the 'modern' we find the belief that anything 'modern' will often be eccentric compared with what has gone before, if only because the modern world takes earlier developments just a little further. This, indeed, would be one way to interpret our claim in this book that the modern understanding of corruption is out of line with the history of Western views of corruption: 'Yes, of course it seems to be eccentric, but that is because it is modern and therefore more advanced!' Yet this interpretation is far from what the editors of this book and our contributors have in mind when we contrast contemporary views of corruption with what has gone before. Our point, to reiterate, is to show that these contemporary views are seriously deficient: it is to insist that what from one modernist point of view might seem to be the most advanced perspective is not necessarily superior to its predecessors.

I noted earlier that contemporary discussion of corruption often reflects an all too common view of the differences between Western and non-Western societies: that the latter are lagging some way behind the former. With regard to corruption, this suggests that while corruption is universal, its most significant impact is likely to be found in developing countries. The assumption here is that 'modern'—that is, already developed—countries have advanced well beyond the level of corruption to be found in countries that are not yet 'modern'.

Leaving this issue aside, however, the three contributions that follow the five historical chapters discussed above address issues that are entirely contemporary in character. First, responding indirectly to the Smithian celebration of the market outlined by Lisa Hill and adopting a less than entirely positive view of 'modernity', John Clammer views corruption from the standpoint of a sociologist with an interest in recent developments in social systems analysis. Clammer sees our globalised world—'modernity'—not simply as a collection of many discrete societies whose responses to the threat of corruption can be compared and contrasted to produce measures of success or failure, but rather as a large-scale system held together, inter alia, by networks of national and international trade. From this perspective, corruption appears as less a product of particular societies—something to be managed by 'better policing, moral education or institutional adaptation'—than a systemic problem arising in large part from dysfunctions in the social system itself. It can be seen as an index or an outcome 'of the entropy of a particular form of socioeconomic system (globalised neo-liberal capitalism)'. 'Modernity' itself generates 'forms of social disorganisation' which, in turn, generate corruption.

In Clammer's view, social subsystems of the contemporary global order interact with each other to produce three key elements in current forms of corruption: 'mal-' (or distorted) 'development', violence and 'capitalist-led globalisation'. Corruption is thus 'built into the system itself'. Distorted 'development' and 'globalisation' are 'expressions both of one another and of the underlying philosophy of neo-liberalism'.

Our collection closes with two contributions that, directly or indirectly, address what, in a different context, might be seen as the link between culture and corruption. I say 'a different context' because the concept of culture has had a chequered history in the social sciences (Bennett, 1998). Culture is normally seen as an ideational unity, a more or less coherent collection of beliefs, injunctions, norms, values and other ideas that is shared by members of a community. A community's culture is thus thought to both unify it and distinguish it from communities with other cultures (Helliwell & Hindess, 1999). Culture, in this sense, can be seen as providing a number of tools that members of a community can use in deciding on a course of action, yet it is often understood in a more directly prescriptive sense—that is, as requiring, justifying or excusing particular actions. This last understanding of culture has been perhaps the most important source of objections to the concept because it suggests that people are 'cultural dopes'—that they are pushed around by their culture (Hall, 1981; Phillips, 2007). A distinctive version of the concept, 'political culture' (Almond & Verba, 1963), was influential for a time in political science. The concept was originally designed to capture differences in attitudes towards political authority between relatively stable democracies (the United Kingdom and the United States) and other less-stable countries, on the assumption that differing attitudes towards political authority would account for significant and observable differences in patterns of political behaviour between these countries. This notion of political culture is predicated on the assumption that cultural differences would, in fact, be reflected in conduct. The concept was later accused of lacking objectivity— that is, of favouring the UK and US experience—and has since fallen out of favour (Elkins & Simeon, 1979; Somers, 1995).

Accordingly, we have made limited use of the concepts of culture and political culture in this collection. Without directly invoking the term 'culture', John Uhr's chapter focuses on the attitudes and values of elected politicians, which could easily be viewed as important components of a society's culture. Attending to these elements, rather than the private interests of officials, Uhr aims to shift our concerns away from corruption in the conventional sense. Rather than offer an alternative account of corruption, he promotes the ideal of an 'ethical politics', of a kind that would strengthen democratic processes, particularly the public discussion of political responsibilities. Uhr argues that analyses of corruption are generally premised on distrust of office-holders. They seek to show how 'external' accountability mechanisms can be used to regulate the behaviour of those holding political office. In contrast, 'ethics analysis' focuses on office-holders' sense of 'personal responsibility'—that is, on their capacity for self-regulation. It builds on trust rather than its contrary and seeks to stimulate the 'praiseworthy political management of official relationships of power'; however, in contrast with the treatment of officials' corrupt conduct as a personal failing, the focus on ethical self-regulation is not simply individualistic. The determination of standards in a democracy requires responsible public deliberation about the conduct of relationships between all those sharing political power, including the basic organising offices of citizen and government.

Uhr builds his argument through the example of the Australian 'children overboard affair', in which ministers and other elected officials misrepresented facts in what they seemed to think were the interests of the ruling party (acting, that is, in what Dennis F. Thompson [1995] calls their 'political' rather than their 'private' interests). Uhr uses this example to illustrate tendencies that, in his view, are corrupting the relationships between government and citizen. In this case, no laws were broken or openly subverted and the 'personal decency' of the politicians involved was not in question. Nevertheless, the government practised a form of deception that many Australians saw as undermining the norms of the various political offices constituting Australian democracy, thereby demonstrating that political corruption can advance in many guises. The chapter concludes that a 'relationship-centred' approach, rather than a 'rule-centred' approach, requires disputes over standards to be 'managed through collective political deliberation over appropriate relationships of power'.

Finally, Peter Larmour considers the way the concept of culture has been used in a recent series of studies of corruption in island states of the South Pacific. Culture is often invoked in the prescriptive sense noted earlier as an explanation for events in the region, which echoes complaints by the anti-corruption NGO Transparency International that the 'myth of culture' has been used as an excuse for corruption. Yet culture is sometimes seen as the thing that is corrupted. Just as the word 'corruption' in English carries a strong sense of decline, so its use seems to presuppose a pre-corrupt golden age. In the Pacific Islands, for example, there is talk of the 'corruption' of traditional cultures and of a loss of standards that had been upheld in the past. Thus chiefs today are said to behave more badly because of the influence of Western culture, institutions or opportunities. At the same time, PNG officials today are thought to behave more corruptly than their colonial predecessors.

One of the difficulties faced by the studies discussed in the chapter is that some of them could find no exact translation for the word 'corruption' in local languages. For example, in Kiribati there were several words with proximate meanings but people used the phrase 'the corruption'. In Tonga the closest word was *angakovi*, which denotes unkindness. In Marshall Islands the opposite was *kien jimwe inmoi*, which translated as uprightness.

Larmour argues that there are differences in the salience and scope of corruption in these countries. The report on Vanuatu found 'very little outcry' about it. In Nauru, by contrast, issues of governance and corruption were 'widely talked about'. There, people defined corruption very broadly to include 'leaders who do not go to church and who party and travel overseas frequently'. Similarly, in Solomon Islands 'street talk' the word *korapt* was often applied to 'personal as well as official indiscretions'. Early publicity for the leadership code in Papua New Guinea showed cartoons of politicians dancing with their girlfriends as well as receiving cash in envelopes. Salience and scope seemed to be the most extreme in Solomon Islands, where systematic corruption growing out of the forest industry had led to what the report called 'insidious tolerance'—namely, it is assumed both that every official is corrupt and that nothing could be done about it. The chapter goes on to consider three crosscutting themes in empirical studies: the contrast between gifts and bribes, petty corruption and the presumed role of ethnic minorities in corruption. The chapter concludes with a discussion of the problematic role of cultural relativism in discussions of corruption.

Conclusion

At the beginning of this introduction, I noted that recent discussion of corruption has been dominated by two assumptions: *first*, that corruption is largely an economic issue in both its content and its most important effects; and *second*, that it involves a blurring of the distinction between public and private. I also noted that these two assumptions often go together with a third that reflects an all too common view of the differences between Western and non-Western societies: that while corruption is universal, its most significant impact is likely to be found in developing countries.

At this point, it is time to sketch the conclusions that the editors believe might be drawn from this book. The first and most important point to make here is that, taken together, the assumptions just noted produce a view of corruption that is narrower in scope than almost any of the earlier views examined in this book. I have argued that broader understandings of corruption, such as the idea of corruption being a form of decay of the body politic, still resonate strongly with current concerns.

Neither the editors of nor the contributors to this book would argue that earlier views of corruption are superior to later views simply by virtue of their coming first. But we do claim that the differences between earlier and later views should give pause for thought. It is at least worth considering what has been gained and what may have been lost in the change from one period to the other. The image of corruption as one or more people behaving badly pales in comparison with the view—advanced by Machiavelli and Ibn Khaldun amongst many others—that corruption is a disease of the body politic that may both encourage improper behaviour on the part of many individuals and discourage those who recognise this behaviour to hold the perpetrators to account. This is not, of course, to suggest that we should not be concerned about people behaving badly. There is much to be said for Richard Mulgan's argument that while it may be appropriate to apply moral absolutes to the conduct of individual public officials, where individual corruption appears to be widespread, the problem is best viewed as a systemic issue—an 'absence of the rule of law or an accountability deficit'—rather than as one of many bad apples.

If the understanding of corruption as men or women behaving badly is an unfortunate narrowing of an earlier, more robust view, the same can be said of the view that corruption is best understood as an economic issue, in both its content and its effects. One familiar problem with the view that corruption is best seen as a matter of individuals pursuing their own private interests is that it takes no account of what Thompson's *Ethics in congress* calls 'institutional corruption', a mode of corruption in which the benefit gained is 'political rather than personal' (1995, p. 7). Thompson also acknowledges that institutional corruption may be difficult to identify 'because it is so closely related to conduct that [it] is a perfectly acceptable part of political life' (ibid.). If it is hard to distinguish between 'corrupt' and 'perfectly acceptable' conduct then current views of what is acceptable would seem to be problematic and to indicate that there is more to corruption than a few individuals behaving badly.

At another level, the arguments of Bruce Buchan and Lisa Hill suggest that the rise of an economistic or liberal-individualistic view of corruption should be seen as a by-product of the emergence of commercial society or perhaps—as the subtitle of Albert Hirschman's *The passions and the interests* (1977) has it— of the 'political arguments for capitalism before its triumph'. It goes without saying, of course, that the existence of such a provenance should hardly be seen as sufficient to undermine the economistic view. Once again, it is worth asking what has been lost, and what has been gained, in the shift from a structural/ political view to an economistic, market-based view of corruption.

The chapters in this collection show that broader understandings of corruption, such as the idea that it is a form of decay of the body politic, still resonate strongly with current concerns. More often than not these concerns are subsumed under the rubric of discourses other than corruption, such as the role of factionalism in political life.

By 'expanding the focus' of conventional understandings of corruption, this collection aims to bridge the gap between two literatures: first, the large and extremely diverse practice-oriented literature devoted to identifying the causes of corruption, assessing its incidence and working out how to bring it under control. Second, the somewhat smaller literature produced by social theorists and intellectual historians that explores the rich tradition of social thought about corruption in the West and in other parts of the world. The latter group of works sees corruption not only as a matter of illegal or improper behaviour on the part of individuals, but also as a societal issue—for example, a disease of the body politic. By opening up discussion of what it is that constitutes corruption we hope to challenge conventional, largely economistic understandings of corruption. The papers included in this volume aim to raise broader questions concerning the ability of citizens to participate in public and political life and to open the vocabulary of the health of the body politic to practitioners who work on the issue of corruption.

Let me conclude this introduction with two further points. The first is to suggest that one important result of the narrow focus of conventional discussions of corruption is the restricted sense of its political significance. Business scandals in the United States, the European Union and Australia suggest that corruption in the private sector can have public consequences that go well beyond the familiar problem of the 'capture' of regulators by the regulated to affect the funding of political parties and of factions within them; the American energy and services corporation Enron was reported to have contributed massively to the US Democrats while President Clinton was in office and later to have contributed to George W. Bush's campaign funds. In this case, what seems at first sight to be economic corruption could also be seen as a disease of the body politic.

Second, it is worth noting the striking results of a survey conducted a few years ago on behalf of TI, whose views on corruption are among the targets of this book. The TI survey examined public opinion in 47 countries around the world and found that, in three countries out of four, people singled out political parties as the institutions from which they would most like to have corruption removed (TI Press Release, 3 July 2003). It seems, and this is my final point, that while the contemporary international anti-corruption movement's treatment of corruption as primarily an economic issue addresses important questions relating to economic development and the eradication of poverty in much of the world, it nevertheless avoids the substance of widespread public concerns about the conduct of political life.

References

Alatas, Syed Hussein. (1990). *Corruption: its nature, causes and functions*. Aldershot: Ashgate.

Almond, Gabriel, & Verba, Sidnay. (1963). *The civic culture: political attitudes and democracy in five nations*. Princeton: Princeton University Press.

Anechiarico, Frank, & Jacobs, James. (1996). *The pursuit of absolute integrity: how corruption control makes government ineffective*. Chicago: Chicago University Press.

Aristotle. (1988). *The politics*. Cambridge: Cambridge University Press.

Bennett, Tony. (1998). *Culture: a reformer's science*. London: Sage.

Brennan, Geoffrey, & Lomarsky, Loren. (1993). *Democracy and decision: the pure theory of electoral preference*. Cambridge: Cambridge University Press.

Buchanan, James MacGill. (1978). *The Economics of politics*. London: Institute of Economic Affairs.

Buchanan, James MacGill, & Wagner, Richard E. (1977). *Democracy in deficit*. London: Academic Press.

Dahl, Robert A. (1989). *Democracy and its critics*. New Haven and London: Yale University Press.

Dahl, Robert A. (1998). *On democracy*. New Haven and London: Yale University Press.

Elkins, David J., & Simeon, Richard E. B. (1979). A cause in search of its effect, or what does political culture explain? *Comparative Politics, 11*(2), 127–45.

Euben, J. Peter. (1989). Corruption. In Terence Ball, James Farr & R. L. Hanson (Eds), *Political innovation and conceptual change* (pp. 220–46). Cambridge: Cambridge University Press.

Euben, J. Peter. (1997). *Corrupting youth: political education, democratic culture and political theory*. Princeton: Princeton University Press.

Farrar, Cynthia. (1988). *The origins of democratic thinking: the invention of politics in classical Athens*. Cambridge: Cambridge University Press.

Goodin, Robert E. (1996). *Theories of institutional design*. New York: Cambridge University Press.

Gray, John. (1982). F. A. Hayek and the rebirth of classical liberalism. *Literature of Liberty: A Review of Contemporary Liberal Thought, 5*(4), 19–67.

Hacker, Jacob, & Pierson, Paul. (2011). *Winner-take-all politics: how Washington made the rich richer—and turned its back on the middle class*. New York: Simon & Schuster.

Hall, Stuart. (1981). Notes on deconstructing 'the popular'. In Raphael Samuel (Ed.), *People's history and socialist theory* (pp. 227–40). London: Routledge.

Helliwell, Christine, & Hindess, Barry. (1999). 'Culture', 'society' and the figure of man. *History of the Human Sciences, 12*(4), 1–20.

Helliwell, Christine, & Hindess, Barry. (2011). Time and the others. In Sanjay Seth (Ed.), *Postcolonial theory and international relations*. London: Routledge.

Hexter, J. H. (1956). Seyssel, Machiavelli, and Polybius vi: the mystery of the missing translation. *Studies in the Renaissance, 3*, 75–96.

Hindess, Barry. (2000). Representation ingrafted upon democracy. *Democratization, 7*(2), 1–18.

Hindess, Barry. (2008). 'Been there, done that'. *Postcolonial Studies, 11*(2), 201–13.

Hirschman, Albert O. (1977). *The passions and the interests: political arguments for capitalism before its triumph*. Princeton: Princeton University Press.

Hume, David. (1987 [1777]). Of parties in general. In Eugene F. Miller Hume (Ed.), *Essays: moral, political, and literary* (pp. 54–63). Indianapolis: Liberty Fund.

International Institute for Democracy and Electoral Assistance. (2008). *Assessing the quality of democracy: a practical guide*. Stockholm: International IDEA.

Johnston, Michael. (2006). *Syndromes of corruption*. Cambridge: Cambridge University Press.

Kalpakian, Jack. (2008). Ibn Khaldun's influence on current international relations theory. *The Journal of North African Studies, 13*(3), 363–76.

Katsiaficas, George. (1997). Ibn Khaldun: a dialectical philosopher for the new millennium. In Claude Sumner & Samuel Yohannes (Eds), Perspectives in African philosophy. Addis Ababa: Eros Effect. Retrieved from <www.eroseffect.com/articles/Khaldun.PDF>

Khaldun, Ibn. (2004). The Muqaddimah. An introduction to history. N. J. Dawood (Ed.). Princeton: Princeton University Press.

Krastev, Ivan. (2004). *Shifting obsessions: three essays on the politics of anticorruption*. Budapest and New York: Central European University Press.

Livius, Titus (Livy). (2006). *The history of Rome. Books 01–08.I*. Project Gutenberg edition [E-Book #19725].

Machiavelli, Niccolò. (1979 [1525]a). Discourses on the first decade of Titus Livius. Extracts *The portable Machiavelli* (pp. 167–418). London and New York: Viking.

Machiavelli, Niccolò. (1979 [1525]b). The history of Florence. Extracts *The portable Machiavelli* (pp. 548–74). London and New York: Viking.

Madison, James, Hamilton, Alexander, & Jay, John. (1987 [1788]). *The federalist papers*. Harmondsworth: Penguin.

Mann, Michael. (1999). The dark side of democracy: the modern tradition of ethnic and political cleansing. *New Left Review, 23*, 18–45.

Phillips, Anne. (2007). *Multiculturalism without culture*. Princeton: Princeton University Press.

Philp, Mark. (1997). Defining political corruption. In P. Heywood (Ed.), *Political corruption* (pp. 20–46). Oxford: Blackwell.

Philp, Mark. (2007). *Political conduct*. Cambridge: Harvard University Press.

Roberts, Jennifer Tolbert. (1994). *Athens on trial: the antidemocratic tradition in Western thought*. Princeton: Princeton University Press.

Rose-Ackerman, Susan. (1999). *Corruption and government: causes, consequences and reform*. Cambridge and New York: Cambridge University Press.

Sachs, Jeffrey D. (2006). *The end of poverty: economic possibilities for our time*. New York: Penguin Press.

Sawer, Marian, & Hindess, Barry (Eds). (2004). *Us and them: anti-elitism in Australia*. Perth: API Network.

Schedler, Andreas (Ed.). (1997). *The end of politics? Explorations in modern antipolitics*. London: Macmillan.

Somers, Margaret. (1995). What's political or cultural about political culture and the public sphere? Toward an historical sociology of concept formation. *Sociological Theory, 13*(2), 113–44.

Thompson, Dennis F. (1995). *Ethics in congress*. Washington, DC: Brookings Institution Press.

Walter, Ryan. (2008). The economy and Pocock's political economy. *History of European Ideas (B), 34*(3), 334–44.

2. Aristotle on Legality and Corruption

Richard Mulgan

Defining corruption

For most people in public policy circles, one suspects, the main problems surrounding corruption are practical. The concept itself is comparatively straightforward and concrete in connotation, referring to certain specific practices such as bribery, cronyism and nepotism. The harmfulness of such practices is taken as self-evident because they are obvious abuses of power. The only question is how to 'stamp it out'.

For a political theorist, however, 'corruption' is a striking and perplexing term. In the first place, it has proved remarkably difficult to define in general terms, beyond a set of leading examples such as bribery, favouritism and nepotism. We may know that it is wrong but we are not quite sure what 'it' is. Experts disagree about what activities are to count as corrupt and about whether activities condemned as corrupt in one political context should be seen as functional in another. Secondly, 'corruption' is a term of unqualified ethical condemnation. To label any person or practice as 'corrupt' is to stigmatise them as beyond the moral pale. It combines the moralism of words such as 'sin', 'evil' or 'wickedness' with added psychological implications of personal depravity and debased character.

This chapter explores the incongruity between these two aspects—between the contextualism and the moralism inherent in corruption—in part through a historical comparison of the use of similar terms by the Greek philosophers, particularly Aristotle.

The problems of defining corruption have been well explored by others (for example, DeLeon, 1993; Heidenheimer, 1970; Heywood, 1997; Philp, 1997). In brief, definitions differ depending on whether they focus on the responsibilities and duties of public office and office-holders, on compliance with law and legally defined standards or more broadly on the clash between illegitimate personal interest and the public interest. While this question can hardly be said to be closed, the most compelling analyses would seem to be those that rely centrally on acting contrary to the common or public interest because it involves the illegitimate pursuit of a private interest (DeLeon, 1993; Philp, 1997). Definitions that depend on compliance with the particular duties of an office or with existing legal rules certainly highlight key factors in identifying corrupt political actions by individual politicians or officials. However, by taking existing duties and rules as given, such definitions are too closely tied to a particular institutional context. They do not provide an external standard by which to assess whether the duties or rules themselves prohibit actions that should be regarded as corrupt. If the definition of corruption is widened to include the illegitimate pursuit of a private interest then it allows an independent judgment of precisely what private interests existing ethical standards and rules ought to preclude. Admittedly, the use of a term such as 'illegitimate' is itself question-begging and does not provide an uncontested criterion for ruling selfish acts in or out, which is why the definition of corruption is so contested.

Corruption needs to be understood in terms of its opposite: the condition of soundness or health that either has subsequently degenerated into corruption or at least provides a standard against which the corruption can be identified (Philp, 1997). In J. L. Austin's (1962) colourful description applied to the term 'real', 'corruption' is a 'trouser' word, being filled and shaped by its complementary counterpart. If we want to give an account of political corruption, we should always begin by asking what uncorrupt—that is, sound or healthy—government looks like.

On the definition given above, uncorrupt politics implies that personal or private interests do not illegitimately override the public interest. At the same time, though the public interest should prevail, private interests are not necessarily ruled out altogether, especially in a liberal pluralist polity. Liberal democratic politics, which provides the moral standard against which corruption is typically characterised in present-day discourse, is based on the legitimate pursuit of self-interest, both by individuals and by sections of the community. True, the rituals of political discourse demand that deliberation about public policy be cast in the language of the public good and that individual or sectional self-interest be suppressed as a reason for acting. At the same time, no-one doubts both the actuality and the legitimacy of political self-interest in liberal democratic politics. To outlaw all self-interested politics would rule out much of the electioneering, lobbying, pork-barrelling and log-rolling on which democratic pluralist politics is premised.

Not that anything goes in the liberal pursuit of self-interest. Liberal pluralism has always adopted some independent, public-interest standards. Some standards are procedural, guaranteeing the political mechanisms by which private interests may compete; others are substantive, limiting the decisions that may be imposed on members of the citizen body. Constitutional and legal rules lay down limits and constraints that competing players must respect. Questions then arise about which types of procedure overstep the line between the legitimate and the illegitimate pursuit of private interests. When does lobbying become bribery and when does bargaining become collusion? When does redistributing resources to one's supporters become an infringement of other people's rights? Opinions differ significantly about what types of self-serving action are to be classed as illegitimate and therefore corrupt. Significant examples of such contested areas include making government appointments for partisan advantage (as in the NSW Metherall affair) or receiving payment for asking parliamentary questions (as in the UK scandal cited by Philp, 1997). At a more mundane level, public servants are clearly at odds over what type of gift may be legitimately received from a public client (ICAC, 2001). Possibilities for disagreement are multiplied when concepts of corruption are applied cross-culturally, for instance in countries where gift-giving or preference for one's own kin or ethnic group is considered appropriate and legitimate.

For present purposes, the important point is not so much the differences in opinion over corruption in liberal democracies but the premises that underlie such disagreement. Any realistic notion of corruption applicable in present-day liberal democratic politics has to recognise that politicians (and citizens) cannot reasonably be expected to be motivated solely by concern for the common good or public interest. Instead, the concept of the public interest is institutionalised more as a set of minimal side constraints—to adopt Nozick's (1974) useful term—on the pursuit of private interests. A condition of sound—that is, non-corrupt—politics is not a polity where everyone pursues the public interest but one where the pursuit of private interests is not allowed to transgress certain minimal public-interest limits. Where public-interest constraints kick in and force private interests to give way is a matter of dispute. As already noted, the boundary between the legitimate and the illegitimate pursuit of private interests is blurred and contested. More fundamentally, however, the judgment is essentially a balance struck between competing values: the pursuit of individual or sectional interests on the one hand, and concern for the common good on the other.

If sound politics is identified as a compromise between selfishness and concern for the common good, corruption then becomes a matter of tipping the balance too far in the direction of selfishness. Such a nuanced view of where the line is to be drawn between non-corruption and corruption may sit awkwardly with the highly moralistic implications of the term itself. 'Corruption', as already noted, carries very strong moral—indeed, moralising—overtones, redolent of 'evil' and 'sin', suggesting both universalistic standards of right and wrong and a sense of righteous outrage at the practices in question. To label a practice as 'corrupt' is to condemn it unequivocally in the strongest possible terms. And yet, we now discover, corruption is not so much a festering disease in the body politic as a possibly minor imbalance between two legitimate forces in the community. 'Corruption' has connotations of moral absolutism (compare with 'swear off the demon drink') whereas, in practice, it seems to refer to striking the right balance ('drink but not to excess').

Corruption in the Greek tradition

An historical digression can help us explore this issue further. In the history of European thought, discussion of corruption in politics and the possibility of achieving non-corrupt politics immediately suggests the Greek philosophers, particularly Socrates and Plato, but also their immediate successors in the late-classical and Hellenistic periods, all of whom agonised about the corruption of politics and the corruptibility of politicians. Socrates rejected the life of the politician as incompatible with the pursuit of knowledge and thus provided the inspiration for subsequent philosophies of quietist withdrawal, such as Cynicism, Epicureanism and the more extreme versions of Stoicism that were to flourish in the Hellenistic age. Plato, in turn, while never renouncing the world of politics, nonetheless located it in the inferior realm of his dualistic universe. Politics was relegated to the world of the senses, the world subject to inevitable change and decay (literally: the world subject to corruption). Aristotle, though less contemptuous of the sub-lunar world of change and contingency than Plato, also never abandoned his Platonic commitment to the superiority of an eternal unchanging realm accessible only to pure reason. Human society was inevitably contingent and liable to variation.

These theorists, then, all held to some form of ontological dualism, in which a world of pure truth and goodness stood opposed to an inferior world of uncertainty and evil. In terms of their approach to government and politics, this dualism took one of two forms. The more radical and deliberately paradoxical path, such as that of the Cynics, involved a total rejection of all government, and by implication a rejection of all human society, as irredeemably flawed; the less radical approach followed by Plato and Aristotle was to devise an ideal form of government that would in some way incorporate the other-worldly values of unqualified truth and goodness. This ideal, in turn, provided a standard against which the performance of everyday regimes could be judged and improvements recommended. For Plato, such an ideal is the rule of philosophers, as depicted in *The Republic* and recalled in later political dialogues such *The Statesman* (293) and *The Laws* (711–2, 875). For Aristotle, the political ideal is similarly the rule of the ideally wise and virtuous (*Pol.* IV 2, 1289a30–2), whether through an outstandingly virtuous individual or family (absolute rule) or through a broader aristocracy of truly virtuous men.

Plato, in *The Republic*, describes the contrast between the ideal and inferior states in terms of an imagined 'decay' or 'destruction', using the word *pthora* (546a), the Greek term later regularly Latinised as *corruptio*. The ideal state undergoes a number of stages of such decay, through timocracy, oligarchy and democracy, culminating in tyranny, which is the worst regime of all. Elsewhere, the contrast between ideal and inferior is expressed in different images. In *The Statesman*, for instance, inferior regimes are said to 'mimic' or copy the ideal constitution (301a, 303c), an image often used by Plato in his epistemology to represent the relationship between the inferior objects of the senses and the objects of true knowledge. Aristotle, in *The Politics*, uses different terminology again, 'correct' (*orthos*) for the good forms of government and 'deviations' or 'perversions' (*parekbaseis*) for the inferior. The implication is in all cases the same: the ideal form of government is conceived as logically prior, and inferior constitutions are defined in relation to it, as being in some sense lacking or deficient.

There is thus a close parallel with the modern concept of political corruption understood in terms of the absence of sound or non-corrupt politics. In Greek, however, the equivalent term to 'corruption' (*pthora*) retains more of its literal meaning and implies actual decay or disintegration. In Aristotle, *pthora* is the standard philosophical opposite of genesis or 'coming into being' and in *The Politics* its main use arises in connection with the destruction of particular constitutions (Bonitz, 1955). In modern English, on the other hand, the metaphor of organic decay is less prominent. We talk of corrupt regimes without necessarily implying that they have degenerated from a former healthy condition. In this respect, corruption is closer in meaning to 'deviant', the term Aristotle himself uses to describe inferior constitutions.

For both Plato and Aristotle, the key feature that the ideal regimes possess as a result of their wise and virtuous rulers is that they are governed in the common interest. Conversely, the leading characteristic that distinguishes deviant regimes from the ideal is that their rulers rule in their own interest rather than the common interest. In *The Republic*, the guardians' training and communal living lead them totally to suppress any notion of self-interest and to find their personal fulfilment in the happiness of the whole (420b–421c). The imagined corruption of the ideal state and its decline to tyranny through descending stages of moral degradation can be read as a gradual assertion of individual self-interest and a retreat from commitment to the common good. Aristotle gives even more prominence to the contrast between pursuit of the common interest and self-interest, making it the only criterion defining the difference between correct and deviant constitutions:

The correct forms of government are those in which the one, the few or the many govern with a view to the common interest: but the governments which rule with a view to the private interest whether of the one, or of the few or of the many are deviations (*Pol.* III 7, 1279a28–32)

Aristotle initially allows three types of correct constitution—namely kingship (rule of one), aristocracy (rule of few) and polity (rule of many)—all in the common interest. Later, however, he concentrates on two varieties: absolute kingship, the (largely hypothetical) rule of one outstandingly able man, and aristocracy, the regime where power lies with a citizen body consisting of virtuous men of property. The third correct option, polity—rule by a virtuous majority— quickly slips down the ranking. A majority of citizens are capable of only a limited, military-style virtue (*Pol.* III 7, 1279b1–2) and polity becomes a somewhat deviant constitution, better than oligarchy and democracy but not fully correct and therefore, by implication, not fully governed in the common interest (*Pol.* IV 8, 1293b22–7). Rule in the common interest rather than in the interest of the rulers remains the touchstone of a correct regime. Aristotle's account of political deviance thus resonates again with modern analyses of political corruption: both establish a nexus between political deviance and the rulers' pursuit of their own private interest against the common interest.

However, despite this conceptual parallel, the ancient and modern views of political corruption exhibit important differences. One such difference concerns the practicality of achieving non-corrupt politics. In the modern conception, corruption is seen as remediable, at least at the systemic level; the best existing regimes, such as those at the top of the Transparency International (TI) table, are considered to be largely free of corruption. Though corruption, like crime, will never be totally stamped out, it can be relegated to the margins as it has been in many present-day polities. In particular, from the perspective of developed donor countries like Australia, political corruption is mainly a problem for 'messy' or 'failed' states, such as Indonesia or Papua New Guinea. Even where more systemic corruption is evident, as in Australian State police forces, such practices can be interpreted as intolerable pockets of corruption to be stamped out by anti-corruption agencies and mercifully absent from other branches of government.

For Aristotle, however, as for Plato, all existing regimes fall on the corrupt or deviant side of the corrupt/non-corrupt line. Plato certainly considered his philosopher's city to be beyond practical reach; he may have intended it to be impossible even in principle. His ideal state in *The Laws* makes more concessions to human frailty but is still clearly an unachieved ideal that is most unlikely ever to be put into practice. In a similar vein, Aristotle considers absolute rule to be practically impossible (*Pol.* VII 14, 1332b, 2207). Even his ideal aristocracy, which contains everything one could wish for but nothing impossible (*Pol.* VII

4, 1325b38–40), though in principle attainable, is an imagined ideal—not a realistic possibility. The function of the ideally best constitution was to provide a moral contrast with the inferior specimens of everyday experience, not to provide some model of constitutional 'best practice' to which struggling nations and failed states should be expected to aspire as a condition of receiving loans from richer countries.

This difference in practicality is also reflected in differences over the meaning of corruption. Modern notions of corruption, as already noted, concentrate on the *illegitimate* pursuit of self-interest in preference to the common interest. In this respect, they establish a balance between the pursuit of public and private interests and do not require governments (or citizens) to be completely dedicated to the common interest. By contrast, Aristotle, like Plato before him, did require such complete dedication. Ideal, non-corrupt states are governed by ideally virtuous rulers who are wholly focused on the common interest and would never consider pursuing their own interests at the expense of the good of the community. Aristotle's ruling aristocrats had their own private lives and personal interests, but insofar as they acted politically they would be wholly devoted to the good of the *polis*. In this respect, the ancient accounts, though more utopian, may be said to be more in tune with the moral absoluteness implicit in the concept of pure, non-corrupt government.

On the other hand, if the standard of non-corrupt government is placed so high as to be unachievable, it could be argued that such conceptual purity is bought at too high a price. In particular, if all regimes are essentially corrupt because all are ruled in the interest of the rulers, what becomes of the distinctions that we want to make between corrupt and non-corrupt regimes, between Finland and Nigeria or between New Zealand and Indonesia? If all are corrupt, what is the point of condemning corruption?

For Aristotle, as for Plato, the fact that all existing regimes are deviant because all are governed in the interest of the rulers does not mean that all are equally deviant. Such a categorical conclusion may have been drawn by the more radical anti-political philosophers, such as the Cynics and Stoics. But both Plato and Aristotle, and particularly the latter, were interested in distinguishing between varying degrees of deviance in everyday politics. That is, the model of the ideal, correct state was used not only to criticise all everyday regimes as fundamentally flawed but also to provide a standard against which everyday regimes could be assessed and found more or less deviant.

Here the key factor was the rule of law. Rulers might all be self-interested, whether they were single rulers (tyranny), the rich few (oligarchy) or the poor majority (democracy). But their rule could be better or worse, depending on whether they were constrained to act within the law or whether they were free to follow their wishes. Plato makes the case most compellingly in *The Statesman* in the context of an argument intended to highlight the weaknesses as well as the strengths of the rule of law (291–300). Law is deficient because rules are blunt and circumstances varied. The true professional, such as a skilled doctor, is not bound by the instructions left for subordinates but assesses each case on the basis of individual judgment. So too the true politicians—the philosopher rulers— will not be bound by general laws but will judge each issue on its merits. However, while the constraint of law curbs the wisdom of the philosopher, it also serves to restrain the selfishness of the ordinary ruler. Amongst inferior regimes that lack the benefit of having philosophers as their rulers, those governed in accordance with law are all superior to those where rulers can rule as they wish. The theme of the value of the rule of law in curbing the self-interest of rulers is developed in much more detail in the dialogue *The Laws* and was also taken over by Aristotle, who uses it as a major criterion in distinguishing between more moderate and more extreme versions of inferior constitutions.

Aristotle, too, recognises that the bluntness of law can create problems and also that laws themselves may be unjust if they are the product of an unjust regime (*Pol*. III 11, 1282b12). Yet lawful rule is on the whole better than lawless rule, because all laws are general and therefore to some extent impartial and a curb on the rulers' self-interest. Ordinary people who are called on to make decisions in particular cases are too likely to be carried away by feelings of friendship or hatred and to be blinded by personal pleasure and pain (*Rhetoric* I 1, 1354a34–b11). This argument is summed up in the famous epigram that 'law is intellect without desire' (*Pol*. III 16, 1287a32). Thus, in each case, the most extreme and worst forms of oligarchy (*Pol*. IV 6, 1293a30–1), democracy (*Pol*. IV 6, 1293a8–10), and tyranny (*Pol*. IV 10, 15–23) are characterised by the absence of the rule of law, whereas the more moderate and more stable are ruled in accordance with law.

Aristotle's argument for the rule of law does not depend on the content of the laws so much as on the nature of any law. Laws themselves can be partial and unjust in their intent. Indeed, all laws in deviant regimes are inevitability skewed in the interest of the ruling group. What makes the rule of law superior (or less inferior) is that any law impartially applied must reduce, though it will not eliminate, the personal benefits that rulers derive from decisions. For instance, laws in an oligarchy will always favour the wealthy and propertied and will always penalise the poor and property-less. But at least the wealthy will be treated equally with one another and in accordance with legal precedents; rulers will not be able to make unpredictable, ad-hoc decisions to suit themselves.

Again there is a parallel with modern accounts of corruption in which legality or the rule of law is sometimes taken as a defining feature. Corruption is often equated with breaking the law for the sake of securing a personal advantage. Anti-corruption campaigners are therefore always putting their weight behind greater respect for the rule of law. However, as already noted, such a conception of corruption is question-begging in that it does not stipulate what types of self-interested action should be considered corrupt and therefore illegal. For instance, a case can be made that some lawful activities, such as corporate contributions to campaign funds, involve an illegitimate pursuit of self-interest and should therefore be outlawed as corrupt. That is, a conception of corruption that is grounded in existing law is open to charges of circularity or moral relativism because it offers no independent standard of what should count as corrupt.

Aristotle, however, avoids this difficulty because he is assuming that all regimes, lawful and lawless, are deviant and unjust, though to varying degrees. He is not, at this point, trying to draw a line between sound and corrupt regimes or between just and unjust laws. He therefore does not face the issue of an independent ethical standard implicit in the modern use of corruption. That issue has been dealt with elsewhere, in the conception of the correct (and unattainable) constitution. Here, he has a more modest aim: simply to mark out a means by which the harmful effects of self-interested (and corrupt) rule may be mitigated. Self-interested rulers constrained by law will deviate less from the standard of good government and do less harm than the same rulers unconstrained by law. The rule of law is thus not overburdened with any moral connotations of being linked with the concept of uncorrupt government. In this case, the question of whether particular laws are good or bad can be more safely left to one side. The main point is that keeping within any law, whether good or bad, will be better and less corrupt than allowing self-interested rulers the freedom to disregard the law at will.

Aristotle is similarly pragmatic in his advice about how best to ensure that members of the ruling groups rule in accordance with law. General commitment to the values of the regime is a key component, to be achieved through public education (*Pol.* V 9, 1310a14–18). But equally important are socioeconomic factors. Citizens who must give most of their energy to making a living will take little interest in politics and will therefore be content to let the law take its course rather than try to impose their own solutions (*Pol.* IV 6, especially. 1293a17–19). Hence, the most law-abiding form of democracy is one where the people are predominantly agricultural without the time or incentive to come into town to attend meetings. The rule of law is under most threat either from the idle rich, with the leisure to use government to enrich themselves still further, or from the indigent urban poor who also have both the time and the incentive to make decisions in their own interests. Those of moderate wealth, on the other hand, can generally be trusted to be law-abiding (*Pol.* IV 11, 1295b2–34).

Aristotle's insistence on the importance of law—any law—in reducing the incidence of political corruption does not provide a defining mark for corruption. Nonetheless, it may be instructive for modern debates about corruption. It resonates, at least, with the practical focus in much anti-corruption work on the importance of preventing government officials from breaking actual laws for personal gain. Most anti-corruption campaigns are concerned with breaches of actual laws and regulations, regardless of the actual content of the laws and regulations in question and regardless of whether such laws and regulations are justified. True, this point begs the broader and more fundamental question about what types of self-interested activity should be treated as corrupt and therefore made the subject of anti-corruption laws and regulations. But for the most part, laws and regulations are taken as given and the task is simply to make sure that those in positions of power and responsibility uphold the law as it stands and are not tempted into breaking it for their own private benefit. Indeed, it is for this reason that many modern accounts of corruption adopt illegality as a defining feature of corruption. Thus, both ancient and modern perspectives agree on the importance of rulers ruling within the law, whatever the law may be. The ancients viewed this more as a task of reducing the inevitable corruption or deviance of all governments, whereas in the modern view the issue of legality marks the difference between corrupt and non-corrupt governments.

Structural weakness and moral failure

So far, we have found reason to criticise modern notions of political corruption because they either do not provide a clear account of what should be considered corrupt/non-corrupt politics or, if they do attempt such an account, inappropriately apply a term of absolute moral condemnation to what is in practice a realistic balance struck between self-interest and the common interest. Aristotle avoids these objections, because the equivalent term for political corruption is clearly applied to all non-perfect regimes and is not used to draw a line between the more or less imperfect. Corruption becomes a matter of degree, a characteristic essential to all existing regimes.

The focus of discussion has been at the general level of the regime as a whole, in the attempt to distinguish a corrupt from a non-corrupt polity. Yet corruption can also be approached at the individual level, from the perspective of the individual politician or official who may or may not break a particular law or code of conduct for personal gain. In this context, the language of moral absolutes appears less inappropriate. We talk often of people of 'total honesty' or 'unimpeachable integrity' who would never 'cross the line' to commit a corrupt act. In such individualised contexts, judging the behaviour of, say, individual tax officers or individual police, black-and-white moralising descriptions such as 'honest' or 'corrupt' seem wholly appropriate. They indicate an assumption that there are important ethical standards which individuals can reasonably be expected to uphold.

Moreover, breaching such standards for personal gain marks an abhorrent betrayal of public trust. In contrast with the collective perspective, judging individual corruption in terms of existing law seems less question-begging. Individual officials cannot be expected to set the standards for themselves and so are appropriately judged in terms of the rules set for them. Entire governments, on the other hand, are properly judged not just on whether their rules are complied with but also on whether they have set the right rules—a much more nuanced judgment where terms such as 'corruption' may be more contestable.

Note that a judgment of individual corruption, although couched in the strongest moral terms, is very context specific. This is not to say that the person concerned is wholly depraved or, more importantly, that the persons not so condemned are moral paragons, wholly dedicated to the common good in all their actions. All it means is that, in relation to the specific range of professional ethical demands that most people can be expected to meet, a particular individual has failed to measure up, and culpably so. For this reason, the sense of moral condemnation implicit in the label 'corruption' is strongest within a context of everyday compliance. We are most comfortable in the allocation of moral blame if the individual has been surrounded by non-corrupt colleagues and therefore has had every encouragement to stay on the right side of the line. By contrast, in contexts where corrupt behaviour is endemic, the very use of the term 'corruption' to describe such individual acts appears more questionable. The behaviour in question is much less obviously due to individual moral weakness but is more a matter of institutional structures and social norms, as Aristotle recognised. For individuals, avoiding corruption is not meant to set heroic ideals, but rather a basic level of honesty that only the very weak or wicked will fall beneath.

Judgments of individual corruption therefore appear less problematic than those made of whole governments, particularly insofar as they take existing standards and general compliance with such standards for granted. Of course, collective assessments of corruption can be made in terms of the amount of individual corruption that occurs. Country A may be less corrupt than Country B, not because its government is more concerned with the common good, but because fewer politicians and officials are on the take. Indeed, most collective assessments, such as those conducted by TI, seem to be of that type. It is for this reason also that definitions of corruption so often concentrate on actual illegality or the duties of an actual office—definitions that fit the individual case much more than the collective.

Perhaps critical political theorists are the only people who want to take collective assessments more literally as implying a moral judgment on the polity as a whole, including its tolerance of sectional interests and where it strikes the balance between private interests and the common good. In this case, as the analysis of Aristotle above suggests, the concept of corruption should perhaps be abandoned as a means of distinguishing everyday regimes from one another. Taken literally—as government in which the common interest is never compromised for private interests—it sets a standard beyond the reach of all practicable regimes. Its use by some regimes to criticise others therefore appears as hypocrisy or special pleading. Moreover, even if corruption is reserved for assessments of the amount of individual illegality, the above analysis suggests that we should use it sparingly when talking of regimes where illegality for private purposes is rife. The concept of corruption entails a charge of moral failing that is unjustified unless it occurs against a background of normal compliance. In other words, once so-called 'corruption' reaches a certain level of prevalence, it is transformed into something else, such as the absence of the rule of law or an accountability deficit. Such faults are no less harmful but they are dependent more on institutional and structural weaknesses than on moral failure.

References

Austin, John Langshaw. (1962). *Sense and sensibilia*. Oxford: Clarendon Press.

Bonitz, Hermann. (1955). *Index Aristotelicus*. Graz: Akademische Druck-U, Verlagsanstalt.

DeLeon, Peter. (1993). *Thinking about political corruption*. Armonk and London: M. E. Sharpe.

Heidenheimer, Arnold J. (1970). *Political corruption*. New Brunswick: Transaction Publishers.

Heywood, Peter. (1997). Political corruption: problems and perspectives. *Political Studies, 45*, 417–35.

Independent Commission Against Corruption [New South Wales] (ICAC). (2001). *Unravelling corruption II: exploring changes in the public sector perspective 1993–1999*. Sydney: Independent Commission Against Corruption.

Nozick, Robert. (1974). *Anarchy, state and utopia*. New York: Basic Books.

Philp, Mark. (1997). Defining political corruption. *Political Studies, 45*, 436–62.

3. To Corrupt: The ambiguity of the language of corruption in ancient Athens

Arlene W. Saxonhouse

Today the language of corruption thrives largely within the framework of moral theory. The most general sense of the term to which most scholarly attention is given seems to be the inappropriate use of public resources for private gain, with the meaning of 'public' branching out from governmental institutions to economic entities such as public corporations. The use of public resources for private gain harms the lives of those who depend on the open and fair distribution and use of public goods. Thus, the moral context enmeshes the language of corruption in a liberal world that distinguishes public from private, and the optimism of Mandeville's private vices leading to public virtues is left far behind. Instead, energies turn to completing the project of Federalist Papers No. 10 (Madison, 1987 [1788]) and developing institutions that acknowledge the ingrained pursuit of private interests but manage to 'control the effects'. Or, in a very different literature—that of communitarianism and its variants— corruption may more generally refer to 'a people' (à la Machiavelli or Rousseau) who lack concern with the welfare of the whole leading to the death of the polity. Private interests draw them away from a concern with the welfare of the whole, and public corruption takes its place against public virtue. Such approaches to corruption offer valuable tools for assessing the potential of democratic regimes committed to popular welfare; however, the concept of corruption fits into other contexts where it may have meanings that are not so centrally dependent on the public/private dichotomy that lies at the heart of current discourses of corruption.

The democratic Athenians of ancient Greece had their own institution to deal with the so-called sticky hand. This was the *euthunê*, which required each public official to render an account before a panel of his peers before he left public office. Thucydides (like the communitarians of today) mourned the decline of popular devotion to the city as the successors of Pericles grasped at supremacy for themselves without attention to the welfare of all. Authors from ancient Athens not so enmeshed in the public/private dichotomy also understood corruption as the dissolution of an institution or practice or way of living distant from what might be seen as its 'natural' form. For Plato there was the corruption of the form—that which exists by nature and not by art or craft, and that which exists in an unchanging world of being. When brought into the world of daily experience and change, the form is corrupted and loses its perfection. For Thucydides, there were the perfection and imagined eternity of the Periclean city described in Pericles' funeral oration, which dissolved with Pericles' death, the pressures of war and, most importantly, the embodiment of the city in the actual lives of its citizens. From such a perspective, these authors offer a very different sense of corruption, one that takes it out of the public/private dichotomies so prevalent today. They place the concept into a much more ambiguous but (I will suggest) richer theoretical world.

Both Plato and Thucydides offer portraits of the perfect city but then point to the necessary corruption of such cities that cannot maintain their perfection, cities that undergo transformations in a world of constant change. There is no eternity for cities; there is no city by nature. Cities are embodied—that is, built out of human beings for whom there is no eternity or perfection. In opposition to the corruption of cities, though, each author offers a new form of knowledge. This newly identified way of knowing requires the corruption of the traditional forms of literary expression. The new forms of expression that both Plato and Thucydides introduce—by transcending the corruptible forms of knowledge and politics itself—illustrate the constructive consequences of literary corruption, achieving an incorruptibility of knowledge, as they see it, which is denied to politics.

Socrates, according to the accusation of the Athenians, corrupted the youth of Athens. In Plato's dialogues, Socrates will often corrupt the texts of Homer through misquotation. Corruption of this sort can and does lead to disorder. There is no secure text of Homer to which we can refer. The youth of Athens 'corrupted' by Socrates no longer support the political agenda of the city—but such efforts 'to corrupt' may allow, even be necessary for, the emergence of the incorruptible. Thucydides' description of the civil war in Corcyra during the Peloponnesian War captures the chaos that results when language itself is corrupted and words no longer provide a stable referent. But despite the corruptibility of words with their inherent malleability, Thucydides writes a work of *logoi* that he claims will be 'a possession for ever' (*kteis es aiei*) (1982, 1.22). In doing so, he affirms the power of words to rise above the potential corruptibility that can result from the vagaries of political conflicts.

Both Plato and Thucydides understood corruption of form in a dual sense. The first is the destruction of any image of the perfection of a city. The second is the corruption of a literary genre as a necessary prelude to the eternal incorruptible forms of knowing. Both authors corrupt traditional genres within their own novel writings: Thucydides with regard to how the past is recorded and presented, Plato with his prose representations of conversations. They both engage in this corruption of literary form, though, in order to establish incorruptible forms of knowledge that will provide a political education impervious to the pressures of a constantly changing world that brings on events like the revolution in Corcyra. The ways of knowing in the past were subject to corruption—by the Sophists, by characters like Socrates, by those whose stories were told with prejudice and self-interest, by the dislocations of war. The new ways of knowing offered by Thucydides and Plato are intended to rise above the impermanence of the old. For Thucydides this knowledge may allow us, as he says, 'to see clearly' (1.22); for Socrates, it may allow us to 'live well'. Corruption of the old, in this fashion, gives birth to what is most valuable—and incorruptible—in life. In this sense, the ancient authors let us take corruption beyond its negative political and moral connotations in order to explore its more positive potential.

Elsewhere I have treated Socrates and the corruption of the young (Saxonhouse, 2004). In this chapter, I want to look at the writings of Plato and Thucydides as they consider how to move beyond the corruptible forms of knowledge that dominate their societies. By exploring these epistemological and genre questions, we see their relation to the political possibilities of incorruptible regimes. Ultimately, I find an ancient pessimism, which I contrast in a coda at the end of this chapter with a modern Hobbesian optimism. Hobbes's optimism, though, leads to questioning the consequences of longing for the politically incorruptible.

Any study that turns to the ancients for insights into contemporary issues must acknowledge that all the literature from that period is in some sense experimental. The literary models were few and opportunities for innovation enormous. Nevertheless, when one turns to the fifth and fourth centuries BCE, literary genres had been established and patterns of expression for offering views concerning the gods, the past, the good life and the polity in which one lived had all found their form: epic, tragedy, comedy, the expansive histories of writers like Herodotus and the now lost Hellenicus and Hecaetetus. Both Thucydides and Plato violate those forms in an effort to offer to their readers truths that exist beyond and above the corruptible knowledge that is based on the experience and discourse of their daily lives. Each believes that by consciously corrupting the literary forms of their times, he reveals a new grounding for knowledge, a knowledge that might be 'a possession forever'. The challenge that exists is whether in their effort to go beyond the corruptible knowledge offered by other literary genres these authors can offer us a politics beyond corruption. I argue that they cannot.

I am here using a very different meaning of corruption than that which dominates the current language of corruption studies. It is the language of corruption that emerges in the classical texts. Many Greek words are commonly translated by 'corruption': *luô*, *stasis*, *metabolê*, *diaphthora*. All imply the loss of some integrity, the loss of form, and suggest the process of change that such loss entails. The Greek words most commonly translated as 'corruption' are *diaphthora* and its derivative, the verbal form *diaphtherein* (to corrupt). The verb *diaphtherein* entails what we think of as 'decay from an original form' or, as in the *Oxford English Dictionary* definition, the loss of unity or integrity. In the Greek, as in the English, this can refer to a body, a political regime or an individual.

Let me begin with an example from *The republic*. Socrates has just proposed that unless philosophers become kings or kings become philosophers there will be 'no rest from ills for the cities…nor I think for humankind' (Plato, 1968, 473). His interlocutors in *The republic* are not as ready to accept the genuineness of this proposal as later readers of the dialogue have been. Surely, they suggest, he cannot be serious. Those who stay with the practice of philosophy, Adeimantus remarks, 'become quite queer, not to say completely vicious; while the ones who seem perfectly decent, do nevertheless suffer at least one consequence of the practice you are praising—they become useless to the cities' (487d). Socrates' response is to insist that they clarify precisely who the philosopher is:

> Won't we make a sensible apology in saying that it is the nature (*pephukôs*) of the real lover of learning to strive for what is; and he does not tarry by each of the many things opined to be but goes forward and does not lose the keenness of his passionate love nor cease from it before he grasps the nature itself (*phuseôs*) of each thing. (490b)

What Adeimantus has seen and used as the basis for his evaluation of the philosopher are the result, Socrates explains, of the 'corruptions of this nature' ('*tês phuseôs…tas phthoras*') (490e). He has looked at how that nature, Socrates says in the next phrase, has been 'destroyed' (*diollutai*, dissolved) by the many. Adeimantus grounded his understanding of the philosopher in his observation of the corrupted nature of the philosopher and thus, looking at the corrupted form of the philosopher, found the philosopher a queer character, useless for cities. Studying the philosophic nature in its pure form offers a very different character, one whose benefits for the city become apparent in the later sections of the dialogue.

In elaborating his response to Adeimantus, Socrates presents numerous examples of how the philosophic nature is corrupted (*diaphtheiromenous*)—by the sophists, by the assemblies, by the theatre (492a–b). At the conclusion of his examples, Socrates tells Adeimantus: 'Such is the extent and character of this destruction and corruption (*diaphthora*) of the best nature (*phuseôs*)' (495a). Socrates begins with the affirmation that there is a nature (*phusis*) that is the purity of the philosophic soul. The forces of the society in which the philosopher matures threaten this purity. The pressures of life in the city corrupt the natural form of the philosopher and make the young men with whom Socrates converses confuse philosophy with its perversions. The philosophic nature needs to be released and protected from the societal corruption if it is to retain its natural purity, just like the plants that must be nurtured on pure soil.

The world in Socrates' story has been turned upside down. The Athenians try Socrates for the corruption of their young men. Here, in *The republic*, Socrates tries the Athenians for the corruption of the philosopher. Each assumes that there is a pure nature that has been corrupted by the influence of the other. For the Athenians it is their youth educated according to their own laws and customs; for Socrates it is the philosophic soul. The challenge for each, as the Athenians and Socrates see it, is to preserve themselves against the destructive forces (Socrates/the Athenians) that threaten their perfection with corruption. The Athenians and Socrates each try to remove the cause of that potential corruption: the Athenians in deed by killing Socrates, Socrates in word by making philosophers kings in his Callipolis and through that exercise making the young love philosophy. Each also imagines a pristine form that experiences corruption and in each case the corruption of that form undermines the security and stability of what is perceived as the good regime, the regime worth defending.

As Socrates continues to explore who the philosopher is, he investigates what it is that the philosopher knows, as he phrases it at the end of Book V. There he says that the philosopher loves 'what is', not the many particular, embodied examples of what it is that he loves. In other words, according to Socrates, one who loves young boys will love the 'form' or 'idea' of the young boy and not attend to whether the boy has a straight or snub nose, noses such as are found in the assorted corruptions of 'the young boy' who exists in the world of daily and sensory experience. More significant than the somewhat salacious example that Socrates introduces at this point is the 'fair' or the 'beautiful' itself that resides in 'nature'. When it manifests itself for our senses to apprehend, it does so only in a corrupted particular form of a boy or a deed or a picture or whatever else we experience with our senses. The famous image of the divided line, which Socrates introduces in Book VI as he continues his search for the philosopher, clarifies further the difference between 'what is' and what, by its existence in the world of particularity, is always a corruption of form and subject to change. It is here that we learn about the famous (or infamous) 'forms', the purity of which serve, according to the language of the image of the divided line, as the beginning points from which all else is derivative or a corruption of that perfection. The highest activity of the intellect is apprehension of the incorruptible, unchanging forms. That deriving from the forms and existing in the corruptible world of change call forth only lower mental faculties such as trust or imagining.

For Socrates, the goal of the philosopher is to attain the forms through the intellect. Otherwise, we all labour in a world of corruption, unable to divine the purity by which we can have true knowledge and by which we can evaluate the good and the bad, the beautiful and the ugly. Thus, for example, in the aporetic dialogues like the *Laches* or *Charmides* or *Lysis* or *Euthyphro*, Socrates searches for an understanding of courage or moderation or friendship or piety, definitions that are pure in their abstraction from the particular expressions in our daily activities. Thus, he rejects Euthyphro's description of acting piously by prosecuting his father as, in any sense, clarifying what piety is. Such a description does not help Socrates to understand the virtue he allegedly lacks and why the Athenians are prosecuting him for impiety. Instead, he tells Euthyphro:

> I didn't bid you to teach me some one or two of the many pious things, but that *eidos* [form, shape] itself by which all the pious things are pious...teach me whatever this idea itself is, so that by gazing at it and using it as a pattern, I may declare that whatever is like it, among the things you or anyone else may do, is pious, and that whatever is not like it is not. (Plato, 1984a, 6d–e)

He looks for the nature (or form) of piety, the pure virtue itself, untainted by particular persons (such as Euthyphro prosecuting his father) or particular actions (such as bringing to justice a parent who allows a slave who murdered another slave to die).

But—and this is the proverbial 'big but'—in the Platonic dialogues and in Socratic discourse, we never actually find those pure forms. We do not know what piety is at the end of the *Euthyphro*, or what courage is after the discussion in the *Laches*, or what friendship is in the *Lysis*, though we may know what all of these virtues are not and certainly understand that the definitions we use are woefully inadequate. In the dialogues Socrates finds himself always distracted by the complex problems that arise when we search for the natural and the pure forms in the corrupt manifestations that engage us in the sensory world of what is particular and embodied. Thus, we learn from Socrates that the pure, incorruptible, unchanging forms may exist in nature, and that that nature is not readily accessible to us. Indeed, knowledge of the pure forms may be an impossible goal. Access to the purity of the philosophic nature and the purity of the forms that rise above the everyday experience of those living in a world of change is an inaccessible aspiration. We are left in the corrupt world where the changeable always marks our distance from a purified nature.

The challenge that Socrates sets forth by affirming that the unexamined life is not worth living is to educate us about the difference between what is natural, pure and uncorrupted and what is corrupted in the world in which we live, without ever taking us to view the uncorrupted beautiful or good itself. In *The republic*, he says to Glaucon, who is eager to follow him in pursuit of the forms: 'You will no longer be able to follow…although there wouldn't be any lack of eagerness on my part…Whether it is really so or not can no longer be properly insisted on. But that there is some such thing to see must be insisted on. Isn't that so?' (533a). The forms may exist, but as we live our lives we are governed by that which is far distant from them. The political world has not brought the forms down into the world in which we live—and the question that plagues *The republic* is whether, given the challenge of ever having access to the forms themselves, we ever could incorporate them into our cities and create the incorruptible polity.

Consider here Thrasymachus's argument in Book I of *The republic*—or, indeed, Glaucon's argument at the beginning of Book II. In both cases, the arguments go: we accept the laws that rule over us as if they existed by nature, as givens. Yet both Thrasymachus and Glaucon reveal that these laws or norms or rules are not in any way according to nature. Rather, they come into being as the result of agreements amongst those who are concerned with their individual welfare, not the welfare of the whole. According to Thrasymachus's phrase—that justice is the interest of the stronger—the strong are the ones who impose the laws and they do so to serve their interests. Thus, obedience to the laws serves the interests of those who made them. In Glaucon's story, the weak are the ones who fear the strong and agree to set down laws as a restraint on the strong. Here the laws serve the interest of the weak. In both accounts, though, the legal system appears as a corruption of nature, constructed against the nature of a justice that serves the welfare of all. To deviate from the laws and norms of the society in which one lives is simply to reject the corrupted system of order established by those who sought their own self-interest in setting up the laws—be they the strong as for Thrasymachus, or the weak as in Glaucon's story.

The founding of Callipolis in *The republic* is Socrates' effort to construct a city that is pure and uncorrupted. But the very effort to found such a pure city that looks to the welfare of the whole and not a part (especially not the rulers who would rather be philosophising than ruling) falters. Besides condemning all other regimes as corrupt, it is itself flawed, existing only through lies, tricks and massive oppression. Only in the original city—called a city of pigs by Glaucon—did we find a city according to nature (*kata phusin*—a phrase repeated frequently in this section of the dialogue: 369b, 370c). But who wants to live as a pig? The purity of the city of Callipolis constructed by Socrates in the middle books of *The republic* may exist as a form of perfection in our dreams, but as Socrates describes the forces necessary to bring such a city into being (such as getting rid of one's own wife, children and property, taking all children under ten away from their parents and sending those older than ten out into the fields), it is clear that we will never find this city in the corruptible world of senses, a world of change, a world of particulars, where we feel an attachment to that which is our own.

Callipolis is Socrates' effort at presenting a perfect regime free from corruption, but he fails, both in terms of the structure of the city itself with all its deceptions and perversions and in the inability to preserve the city over time. In Book VIII, we learn that even this regime created in speech cannot escape corruption. The philosophers so thoroughly trained in the mathematical arts through astronomy and harmonics find that their mathematics fails them and they miscalculate the correct timing for the mating cycle. From the unpropitious births resulting from those miscalculations come those who care more for honour than philosophy, and the form of the city is corrupted, dissolving into other regime forms, including tyranny.

Thucydides, in his turn, has his Pericles portray a version of the perfect city—his Callipolis, so to speak—as he delivers his funeral oration for the Athenians who have died in the first year of the Peloponnesian War. Pericles speaks of the wonders of Athens, a city where

> the elegance of our private establishments form a daily source of pleasure and helps to banish our cares; and the magnitude of the city draws the produce of the world into our harbour, so that to the Athenian the fruits of other counties are as familiar a luxury as those of his own. (1982, 2.38)

The city for which the young men have died, Pericles tells his audience (and Thucydides' readers over the centuries), is 'the school of Hellas' (2.41). But Pericles not only offers praise of the city that he leads in the last third of the fifth century, he also points to its eternity in the hearts and minds of men all over the world:

> For this offering of their lives made in common…[the dead] received that renown which never grows old, and for a sepulchre, not so much that in which their bones have been deposited, but that noblest of shrines wherein their glory is laid up to be eternally remembered upon every occasion on which deed or story shall call for its commemoration…and in lands far from their own, where the column with its epitaph declares it, there is enshrined in every breast a record unwritten with no tablet to preserve it, except that of the heart. (2.43)

Thus, Pericles imagines the unchanging eternity of his Athens in the incorruptible memory of future generations, in the thoughts and hearts of men rather than in the practices of everyday life. By lifting his Athens out of everyday experience, he removes it from the taint of dissolution just as Socrates attempted to do with the forms and his own Callipolis. Ultimately for Plato's Socrates, the Callipolis he so praises can exist only in the unseen soul, not in the practices of living beings organised into a political unit. Thucydides, though, found no such place for Pericles' Athens—except in the volume that he wrote.

Neither Pericles' Athens nor Socrates' Callipolis survives unblemished. Callipolis dissolves under the pressures of reproduction, when mathematical calculation goes awry. Pericles' city dissolves under the weight of the plague, which tells citizens (and readers) that their city does not live only in the hearts and minds of those who carry the image of the city in them. It also exists in corruptible bodies, bodies that suffer from diseases, where tongues become bloody and the breath is fetid, where pustules and ulcers surface and mar the skin, where retching prevents nourishment (2.49). There is no such 'unfelt death' as Pericles imagines in his oration (2.43). Thucydides' placement of his description of the plague in such close proximity to the funeral oration has drawn forth its share of scholarly notice, but it is worth remarking again how Thucydides' compositional technique underscores the inevitable dissolution of the images of perfection when brought into the physical existence of the city. Corruption is the corrective to the unattainable *political* ideal of eternity. Both Thucydides through Pericles and Plato through Socrates look for perfection in the city, and both acknowledge the inaccessibility of that perfection. Corruption inevitably occurs.

Neither author, then, allows us to escape political corruption. Yet, despite the distance at which both Plato and Thucydides put us from such political perfection, they do offer us something to replace that world of inescapable corruption in the very texts they compose and the knowledge they offer through those texts, texts that we still read millennia after the cities they wrote about disappeared (or, indeed, were never founded). But they understood that in order to give us these lasting texts, they themselves had to corrupt what had been given. Only through such corruption could they present their new ways of knowing, which offered a form of knowledge that they could not find in politics. As we all know, Plato wrote dialogues, but before him there were no dialogues except for the peculiar Melian Dialogue in the midst of Thucydides' *History*. The radical nature of these dialogues, so familiar to us now, easily escapes us. In offering these works—also intended as homage to his mentor, Socrates—Plato is shattering the traditional genres and modes of expression for his audience.

The dialogues are not theatre intended to be performed on stage after selection by the citizens and produced with the resources of wealthy citizens. Nor are the dialogues epics telling stories in metred verse recited by the *rhapsode* to an engaged audience. Often the characters will make it clear that they are characters in a revised literary form, and that they are also distorting the content of the Homeric poems. In the *Apology*, for example, the grand Homeric hero, the beautiful Achilles, standing firm in battle, is simply a foreshadowing of the new hero, Socrates. The courageous Achilles is replaced with the stooped, bug-eyed Socrates wandering through the stage of Athenian politics, rather than on the battlefields outside Troy. The vision of Homeric heroism is corrupted to serve the new interests of the Platonic dialogue. Or in Book X of *The republic*, Homer is dismissed because he had only 'few followers of his ways' (though all of Greece may have read/heard his poem) and his Odysseus, who had travelled widely and experienced much and expressed the desire to continue such adventures at the end of the *Odyssey* in Socrates' rendering, seeks the quiet life ignored by all those souls eager for fame and discovery. The leading characters of the poets are rendered useless for their original roles in Plato's writings, where they become Socratic characters rather than epic ones. The poets themselves are shown to be contradictory (see Adeimantus's speech in Book II and the whole of the *Protagoras*) and unreliable, worthy of little more than consistent scorn. In writing his dialogues, Plato corrupts both the forms that these poets have employed and their protagonists. In doing so, he corrupts the old ways of gaining and, most significantly, transmitting knowledge, replacing those ways with his novel dialogues.

The dialogues themselves were neither performed nor read aloud as was most of the earlier literature. Thus, they allow for the private experience we all take for granted when we read our books now. They are not public performances but are experienced by those who can read and who are drawn into conversation even when there is no one physically present with whom to speak. While our reading of the dialogues may be private, they turn us into eavesdroppers on conversations which in themselves leave us uncertain about the answers to the questions posed. The lessons learned from reading these dialogues are not precise, but rather foster the critical perspective of a Socratic questioner, the one who will not allow the traditions of a society to stand uncorrupted. With a literary form that undermines the established forms of the public recitations and the performances that tend to re-enforce (or, as with Euripides, question) the societal values of the time, Plato offers a new way to undermine those values. But in doing so—in corrupting the old forms—Plato insists that we learn the importance of the search for the incorruptible knowledge that escapes the contradictions of the changeable opinions that can wander away from us. In the *Euthyphro*, Euthyphro finds his beliefs walking away from him. Socrates imagines that if he had spoken as Euthyphro, Euthyphro would accuse him 'by saying that after all it's because of my kinship with him [Daedalus] that my works in speech run away and aren't willing to stay where someone sets them down' (1984a, 11c). Opinions disappear, lacking the permanence that knowledge of the incorruptible forms might offer.

As suggested above, we might never achieve knowledge of those forms and, to be sure, as the story of *The republic* makes clear, we cannot bring them uncorrupted down into the world of our daily experiences. But to be human and not a sleeping horse (as he suggests Athens is in the *Apology*: 30e) or a pig living in the 'natural' city of Book II of *The republic* requires the examined life. Examining, though, means corrupting what society offers as given and engaging others in this process, just as Socrates the corrupter of the young does. It is the dialogue form that teaches us a practice of examination that makes us aware of the inconsistencies in our beliefs and makes us long for the incorruptible forms that lie beyond that which we can find in our daily experiences. To accomplish this, the new literary form that destroys the old is essential. Only by corrupting what has been can we escape from the old forms of knowledge offered by the poets and by the strong to serve their own self-interest.

Jacob Klein (1965) writes a book that analyses in detail the Platonic dialogue entitled *Meno*. He prefaces this work with a study of the Platonic dialogue itself as a tool of Platonic philosophy. Drawing on the discussion of writing in the *Phaedrus*, Klein focuses most specifically on the playfulness of the written words—a quality that makes them 'unreliable', unable to defend or explain themselves. Thus, Klein argues, 'a written text is necessarily incomplete and cannot teach properly' (p. 11). But, consistent with the themes of the *Memo*, Klein continues to develop the point that words serve as 'reminders' for those who know of the forms of knowledge, though they can never capture the whole of knowledge in themselves. Instead, as Klein suggests, a 'properly written text' will initiate an intellectual movement that tries to continue the conversation begun in the text and expressed by words which in themselves are playful and variable, but which can also make us aware of a knowledge that goes beyond speech (p. 11). Klein's analysis points to the need for the dialogue as a tool that can rise above corruptible words so subject to change and manipulation—as Thucydides makes us realise in his description of the corruption of language at Corcyra (3.88) or Plato when he writes about the variability of language in democracies (8.560e–561a). The dialogue form is a necessary antidote to the potential corruption of the words out of which it is constructed. Only by being able to use the dialogue to escape the playful words that always change their meaning can we move towards a Platonic vision of incorruptible, unchanging knowledge.

Thucydides, too, confronted the challenge of finding a source of permanent knowledge given his own sensitivity to the fluidity of language and the prejudices of those who used it. Before Thucydides, Herodotus had come to dominate the practice of *historia*, the investigation into deeds performed and speeches spoken in the past. He reported those deeds and speeches so 'that the things that have been done amongst men may not be forgotten over time, and that the great and wondrous deeds performed by Greeks and by the barbarians may not be without fame, and other things and through what cause they went to war with one another' (I.1). To accomplish his goals, Herodotus reported the widely varying, generally charming and occasionally disturbing stories that men tell of past deeds and characters. Some of the stories (*logoi*) he believes; others he questions. But he is a glutton for a good tale and delights in telling a good story even if he does not believe it. Thucydides rejects all this. He will not, he tells us, write a work filled with myths. It may be less pleasurable to read his work for this reason, but because of his efforts to weigh and test the evidence and speeches of others (recognising their biases and favouritism), he will enable his readers 'to see clearly' what has occurred in the past and will occur again in the future 'according to human nature' (1.22). In this way, through his careful efforts to test the information that he gets from others, the knowledge he offers will be an unchanging 'possession for ever' (1.22). He does not compose a work for the pleasure of the moment, as (by implication) did Herodotus and those who preceded him. The truths Thucydides offers will not fade or change with the times—just as the Platonic forms remain unchanging. Though the actors may change and the circumstances will change and cities will rise and fade, though even words will change their meaning as they do during the social and political chaos at Corcyra, the knowledge gained from the study of the particular war about which Thucydides writes will enable us to know all wars, all states, all political leaders as they come into being across time and space. In Thucydides' case, the permanent truth does not come from access to the Platonic forms, but from the hard work of testing the speeches of others to distil an accurate knowledge of events and circumstances, which Thucydides then writes down in his history of the Peloponnesian War.

Thucydides' history, for the most part, follows a severe chronological order as he takes his reader successively through the almost three decades of the war. Occasionally, he deviates significantly from that order, twice specifically to recall the actions of the so-called tyrannicides, Harmodius and Aristogeiton (1.20 and 6.54). For the Athenians, these tyrannicides had become heroes of their democracy, defenders of freedom, to whom the Athenians attributed the overthrow of the Peisistratid tyranny. Twice Thucydides recalls the stories surrounding the tyrannicides and twice he affirms the inaccuracy of the tales as most people recited them. In particular, the stories told about Harmodius and Aristogeiton beautify their motives—the Athenians imagine them as acting out of a noble love of freedom. In fact, Thucydides emphatically tells his readers, they acted for petty personal interests, specifically jealousy and shame—so too with the expedition of the Greeks to Troy. It was not an oath of loyalty that brought the thousands of Greek ships to the beaches outside Troy. It was the might of Agamemnon's army (1.9). Thucydides' challenge is to demonstrate how the untested—albeit pleasing—stories that marked the histories of the past, whether presented in prose by the historians or in verse by the epic poets, offered only fallible opinions that were no more secure than (to adopt Socrates' simile) Daedalus's statues. The incorruptible knowledge he teaches is neither hardly so pleasant nor so easily accessible, but it is unchanging, true across time and space, and worth the effort that he has put into it and that he demands of his readers.

For Plato and Thucydides, the incorruptible cannot be found in politics, in the particular states in which they live or in the imagined polities of Callipolis or the Athens of Pericles' funeral oration. Neither of those cities of invented perfection can last. Rather, the incorruptible lies in the intellectual access to the truths to which their novel literary products lead us. There we can aspire to the permanence that eludes the political, corruptible world of constant change.

Coda

In the work of the ancient authors discussed above, we see a political pessimism. Polities are not the venue in which we can find the incorruptible. And both Socrates and Thucydides suffered at the hands of the political world. Socrates, of course, was executed and Thucydides was exiled. Plato and Thucydides offered instead a world of escape in the incorruptible knowledge towards which they directed their readers. If we jump ahead two millennia, though, and encounter the thought of Hobbes, we find a theorist who wishes to offer both truths and polities that are able to withstand the corrosive forces that brought down the cities of Thucydides and Plato. Hobbes's writings contain an optimism that polities—through the practice of an unchanging political science that abstracts from time and space—can escape what others saw as the inevitable corruption of cities. For Hobbes, the polity can become what he calls a 'mortal God' (1994 [1651], p. 109). The mortality of that God comes not from the inherent corruptibility of the physical world, as in Socrates' story of the decline of Callipolis, but from the failure to apply the science of politics fully.

> Though nothing can be immortal which mortals make, yet if men had the use of reason they pretend to, their commonwealths might be secured at least from perishing by internal diseases. For by the nature of their institutions they are designed to live as long as mankind, or as the laws of nature, or as justice itself, which gives them life. Therefore, when they come to be dissolved, not by external violence but intestine disorder, the fault is not in men as they are the *matter*, but as they are the *makers* and orderers of them. (p. 210)

Barring external forces, the mortality of the regime can be addressed by the truths that Hobbes teaches—truths that will make the polity as immortal as a god.

Hobbes devotes all of Chapter 29 of *Leviathan* to 'those things that weaken or tend to the dissolution of a commonwealth' (p. 10). He discusses a whole range of causes for the dissolution of commonwealths—from the belief that 'whatsoever a man does against his conscience is a sin' to the insistence on the sanctity of private property and the dividing of sovereign power to reading the books of Greeks and Romans, and so forth. But it is in the phrase that the cause lies 'not in men as they are the *matter*, but as they are the *makers* and orders of them [commonwealths]' (p. 210) that Hobbes summarises all his other points. Nothing in human nature precludes the creation of an incorruptible polity; only the science or knowledge that men use to structure those polities prevents it. With the science that Hobbes teaches we *can*, he assures us, turn those mortal gods into immortal ones. The challenge is to learn his simple science. As he hopefully ends the first part of *Leviathan*:

> [W]hen I consider again, that the science of natural justice is the only science necessary for sovereigns and their principal ministers; and that they need not be charged with the sciences mathematical (as by Plato they are) further than by good laws to encourage men to the study often; and that neither Plato, nor any other philosopher hitherto, hath put into order...proved all the theorems of moral doctrine, that men may learn thereby both how to govern and how to obey; I recover some hope that, one time or other, this writing of mine may fall into the hands of a sovereign who will consider it himself (for it is short, and I think clear,) convert this truth of speculation into the utility of practice. (pp. 243–4)

Hobbes expresses in his *Leviathan* the arrogance of a knowledge that can lead to regimes that will never disappear; the only challenge is to use our reason correctly in implementing that knowledge. Hobbes's legacy here to the modern world is the faith in a reason or science that rises above the corruptibility of the physical world. Plato and Thucydides, who also see knowledge as needing to rise above the corruptible world, serve as a corrective to this optimism. The incorruptible wisdom that they offer may be the knowledge that this world is constantly subject to corruption, but the truths they offer in their own writings give one the tools to understand and assess that world, to know it, but not to dream—as Hobbes did—of a permanent polity that can derive from and match the universal, unchanging truths he claims to teach. Their texts achieve immortality by contrast with the corruptible from which they try to rescue us; Hobbes's text tries to unite the knowledge he imparts with the practice of politics itself. We find in the writings of Plato and Thucydides an ancient pessimism in contrast with a modern optimism concerning the challenges of political corruption. Hobbes sees the unity between incorruptible knowledge and the polities we can build for ourselves. Plato and Thucydides are far more timid in their claims about the powers of any knowledge that might be 'a possession for ever (*kteis es aiei*)' to transform and improve the political world in which we live.

References

Hobbes, Thomas. (1994 [1651]). *Leviathan*. E. Curley (Ed.). Indianapolis: Hackett.

Klein, Jacob. (1965). *A commentary on Plato's* Meno. Chapel Hill: University of North Carolina Press.

Madison, James. (1987 [1788]). Federalist papers No. 10. In James Madison, Alexander Hamilton & John Jay (Eds), *The federalist papers*. Harmondsworth: Penguin.

Plato. (1968). *The republic of Plato* (Allan Bloom, Trans.). New York: Basic Books.

Plato. (1984a). Euthyphro (Thomas West & Grace Starry, Trans). *Four texts on Socrates* (pp. 41–62). Ithaca: Cornell University Press.

Plato. (1984b). Four texts on Socrates (Thomas West & Grace Starry, Trans). *Four texts on Socrates*. Ithaca: Cornell University Press.

Saxonhouse, Arlene W. (2004). Corruption and justice: the view from ancient Athens. In William C. Heffernan & John Kleinig (Eds), *Corruption: public and private* (pp. 25–51). Lanham: Rowman & Littlefield.

Thucydides. (1982). *The Peloponnesian War* (Richard Crawley, Trans.). New York: Modern Library.

4. Rule by Natural Reason: Late Medieval and early Renaissance conceptions of political corruption

Manuhuia Barcham

This paper argues that, from about the eleventh century CE, a new and distinctive model of corruption accompanied the rediscovery and increased availability of a number of classical texts and ideals, particularly those of Cicero and the Roman Jurists. This new model of corruption accompanied a renewed emphasis on classical ideals in theorising the political, and a subsequent change in the way in which political life was conceived in Europe. Combining the medieval Christian focus on the importance of moral values with the classical emphasis on the value of reason, this tradition merged political and moral reason such that they became conceptually identical and indistinguishable from one another. The polity was thus seen as a Christian community living under laws agreed on through reason, ruled on behalf of the common good by a ruler who was bound and constrained by these same laws. In this new conceptual model, corruption was perceived largely in terms of the adverse consequences of action occurring without regard to natural reason, in contrast with the previous Augustinian approach that had viewed our entire earthly life as corrupt and without possibility of redemption.

The Augustinian context

Following the collapse of the Western Roman Empire in the fifth century, an Augustinian approach to the concept of the political as order provided the most influential framework within which political life was discussed and studied in Christian Europe. Augustine's work presented a political theory that placed earthly political institutions within the context of Christian theology. Probably his most radical departure from the classical tradition consisted in rethinking the role of politics and political institutions in human affairs. Augustine viewed earthly life in the wake of the Fall as inherently corrupt. He differed from earlier classical conceptions in viewing politics and political life as necessary evils requisite to achieve a semblance of order in earthly life. In Augustine's work, the idea of the 'good' life achievable on earth—so important to classical conceptions of the political or its corruption—was dropped from the vocabulary of European political discourse. For Augustine, politics was concerned merely with preserving external peace and order—not with shaping the moral character of the citizens. At best, all laws could do was secure civic order. It is this Augustinian background that provided the framework for much political thought in medieval Europe.

Medieval Europe

Medieval Europe consisted of an assortment of secular realms existing in accord with the Catholic Church under the wider rubric of the greater Christian commonwealth (*res publica christiana*). Europe was seen as a single Christian society governed by two powers with different but complementary roles: the *regnum* (secular government) dealt with temporal matters and the *sacerdotium* (ecclesiastical government) dealt with spiritual matters. Within this Christian commonwealth, both secular and ecclesiastical rulers were seen as deriving their power from God.

During this period, secular and ecclesiastical authorities were intricately intertwined; however, the church lacked a machinery of government and so the Pope had little jurisdictional or coercive power. Thus the Pope depended on the goodwill and piety of secular rulers to implement ecclesiastical policies. To facilitate this process, the church had become increasingly involved in secular government. Discontent from various quarters within the church with this increased involvement in secular affairs led, from the tenth century, to various popes initiating a number of programs of reform designed to refocus the church on matters of theology and away from the secular powerbrokering role that the church had increasingly held.

A consequence of this broad movement of reform over the tenth to twelfth centuries was an increase in the tensions and conflict between *regnum* and *sacerdotium*. As will become clear later in this chapter, religious interference in the political came to be seen as a form of corruption, based on the belief that these two spheres of human interaction should be distinct.

The conflict between *regnum* and *sacerdotium* came to a head in the late eleventh and early twelfth centuries, in the form of the investiture controversy. Conflict over lay investiture and the accompanying charges of simony (the act of buying or selling ecclesiastical benefices or emoluments) led Pope Gregory VII to declare sacerdotal and secular supremacy over all princely sovereignties. Simony was seen as a form of corruption, not because it represented the transfer of funds and favours in exchange for a particular outcome, but rather because it represented the encroachment of temporal affairs into the concerns of ecclesiastical government. King Henry IV of Germany considered that Pope Gregory VII's decree abridged his authority over the episcopacy and impinged on his rights as king. The resulting controversy came to an official end only in

1122, when Henry V and Pope Calixtus II agreed at the Concordat of Worms that secular rulers would only invest bishops with the symbols of their temporal possessions and leave the ecclesiastical establishment to invest them with the symbols of ecclesiastical authority.

Despite apparent conclusion, this controversy had opened up a debate over the relationship between *regnum* and *sacerdotium* that was to continue on and off for the greater part of the next five centuries. The major issue in this debate concerned the extent of the church's jurisdictional authority. One of the early claims by papacy supporters was the Augustinian-derived assertion that the only way to redeem earthly government from being wholly sinful would be the complete submission of earthly princes to the papacy's guidance (Tierney, 1964, pp. 33–95). In arguing this, the papacy supporters used the two-swords doctrine to support their hierocratic claims that the church exercised ultimate authority over the governance of temporal affairs (Robinson, 1991).[1]

The continuing conflict between *regnum* and *sacerdotium* over these issues was to have important consequences for the way in which political life was approached and theorised. Underlying these developments was a particular approach to the concept of politics and political life, which had emerged out of the confluence of the extant classical—particularly Ciceronian—tradition and the strongly Augustinian-influenced Christian tradition.

Political life and natural reason

In the work of John of Salisbury we see a mixing of the Ciceronian republican tradition with Christian doctrine. In his writings, the Christian ruler was limited in the exercise of his power through the use of the Ciceronian notion of the *utilitas publica* (public good), which John used to elaborate the Christian ministerial idea of rulership. As a public power subject to the rule of law, the ruler was thus the minister of the common good and the servant of equity.[2] If the king ruled in accord with the law, he was a just prince; however, if he broke the law, the ruler ceased to be a monarch, becoming instead merely a tyrant, with the rule of a tyrant seen as a corrupted form of monarchic rule (John of Salisbury, 1990

---

1 The two-swords doctrine concerned the division of earthly power between temporal and religious authorities. It was articulated first by Pope Gelasius I, who claimed that power was to be equally divided among these two aspects of the Christian world, but that true primacy lay with the church. This doctrine was to be the basis of dispute between temporal and religious rulers until the collapse of the Christian commonwealth in the wake of the Reformation and the Wars of Religion.

2 When talking about the nature of rule and discussing the character and roles of the ruler in the *Policraticus*, John of Salisbury uses the Latin term *principes* (leading statesman) rather than the term *regis* (king). This distinction is an important one for the purposes of this paper. In using this distinction, John of Salisbury signalled the continued existence of a distinction within European thought between rule for oneself and rule for the sake of the community.

[c. 1159], VIII, 17). Thus, although unfamiliar with Aristotle's *Politics*, John of Salisbury developed a conception of rule easily identifiable with earlier classical conceptions of rule. John of Salisbury differed, however, from the classical texts when, following the received dogma of the time, he argued along hierocratic lines that temporal rulers received their authority through the church, because kingship was a gift conferred by divine grace (John of Salisbury, 1990 [c. 1159], VIII, 14).[3] One of the key results of this claim was that John of Salisbury made no mention of the possibility of any other form of rule apart from monarchy, and his discussion of government focused almost entirely on the moral character and fortitude of the prince, making explicit the notion that only a good man could be a good ruler (John of Salisbury, 1990 [c. 1159], VI, 29).

This image of the political man—the ideal ruler—and the virtues he possessed was a key focus of works of political analysis from the eleventh to the thirteenth centuries. Writers during this period argued that governing should consist of restraining and moderating men so as to protect them from their own excesses, as only a man capable of submitting his own passions to reason could succeed in keeping a kingdom peaceful and united (Giles of Rome, 2001 [1277], I, 1.2). The political and the moral were therefore intricately connected, with the moral quality of rulers having direct impact on the quality of their rule 'because the lord is like the head of the citizens, and all men desire to have a healthy head, because when the head is sick, men must above all things try to have a governor who will lead to a good end according to law and justice' (Latini, 1939 [c. 1266], III, 75). Of all the virtues that leaders should have, prudence—that is, rule according to the dictates of natural reason—was the first and most important, although the virtue of justice was close behind prudence in terms of importance, because the good prince must also be the guardian of the laws (Latini, 1939 [c. 1266], II, 70–1). A man without the correct moral character would corrupt a city by bringing about division and conflict through the promotion of his own welfare rather than the common good. Such a leader would be a corrupted public figure—a tyrant.

Until the early thirteenth century, political analyses thus focused on the virtues and character of the ruler; however, the reintroduction of Aristotle's political and ethical works in the mid-thirteenth century shifted the focus of political inquiry away from the qualities of the ruler and towards an increased focus on the comparative merits of various regime types. Giles of Rome thus argued in his *On the rule of princes* that monarchy was superior to republican forms of self-government because political rule led to discord and war while monarchical rule resulted in concord and peace (2001 [1277], III, 2.3). The other major

---

3   For more on the hierocratic interpretation of the Pope as the source of both spiritual and temporal power, see Ullmann (1972, p. 223).

consequence of the reintroduction of Aristotelian works was the recognition that, contrary to the received Augustinian view, politics was a natural form of human interaction that could be seen as a good in and of itself.

Yet this reintroduction of the classical idea that politics was a good in and of itself should not be seen as a simple refutation of the Augustinian notion of politics. In fact, the relationship between these two traditions of the political was rather complicated. The reintroduction of ideas from the older conceptual political schema did not necessarily lead to their wholesale adoption but, rather, to a novel form of synthesis where the older ideals were adapted to serve contemporary concerns and interests.

One important consequence of this reintroduced Aristotelian corpus was the space it created for the belief in the existence of a form of earthly good—a form of earthly beatitude—without removing the ideal of a final Christian beatitude. This belief had been explicitly denied to humanity in the Augustinian tradition. The idea of the two-ends of man would go on to play a vital role in the shaping of political thought within Europe in the next 400 years, with its influence felt nowhere more keenly than in the ongoing battle for dominance between *regnum* and *sacerdotium*. Among the many who began to explore the various implications of these ideas none was more famous, or more influential, than Thomas Aquinas.

Earthly beatitude

Following Aristotle, Aquinas argued that humanity's rational and social capacities were what led to political government, not human sin (Aquinas, 1964 [c. 1273], Ia.XCII:1 ad 3, Ia.XCIV:4 resp). Politics was thus not an activity to be shunned but one that should be embraced as an important aspect of individual and collective moral growth and wellbeing (Aquinas, 1997 [c. 1265], 1.15.6).

In the late thirteenth century, Aquinas's Aristotelian-influenced writings were central to the renewal of the classical belief that humanity was endowed with certain earthly potentialities that could only be achieved within a human community. Civic life allowed humanity to live together in justice and virtue, thereby providing the medium by which humanity would be able to attain the moral excellence that was humanity's earthly end.

Aquinas argued that, in order to achieve this earthly end, men must practise their political virtues (Aquinas, 1964 [c. 1273], Ia–IIae.LI:2 resp). Natural law provided the framework within which the good life could be achieved, as law was 'an ordinance of reason for the common good made by the authority which has care of the community and promulgated' (Aquinas, 1964 [c. 1273],

Ia.CIII:3 resp). The ruler was obliged to keep the common good in mind when he legislated, and corrupt governments were those that were directed towards the private good of the ruler rather than the common good of the community (Aquinas, 1964 [c. 1273], Ia–IIae.XC:2). For Aquinas, as for John of Salisbury before him, a ruler concerned with his own wellbeing rather than with the common good was nothing more than a tyrant. Unlike earlier medieval authors, however, Aquinas did not place exclusive emphasis on the necessary qualities required for a good ruler, although he did agree that the good ruler was also necessarily a good man.

One of the major consequences of the Aristotelian turn in the writings of Aquinas and the other scholastics was a renewed focus on constitutional form when considering the ends of government. Following Aristotle, Aquinas argued that political regimes dissolve and become corrupt when the citizenry is oppressed by a tyrant or when factions disrupt civic concord and fight over control for the city. Since the political community must above all else be peaceful and unified, the best form of government is that which most easily secures those ends. For Aquinas, this was monarchy, as government by a multitude was prone to disunity. Hence his claim that 'unity or peace is the aim intended by the ruler of any group…for this reason any group is better governed by one person than by many' (Aquinas, 1964 [c. 1273], Ia.CIII:3 resp). For Aquinas, the best order is achieved in a monarchy where the people actively participate in the election of the ruler.[4]

Aquinas's belief in the natural superiority of monarchy should not give the impression that all scholastic authors thought along the same lines. Ptolemy of Lucca argued instead for some form of popular rule (Ptolemy of Lucca, 1997 [c. 1300], 2.8 and 4.1); however, one thing Aquinas did agree on was that peace was best maintained within the community where all were involved in public affairs (Aquinas, 1997 [c. 1265], 1.2 and 1.5).

Good rulers, however, still needed to carry out their duties for love of God and not for personal glory. It is at this point that the key difference between the classical reading of the Aristotelian need for virtue and the medieval concern for Christian morality becomes apparent. A number of classical virtues were still seen as vices in the Christian tradition and so, despite the adoption of many classical ideals by medieval authors, they still perceived the pursuit of *eudaimonia*—so central a concept to classical political and ethical thought—as a form of sinful self-pride.

Thus, the need for the good ruler or person to cultivate the Christian virtues always existed in a form of tension with the Christian perception of self-love as

---

4   Aquinas calls this type of elected monarchy political rule as opposed to regal rule, which was typical of monarchical forms of government where the people do not participate in public life.

a type of sin. Although Aquinas adopted many classical ideals, his writing was still conceived *within the context of a living Christian tradition*. The scholastic adoption of older classical ideals of the political was only ever at best partial and incomplete.

Discord and conflict in the Christian commonwealth

The emergence of scholastic thought in the thirteenth century coincided with the growth of the temporal power of the papacy. Polemical attacks continued as papacy and empire struggled over the nature of relationship between *sacerdotium* and *regnum*.

In the twelfth and thirteenth centuries, the key issue dividing papacy and empire was the Emperor's claim over Italy (Tierney, 1964, pp. 97–115). To the papacy it seemed that if an emperor claimed sovereignty over Rome, the inevitable next step would be the resumption of temporal control of the papacy—something the papacy was determined to prevent. This matter was complicated somewhat, because from about the tenth century a number of urban communes in northern Italy had begun to resist the claims of the German kings by establishing their own republican forms of government. These city-states were unprecedented at this time. Republican self-government was a form of political life completely at odds with the generally held assumption that all properly constituted political societies must take the form of hereditary God-given lordships. Conflict thus ensued between these states and the Holy Roman Emperor.

During the ongoing struggle with the Empire, the papacy had been the major ally of the city-states; however, the danger of this alliance for these republican cities was that the popes might begin to aspire to rule the northern Italian city-states themselves—and this is precisely what happened. From the early thirteenth century, successive popes began increasingly to dabble in the internal politics of the city-states. The result of this internal meddling was that, by the end of the thirteenth century, not only was a large part of central Italy under the direct control of the papacy but the curia also exercised a large degree of influence over many of the major northern city-states (Skinner, 1978, pp. 9–22). Rediscovered Aristotelian works provided the political vocabulary and conceptual apparatus through which these oppositional ideologies and legitimating claims were constructed. And, in constructing their arguments, the apologists for these new republics used a political concept that had not often been used before—that of liberty (Skinner, 1978, pp. 6–12).

The situation was more complicated, however, for apologists for republican rule than having simply to legitimate their independence and continued liberty. The continuing struggle between papacy and empire, as well as the growth of the commercial classes in twelfth and thirteenth-century Europe, introduced a number of complicating factors. Issues of faction and civic discord came to be identified by many writers of this period as major threats to the continued existence of the republican city-states. Faction was viewed as being anathema to the realisation of the goal of liberty because faction was a form of domination by others—not too dissimilar from tyranny. Faction was especially corrupting of political life because of the discord and divisiveness that inevitably arose from its existence.

Often posing this problem in terms of the ongoing struggle between *regnum* and *sacerdotium*, a number of these authors argued that the papacy was the root cause of much of the internal discord and factionalism within the Italian city-states. Thus, Marsilius of Padua claimed that 'the singular cause which has hitherto produced civil discord or intranquility in certain states and communities…is the belief, desire and undertaking whereby the Roman bishop and his clerical coterie, in particular, are aiming to seize secular rulerships and to possess excessive temporal wealth' (Marsilius of Padua, 1956 [1324], 3.1). The corruption of the church about which Marsilius writes harks back to an older argument over the correct relationship between the *regnum* and the *sacerdotium*. In their writings, apologists for both sides had accused one another of corrupting the proper relationship between the two aspects of Christian government. Marsilius's arguments about the corrupt nature of the church can be seen as yet another example of this form of boundary-keeping, which saw the intrusion of the ecclesiastical into temporal affairs as a form of corruption.

Similarly, Dante Alighieri in his treatise on *Monarchy* argued for the independence of the empire from ecclesiastical rule. In arguing this, he drew on the same basic assumptions of the ongoing debate between *regnum* and *sacerdotium* that Marsilius of Padua and the other opponents of the temporal tyranny of the papacy had utilised. Dante placed particular emphasis on his argument that the two-swords doctrine had been wrongly interpreted (Alighieri, 1996 [c. 1313], 3.9). While these theorists were predominantly hostile to the papacy, they were nonetheless still concerned with the preservation of the Christian commonwealth and the idea of Christendom—even though the church should confine its concerns to the immortal souls of the community (Alighieri, 1996 [c. 1313], 3.16). To do otherwise was to corrupt the correct relationship between temporal and ecclesiastical government.

Popular rule and the rise of *podestà*

As Quentin Skinner (1978) has argued, the most original aspect in the writings of these apologists for the Italian city-states was their assertion that popular rule was itself the best form of government (p. 61). The safest plan to ensure the preservation of peace, and thereby maintain concord within the community, would be to vest the power of government in the hands of the people (Bartolus of Sassoferrato, 1997 [c. 1330]a, 420; Marsilius of Padua, 1956 [1324], 1.12.3; Ptolemy of Lucca, 1997 [c. 1300], 4.23). If one hoped to forestall the development of factions or divided jurisdictions, the people must serve as the sole judicial, as well as the sole executive, authority within their polity (Marsilius of Padua, 1956 [1324], 1.12 and 1.17). If peace and the means to live the good life were to be preserved, the body of the people must thus remain sovereign at all times (Bartolus of Sassoferrato, 1997 [c. 1330]b, 16, 34).

While these various authors were writing to defend and legitimate the particular constitutional forms of the northern Italian city-states, a change was taking place within many of these republics. Continued strife and factionalism within the northern Italian city-states in the late thirteenth century eventually led many of them to elect individual leaders, known as *podestà*, in order to quell the discord and unrest that the continued conflict between factions within the cities was causing. The result of this continued conflict was that, by the early fourteenth century, almost all the city-states of northern Italy had moved away from their original popular forms of government towards princely rule. One consequence of this move was the emergence of a new body of literature designed to legitimate the emergence of these new princely governments.

Although this emergent body of literature celebrated the rise of *podestà* at the expense of the older forms of popular rule, it nonetheless maintained a familial resemblance to the earlier political tracts. The common good, achieved through a pacific harmony within the city, was still seen as the goal of government, and the writers of this new literature also agreed on the necessarily destructive consequences of civic discord within the body politic and that corruption would ensue if the ruler placed their own interests above those of the commonwealth (Petrarch, 1978 [c. 1350], pp. 46, 55). In fact, although the *podestà* was expected to rule for the common good and in the interests of peace, the continued discord and conflict of factionalism convinced many within these city-states that only rule by one could provide peace (Skinner, 1978, pp. 24–6).

These authors thus associated peace with good government, whereas discord was equated with tyranny and the loss of liberty (Marsilius of Padua, 1956 [1324], 1.3, 1.5). Political rule, these authors argued, was prevented from descending into factionalism and conflict through the rule of virtuous rulers and the right ordering of the various parts of the polity: 'just as a building is stable when its parts are well laid down, so also a polity has firmness and perpetuity when all, whether rectors, officials, or subjects, work properly in their own ranks, as the action of their condition requires' (Ptolemy of Lucca, 1997 [c. 1300], 4.23).

Politics, then, was primarily the art of making good laws that were conducive to the achievement of the common good. Civic harmony and concord were necessary in achieving this end and so the unity of the citizens had to be the final aim of a ruler,

> for if there is a single, corrupt humour which predominates in the whole body, that is bad; but if all the humours were corrupted, and were to struggle against each other, that would be the worst. Woe, therefore, to the city with many tyrants who did not aim at a single end. (Bartolus of Sassoferrato, 1997 [c. 1330]a, p. 36)

Despite their differences, both groups of authors still recognised a clear division between political and tyrannical rule. Political rule was rule according to right reason for the common good and not according to the passions of the ruler. In contrast, a tyrant was 'someone who acts tyrannically, that is, his acts tend not toward the common good but to the particular good of the tyrant. For this is ruling unlawfully' (Bartolus of Sassoferrato, 1997 [c. 1330]b, 59).

The emergence of humanism

In the fourteenth century, the debates between the apologists for the rule of the *podestà* and the supporters of popular rule took a new turn. Across Europe, but particularly within the Italian territories, a renewed focus was being placed on the study of the classical Roman authors—especially those from the late Republican period (Pfeiffer, 1976, pp. 3–16). Two key questions lay at the base of this new body of thought. What was the relationship between the general moral nature of the population of the city as a whole and good government? And how was the ruler of the city to be properly trained so as to possess the correct moral virtues for rule?

Humanists extended the notion of the virtuous leader to include the population of the polity as a whole. They began to argue that only when the population as a whole acted in a virtuous manner could the true ends of earthly government be achieved. The humanist authors therefore placed particular emphasis on the continued participation and interest of the general citizenry in the process of government. Not to act as a citizen was to promote the corruption of the republic and so was itself a form of corruption. In this nascent civic humanist tradition, then, as for all the earlier authors discussed in this chapter, corruption or tyranny (as it was sometimes described) arose when a private interest displaced or distorted the public interest and so disrupted the concordant nature of political life.

Despite this concern, the humanist literature of the fourteenth, fifteenth and sixteenth centuries argued that the general population neglected to cultivate virtue. So they must look to those who were more noble—those who possessed virtue—to rule them. In this view, the ends of earthly government depended on men of ability to lead the state (Morosini, 1992 [c. 1500], p. 70). An interesting example of the humanists' linkage between virtue and good rule is their treatment of the issue of avarice or greed. Combining the teachings of Roman Stoicism with Franciscan asceticism, humanist authors such as Petrarch and Salutati argued that external riches did not lead to virtue (Kohl, 1978, p. 231). Since avarice was a sin in the Christian moral tradition, the virtuous ruler ought to avoid excessive greed, as to do otherwise was to lead to political corruption (Petrarch, 1978 [c. 1350], p. 63).

The avoidance of morally repugnant practices such as avarice was of key importance in the development of the good prince, because the city's virtue depended upon its ruler's virtue. Combining the medieval Christian focus on the importance of moral values with the classical emphasis on the value of natural reason, the issue of avarice demonstrates the way in which political and moral reason were merged in Renaissance conceptions of the political, such that they became conceptually identical and indistinguishable from one another. The challenge of politics, then, was not to improve laws or institutions but to improve the moral quality of the ruler. The best way to achieve this was to train rulers in 'virtue and eloquence through the prolonged study of the ancient authors' (Petrarch, 1978 [c. 1350], p. 42).

Honour, glory and liberty

Like the earlier scholastic authors, these humanist authors believed that security and peace were among the main values of political life and so achieving them was the highest aim of government. They had different views, however, about how this aim might be achieved.

The scholastics argued that, in order to provide peace and security in his city, the good prince merely needed to possess the older political virtues combined with an inward devotion to God. The quest for honour and glory would inevitably lead to conflict and discord and so should be avoided at all costs. In contrast, the humanists argued, like the Romans before them, that glory was achieved through the pursuit of virtue and, since the achievement of virtue was at the basis of living the good life, the pursuit of glory was entirely compatible with the achievement of good government.

In reviving these older Roman ideals, these humanist authors also revived the older ideas of *virtus* and *fortuna*.[5] This revival opened the way for an increased sense that human choice played a greater role in the events of the world than had previously been thought. The humanists thereby weakened the Christian idea of divine providence that had so firmly underpinned previous political thought and writing—though the humanists still wrote firmly within the Christian context of the final salvation and the goal of eternal beatitude.

In their writings, the humanist authors also strengthened the linkage between liberty, leading a virtuous life and good government, which had been developed by the supporters of popular rule in the northern Italian city-states during the twelfth and thirteenth centuries. According to the humanist authors, a person living his life according to reason was morally free and virtuous, since the rule of the passions over reason was a form of moral slavery. In a tyranny, the ruler, who was himself a slave to his passions, dominated free men like a master dominated bondsmen. In such a society, morality would degenerate and civic life would become corrupted. Of the various forms of government available, they argued, only that which produced maximum liberty would guarantee virtuous activity. Liberty for the humanist authors, as for earlier apologists for the Italian city-states, was the potential to live in freedom within the limits of both custom and law (Rinuccini, 1978 [c. 1479], pp. 193–222).

The greatness of a city was thus held to be a direct result of the liberty found within its walls. Florence, an example oft-quoted by these authors, was free from external conquest and free from faction, and so was able to speak with one voice—concordant and united. Like other humanist authors, Bruni (1978 [c. 1403]) felt that unity within a city was of the utmost importance. Unity was best promoted when the state alone was the font of honour. The creation of an ethic of public service, and hence love of the state, would be lacking if there were other sources of honour.

The notion of the primacy of the state reflected the collapse of feudalism and the disintegration of the conceptual union between *regnum* and *sacerdotium* that was occurring in the fourteenth and fifteenth centuries. This process led to the gradual transfer of political power away from these other estates and towards the emergence of an apparatus of government that existed independently from the person of the ruler—the beginnings of what we in the modern West would later know as the state (Skinner, 1978, 2002).

---

5   Augustine had refuted the existence of the twin goddesses of Virtus and Fortuna through the claim that there existed no conception of fate separate from God's providence.

The art of politics and the art of the state

Machiavelli and Guicciardini both agreed with earlier humanist writers that the pursuit of the common good—and not the pursuit of private interests—was the cause of greatness in cities (Guicciardini, 1994 [1527], p. 87; Machiavelli, 1989 [1525], 1, 2.2). For Machiavelli, to be a corrupt citizen was to place one's own ambitions, or the ends of faction, above the common good, because to act in this way was invariably fatal to liberty and hence greatness (Machiavelli, 1989 [1525], 1, 2.2; Skinner, 1990, p. 138). As for earlier authors, for these, a corrupt city was one where laws were disobeyed and people lived only to further their own self-interest.

The maintenance of a virtuous and free population was, for Machiavelli, as for earlier humanist authors, the key to good government because it was believed that it was both impossible for a tyranny to be established when the city was virtuous and impossible for a corrupted people to establish a virtuous government. Machiavelli wrote 'that where the matter [the population] is not corrupt, uprisings and other disturbances do no harm. Where it is corrupt, well-planned laws are of no use, unless indeed they are prepared by one who with the utmost power can force their observation, so that the matter will become good' (Machiavelli, 1989 [1525], 1, 1.7). Nonetheless, he believed that this good government did not always come merely through the existence of good laws or just rule. It sometimes required employing force. He saw more clearly than other writers of his time the implications of Cicero's belief that the survival and advancement of a republic should take precedence over all things, even at the expense of conventional virtuous and moral behaviour (Tuck, 1993, p. 20). The problem, as Machiavelli puts it, is that a good man must become bad in order to achieve the goal that the good man ought to pursue (Viroli, 1992, p. 175). In a corrupt city, despotic power is the only way out of corruption and so government becomes a quest for security (Machiavelli, 1989 [1525], p. 66).

Machiavelli's contemporary, Guicciardini, was even more pessimistic in his assessment of the hopes for reform of a corrupt city. Like Machiavelli, he argued that persuasion on its own would not work because people within a corrupt city are too accustomed to the type of corrupted life they lead. Nonetheless, he also thought that trying to find a good man to rescue the constitution by force was a risky proposition. For Guicciardini, to ensure that the city did not sink again into corruption, the 'good' man would need to stay in power for a considerable time—and would probably become accustomed to that power and so not want to step aside—thus becoming merely a tyrant, itself a corruption of good government (Guicciardini, 1994 [1527], p. 139).

In light of this problem, Guicciardini argued that ruling or reforming a city required the same competence that citizens acquired through the practice of commerce and the administration of their estates. He went further than his contemporary Machiavelli in addressing the way in which rulers in the sixteenth century could maintain their position through bribery and manipulation. In doing so, he weakened the previously necessary connection between the private morality of the prince and the quality of his rule.[6] Guicciardini argued far more explicitly than Machiavelli that politics—by which he meant restraining private loyalties and reinforcing impersonal attachments such as love for liberty, justice and one's country—was sometimes not enough to ensure the survival of the city. So the ruler of a republic must sometimes, in extreme circumstances, resort to the 'art of the state'—the art of consolidating and creating private loyalties— in order to ensure the survival of the city.

In saying that there was a reason of state that transcended moral reason, Guicciardini should thus be understood as arguing that the language of politics was only appropriate within certain bounds: a republic understood as a community of citizens. Guicciardini makes the innovative and truly revolutionary leap *that in extreme circumstances governmental reason may actually justify cruelties and injustices*. This intellectual leap can be understood better through reference to Mark Phillips' argument that, whereas Machiavelli was motivated in his writings by a concern for liberty, Guicciardini was more concerned with the achievement of order (Phillips, 1977, p. 85).

In the writings of Machiavelli and Guicciardini, then, we see a number of important changes in the way in which the conduct and process of government were theorised in relation to conceptions of corruption. In their writings, the traditionally necessary connection between the individual morality of the ruler and the quality of his rule was uncoupled for the first time. This uncoupling led, in turn, to the emergence of a novel notion of political morality, whereby political morality began to be seen as separate and not necessarily connected to individual morality. Political prudence and virtue were thus no longer necessarily connected aspects of civic life; however, this disconnection was something that happened only in an extreme state of affairs. Political or civil life, for both Machiavelli and Guicciardini, was still seen as the opposite of tyranny and corruption (Machiavelli, 1989 [1525], 1, 1.25, 1.55, 3.8).

---

6   Machiavelli also argues along these lines that it is safer at times for a ruler to be feared than be loved.

The northern Renaissance and the Reformation

While Machiavelli and Guicciardini pushed the traditional notion of government to its limit, the majority of thinkers across Europe in the fifteenth and sixteenth centuries continued to write within the broad context of the humanist tradition. The private morality of the ruler and the quality of his rule were thus seen as being necessarily connected (Erasmus, 1997 [1516], p. 21); however, as humanist writers of the northern Renaissance were composing these last and greatest humanistic treatises on good government, an additional intellectual revolution begun by Machiavelli and Guicciardini was gathering force. This intellectual revolution was set to reshape the political make-up of Europe and irrevocably alter the way in which the political itself in Europe was theorised.

With the publication of his 95 theses in 1517, the young Martin Luther set in train a course of events that was to rock Europe to its very core. Dissatisfied with what he saw as the irredeemable corruption of the Catholic Church brought about by its involvement in temporal affairs, Martin Luther and others, such as Jean Calvin who followed in his wake, used their writings to repudiate the temporal jurisdiction of the church. Arguing that the church was nothing more than the community of the faithful rather than the institutional structure that had claimed this role, Luther liberated Christians from the church's claims to mediate the relationship between God and the individual. In so doing, Luther effectively denied the church any jurisdictional power over temporal affairs.

These early Reformation writings had three major consequences for the model of political life discussed in this chapter. First, the return to a conception of politics as order—and thereby divorced from all ethical and moral content—helped provide theoretical support for the separation of politics and morality that writers such as Machiavelli and Guicciardini had began to explore. Second, the repudiation of any need for a specific institutional structure for the church that these writers espoused meant that the traditional separation of the Christian commonwealth into *regnum* and *sacerdotium* had collapsed, leading in effect to the collapse of the very concept of a Christian commonwealth. And finally, the wars of religion that resulted from questioning the Catholic Church in Luther's writings introduced a period of violence, conflict and instability unlike anything Europe had seen before. In the late sixteenth and early seventeenth centuries, these three factors led many across Europe to the study of the art of the state.

Raison d'état triumphant

Within this context of sectarian conflict and religious war, the writings of Justus Lipsius, Michel de Montaigne, Jean Bodin and others in the late sixteenth century augured an entirely new conception of politics. This new conceptual framework finally severed the Thomistic unity of public and private morality that was first put to the test in the writings of Machiavelli and Guicciardini. The new discourse of politics no longer described the conflict between moral reason and the interests of the state as a divergence between reason and the practice of statecraft. Instead, it was a conflict between moral reason and reason of state. For these authors, the maintenance of justice no longer always took precedence over the preservation of the polity itself (de Montaigne, 1946, p. 388).

In this new conception of politics and political life, governmental prudence was no longer seen as right reason acting in accord with justice. Instead, it was merely the capacity to decide what was most appropriate for the preservation of the state. People began to speak of the political prudence of tyrants—something previously unthinkable. The uncoupling of moral reason and political reason was the final death knell for the model of politics discussed in this chapter. With its uncoupling, the distinction between tyrant and monarch—of key importance to this understanding of political life—collapsed. Without this distinction, the model of corruption that had flowed from this understanding collapsed as well.

Conclusion

A distinctive model of political corruption, and thus politics, emerged in Europe from the early eleventh century. In this model, the medieval Christian focus on the importance of moral values was combined with the classical emphasis on the value of reason. This synthesis gave rise to the belief that natural reason provided the principles by which human life ought to proceed. By extension, a life not led in accord with these principles was seen as being necessarily corrupt.

The clearest example was the notion of prudence. For the authors who wrote within this tradition, prudence meant ruling according to the dictates of natural reason. Appeal to natural reason led these authors to intuit that only a good man could be a good king, since the necessarily all-encompassing nature of natural reason meant that political and moral reason must be identical. A ruler who lacked the requisite moral fortitude was a corrupt ruler—a tyrant—who could not be trusted to rule in terms of the common good.

Political corruption in this notion of politics was, therefore, intricately connected to natural reason. Actions that went against the principles of natural reason—principles that every right-regarding person would be able to intuit—were necessarily corrupt. This model of political life was initially relatively stable, because the Christian and classical traditions were seen as relatively complementary; however, towards the end of the Renaissance, the increasing influence of a number of late Roman Republican authors and their focus on issues of honour and glory began to place this model under strain. The subsequent separation of church and state in the wake of the Reformation, and the concomitant separation of moral reason from political reason in the writings of the *raison d'état* authors, eventually led to the complete collapse of these understandings of political life and the associated notion of political corruption. The belief that these aspects of human life possessed their own intrinsic rationality effectively denied the possibility for any appeal to the dictates of natural reason, and so the model of corruption that flowed from this understanding also collapsed.

References

Alighieri, Dante. (1996 [c. 1313]). *Monarchy* (Prue Shaw, Trans.). Cambridge: Cambridge University Press.

Aquinas, Thomas. (1964 [c. 1273]). *Summa theologiæ*. London: Blackfriars with Eyre & Spottiswoode.

Aquinas, Thomas. (1997 [c. 1265]). On the government of rulers (James M. Blythe, Trans.). *Ptolemy of Lucca. On the government of rulers: de regimine principum*. Philadelphia: University of Pennsylvania Press.

Bartolus of Sassoferrato. (1997 [c. 1330]a). *Treatise on the government of a city*. Oxford: Oxford University History Faculty.

Bartolus of Sassoferrato. (1997 [c. 1330]b). *Treatise on the tyrant*. Oxford: Oxford University Press.

Bruni, Leonardo. (1978 [c. 1403]). Panegyric to the city of Florence. In Benjamin G. Kohl, Ronald G. Witt & Elizabeth B. Welles (Eds), *The earthly republic: Italian humanists on government and society* (pp. 135–78). Manchester: Manchester University Press.

de Montaigne, Michel. (1946). *The essays of Montaigne*. New York: Random House.

Erasmus, Desiderius. (1997 [1516]). *The education of a Christian prince with the panegyric for Archduke Philip of Austria* (Neil M. Chesire & Michael J. Heath, Trans). Cambridge: Cambridge University Press.

Giles of Rome. (2001 [1277]). On the rule of princes (selected). In A. McGrade, John Kilcullen & Matthew Kempshall (Eds), *The Cambridge translations of medieval philosophical texts: ethics and political philosophy* (pp. 200–15). Cambridge: Cambridge University Press.

Guicciardini, Francesco. (1994 [1527]). *Dialogue on the government of Florence* (Alison Brown, Trans.). Cambridge: Cambridge University Press.

John of Salisbury. (1990 [c. 1159]). *Policraticus* (Cary J. Nederman, Trans.). Cambridge: Cambridge University Press.

Kohl, B. G. (1978). Poggio Bracciolini: introduction. In B. G. Kohl & Ronald G. Witt (Eds), *The earthly republic: Italian humanists on government and society*. Manchester: Manchester University Press.

Latini, Brunetto. (1939 [c. 1266]). *The book of the treasure (Li Livres dou Trésor)*. New York: Garland Publishing.

Machiavelli, Niccolò. (1989 [1525]). Discourses on the first decade of Titus Livius. In A. Gilbert (Ed.), *Machiavelli: the chief works and others*. Durham: Duke University Press.

Marsilius of Padua. (1956 [1324]). *The defender of the peace*. New York: Harper & Row.

Morosini, Domenico. (1992 [c. 1500]). Radical proposals by an aged patrician. In D. Chambers, Brian Pullan & Jennifer Fletcher (Eds), *Venice: a documentary history 1450–1630*. Oxford: Blackwell.

Petrarch, Francesco. (1978 [c. 1350]). How a ruler ought to govern his state. In Benjamin G. Kohl & Ronald G. Witt (Eds), *The earthly republic: Italian humanists on government and society* (pp. 35–81). Philadelphia: University of Pennsylvania Press.

Pfeiffer, Rudolph. (1976). *History of classical scholarship from 1300 to 1850*. Oxford: Oxford University Press.

Phillips, Mark. (1977). *Francesco Guicciardini: the historian's craft*. Manchester: Manchester University Press.

Ptolemy of Lucca. (1997 [c. 1300]). *On the government of rulers*. Philadelphia: University of Pennsylvania Press.

Rinuccini, Alamanno. (1978 [c. 1479]). Liberty. In Renee Neu Watkins (Ed.), *Humanism and liberty: writings on freedom from fifteenth century Florence*. Columbia: University of South Carolina Press.

Robinson, Ian Stuart. (1991). Church and papacy. In J. H. Burns (Ed.), *The Cambridge history of medieval political thought c. 350 – c. 1450* (pp. 252–305). Cambridge: Cambridge University Press.

Skinner, Quentin. (1978). *The foundations of modern political thought.* Cambridge: Cambridge University Press.

Skinner, Quentin. (1990). Machiavelli's *discorsi* and the pre-humanist origins of republican ideas. In G. Bock, Quentin Skinner & Maurizio Viroli (Eds), *Machiavelli and republicanism.* Cambridge: Cambridge University Press.

Skinner, Quentin. (2002). From the state of princes to the person of the state. In Quentin Skinner (Ed.), *Visions of politics: Renaissance virtues* (Vol. 2). Cambridge: Cambridge University Press.

Tierney, Brian. (1964). *The crisis of church and state 1050–1300.* Englewood Cliffs: Prentice-Hall.

Tuck, Richard. (1993). *Philosophy and government 1572–1651.* Cambridge: Cambridge University Press.

Ullmann, Walter. (1972). *A short history of the papacy in the Middle Ages.* London: Methuen.

Viroli, Maurizio. (1992). *From politics to reason of state: the acquisition and transformation of the language of politics 1250–1600.* Cambridge: Cambridge University Press.

5. Changing Contours of Corruption in Western Political Thought, c. 1200–1700

Bruce Buchan

While the concept of 'corruption' has played a prominent part in the history of Western political thought, it has rarely excited sustained analysis. Today, corruption is usually used to refer to a particular kind of misdemeanour in public office. In contemporary neo-liberal economic thought, a primary aim of governments is to secure the requirements for a healthy domestic economy underpinned by foreign investment, and among these requirements is the elimination of 'corruption' (see International Monetary Fund, 1997). Corruption here denotes forms of behaviour that threaten to subvert the separation of government and economy, and impose wasteful costs (Dearden, 2003). This technocratic view of corruption is well entrenched in recent literature (Nicholls, et al., 2006; Nye, 2002; Rose-Ackerman, 1999; Shah, 2006). The term itself is most often used today to describe those activities, such as bribery or other private inducements offered to determine public decisions, in which public officials violate rules or laws for the sake of private, usually pecuniary, gain.

One criticism of this approach is that it obscures the normative dimension of the term 'corruption'—that is, it is a term that is defined by a prior conception (or assumption) of an *un*-corrupted condition, and hence of a particular vision of the boundaries supposed to have prevented the contamination of corruption. As Philp (1997) suggests, identifying political corruption assumes an ideal image of an uncorrupted politics. Rather than a self-evident category of conduct, corruption is a political concept whose parameters are set by an implicit vision of what the political realm actually is. It will be argued in this chapter that the concept of corruption has played an important role in Western political thought in helping to define the nature of politics itself. Over time, however, the conceptual contours of corruption have shifted, as have the ideas of politics with which corruption is entwined. In medieval political thought, corruption was a term used to trace the 'health' of the community to its moral qualities, and especially to the emulation of virtue among its members. A new language of politics began to emerge in parts of Europe in the seventeenth and eighteenth centuries, partly in response to the growing influence of commerce and trade (Hirschman, 1977, pp. 39–40). In this new language, the polity came to be conceived as an artefact of governmental activity premised on the separation of public and private interests. Importantly, this meant that the 'political health' of the polity was not held to depend on virtue (or 'political disease' on vice), but on the governmental management of separate but interdependent political, social and especially economic realms (Doyle, 2004, pp. 86–7, 93–4). In tracing this shift, corruption emerges as a very elastic term but an important indicator of the development of early modern European political thought.

The moral physics of corruption

It is a commonplace of the literature on corruption that modern usage of the term to denote the use of public office for private (pecuniary) gain has substantially changed from ancient Greek and medieval usages. In ancient Greek thought, Euben (1989) maintains, corruption was understood to refer to the process and effects of change, but specifically denoted decay or degeneration. Degeneration could be both physical and moral. In his *Ethics*, for example, Aristotle (384–322 BC) likened moral decay to physical decay by contrasting it with the optimal condition or mean:

> [B]oth excessive and insufficient exercise destroy one's strength... whereas the right quantity produces, increases and preserves it. So it is the same with temperance, courage and other virtues. The man who shuns and fears everything and stands up to nothing becomes a coward; the man who is afraid of nothing at all, but marches up to every danger, becomes foolhardy. Similarly the man who indulges in every pleasure and refrains from none becomes licentious...Thus temperance and courage are destroyed by excess and deficiency and preserved by the mean. (Aristotle, 1976 [335-323 BC], II 2, 1104a)

In moral terms, then, virtue denoted a carefully judged mean between excess and deficiency. Thus 'corruption' might refer to the process by which a virtue such as liberality gives way to vices such as prodigality (wastefulness) or illiberality (meanness). Aristotle (1976 [335-323 BC], VII 1, 1145a–b) seems not to have used the term 'corruption' to refer to any particular vice, but to refer to the fact that a virtuous person can be 'corrupted' by vice. Aristotle referred to vices that have come to be associated with corruption as a particular form of action, such as greed or avarice, as vices of licentiousness and prodigality. The licentious, he argues in the *Ethics*, are especially to blame because they voluntarily surrender to pleasure, while the prodigal are so desirous of making money that they 'take [it] from the wrong sources', and indeed are also licentious in their 'self-indulgence' (1976 [335-323 BC], IV 1, 1120b, 1121b).

In politics, the problem of personal vice is important because the inability (or unwillingness) to make wise and balanced judgments leads people to harbour grievances and form factions (due to envy or malice), and this, Aristotle maintained, was the chief cause of constitutional change (1962 [335-323 BC], V, 1302a34). Aristotle's political thought was coloured by the need to preserve the political community by balancing the ever-present tension between the rich and the poor. Rather than opting for a simple ideal type of regime, he appears to have favoured the supreme need to preserve the political community from dissolution, even to the extent of proffering advice to tyrants on how best to preserve their rule (Aristotle, 1962 [335-323 BC], V, 1313a18 – 1315a40). The political 'mean' Aristotle endorsed was a kind of mixed constitution in which democracy, monarchy or aristocracy alone did not prevail, but the finished form or 'polity' borrowed and combined elements of each. Although such a community could be described as imperfect, it had the greatest chance of preservation and longevity, and therefore of staving off the horrors of political dissolution (Aristotle, 1962 [335-323 BC], 1288b). For Aristotle, then, the political problem of corruption was not defined by private misuse of public funds, though he recognised this as a problem, but the larger problem of how to prevent the 'corruption' (understood as the degeneration or dissolution) of the polity itself.

For Cicero (106–43 BC), too, corruption could denote both a moral and a political problem. Among the injustices citizens may commit through fear or desire, he singled out the danger of avarice or the 'desire for money [that] has become unlimited' (*infinita cupiditas pecuniae*) (1991 [44 BC], 1.8). Among those charged with 'care for the whole body of the republic', it was necessary that virtues (chiefly liberality, beneficence, faithfulness and gentleness) be emulated to prevent the 'corrupting influence' (*corruptelam*) of money (1991 [44 BC], 2.15). Cicero's concerns here related to the inappropriate uses of money as gifts, presents or bribes (*pecuniae*) to sway popular opinion, but also included some criticism of the inappropriate use of patronage relations to manipulate judicial decisions by favouritism (*gratia*). It even encompassed his critique of 'maritime cities' (such as Carthage and Corinth), whose exclusive focus on trade led to luxury, idleness and 'corruption (*corruptela*) and alteration of character' (Cicero, 1999 [c. 51 BC]). For Cicero, then, corruption could be said to denote a range of moral, legal and political distortions caused by the inordinate love of and misuses of money (*avaritia*). Yet at all times corruption was a danger that could be circumvented or arrested by the proper cultivation of virtue (Nederman, 1988, p. 5).

For later Christian thinkers such as Saint Augustine (354–430), arresting corruption was a near impossibility, a conclusion to which he seemed 'resigned' (Kaufman, 2009, p. 56). Augustine's pessimism about corruption was coloured by the problem of original sin—the 'corrupt root' of human nature (Saint Augustine, 1998 [413-26 AD], p. 556). A key problem for medieval Christian thinkers was therefore how to reconcile the Ciceronian and Aristotelian emphases on human reason and moral judgment with the Christian doctrine of sin. In medieval European thought, forms of pecuniary impropriety such as venality or simony could be denounced not only as moral failures, but also as spiritual failures carrying strong connotations of the sin of avarice (McCall, 1979, pp. 24–6). According to Coleman (1988), the problem of avarice in medieval political thought consisted in the immoderate love of money supplanting the love that human beings should have for God or for each other (p. 624). The solution to the problem of avarice, however, could be framed in distinctly Aristotelian terms, requiring the restoration of the 'right order of things' by the exercise of virtues such as liberality. Consequently, the key to the public, political wellbeing of the community lay in the exercise of the appropriate virtues by its members. Historians have argued that this conception of the direct relationship between virtue and politics precluded a conception of public office or 'politics' as a distinct field of activity characterised by its own norms of disinterested and 'rational' conduct (see Génaux, 2002, pp. 107–8; Swart, 2002, pp. 96–7; Waquet, 1991, pp. 10–14). Medieval understandings of politics were often expressed in terms of an organic unity of the entire community (Harvey, 1999, pp. 85–93; Kantorowicz, 1957, p. 199; Von Gierke, 1958 [1900], p. 8). This image was often expressed through the analogue of the 'body politic'—an image that could be used to reinforce hierarchical notions of the supremacy of the monarch ('the head') or to emphasise the interdependence of each part in the whole (Nederman, 2000b, 2004, p. 61). As John of Salisbury (c. 1115–80) described it, the political community could be thought of as consisting of several connected members, just like a human body. Most importantly, John's body politic made special mention of the treasury and the need to regulate it: 'Treasurers and record-keepers…resemble the shape of the stomach and intestines; these, if they accumulate with great avidity and tenaciously preserve their accumulation, engender innumerable and incurable diseases so that their infection threatens to ruin the whole body' (John of Salisbury, 1990 [c. 1159], p. 67).

Importantly, John identified finance as crucial (for nourishment of the body) but dangerous if not properly regulated (causing disease and infection in the body).[1] While John thought it expedient for the ruler to be wealthy, he argued that the ruler must count their wealth as the people's (p. 40). John also stipulated that no-one 'who governs is to accept a present or gift, except of food or drink', although they ought not to refuse gifts entirely but to exercise moderation (p. 97). His reasoning here was that it would require 'an inhuman strength to accept from no one; but to accept indiscriminately is most vile; and for all things,

---

1 John's use of the 'body politic' metaphor (along with Christine de Pizan's later use of a similar metaphor) here reinforced the importance of wealth creation to the health of the polity, and the need to differentiate appropriate wealth creation from the potentially corrupting influence wealth might have on the exercise of public authority (Pizan 1994 [1404-07], pp. 103-4).

most avaricious' (ibid.). He was clear here also that acceptable gifts included 'perishable', consumable items, and anything in the way of money or property must not 'take on the character of remuneration' (ibid.).

These concerns certainly pertain to what we would consider today as 'corruption', but as a churchman John was also concerned with the spiritual dimension. In this vein, he spoke of corruption in the rubric of 'avarice', indicating both a sin against God *and* a failure of moral judgment. Above all, corruption was linked to the cardinal sin of pride, which he described as the 'root of all the evils that feed mortality', a 'poisonous vice' or 'virus of mortification' capable of 'infecting the vital organs' (p. 17). Those infected with pride turned away from God and towards transient and perishable desire, sensuality, money or earthly power— in short, all 'things…corruptible and false' (*corruptibilium et corrumpentium*) (p. 18). Hence, the avaricious 'love of money' that led to corruption was opposed to the godly 'love of incorruptibility' (*incorruptionis*) (p. 101).[2] In this sense, corruption could denote not simply a particular act or abuse of public office, but a whole process of spiritual, moral and bodily decay (Binski, 1996, pp. 134–8). This image of corruption, Gonzalez (2005) contends, also had strong theological overtones in medieval Roman Catholic doctrine. Corruption, so it was thought, was the fate of all human beings: the physical decay of the body was the necessary step to the resurrection of the soul and, at the last judgment, to the triumph over corruption when the 'dead shall be raised incorruptible'. Tales of the apparent lack of physical corruption in the remains of the saints was interpreted as a sign of their holiness, of their having triumphed over death and corruption and that their 'spirits live with God' (Saint Augustine, 1998 [413-26 AD], p. 1135).

The political problem of sin or vice in the 'body politic' was that if it took hold in one segment of the 'body politic' it may cause the 'disease' to spread, disrupting the relationships between its various parts.[3] While the corruption of the individual's body was something to be embraced, Génaux (2002, pp. 115–16) points out that the corruption of the body politic was something to be avoided. If it were to be avoided, some way had to be envisaged to prevent potential sources of corruption in the body politic from infecting all the other members. Marsilius of Padua (1275–1342) marshalled an Aristotelian scheme of 'temperate' and 'intemperate' polities in order to argue that 'bad' polities were those in which public authority was under the sway of those who were not motivated by or able to protect the common good. He spoke of regimes as either 'well-tempered' or 'flawed' (2005 [1324], I.vii.2). The difference between them

---

2   John of Salisbury (1909, §587c, p. 367).

3   The problem was further complicated by the doctrine of the monarch's two bodies: the individual person who passes away, and the person as embodiment of the state or *dignitas* that lives on beyond the individual's death (Kantorowicz, 1957, pp. 30-40, 407).

consisted in how well distinct and identifiable boundaries between spheres of responsibility were maintained, and especially the boundaries between secular and religious authorities (II.ii.2). Possibly betraying his medical schooling, Marsilius tends to phrase his arguments in medical terms. Hence, for example, civil strife is 'diagnosed' (*dignoscitur*) as a 'contagious' (*contagiosa*) 'illness' or 'indisposition of a civil regime' (*civilis regiminis disposicio*) (I.i.3).

When his attention shifts to analysing the specific problems presented by the unwarranted claims of the church over secular rulers, there is a detectable shift in Marsilius's tone. One of his chief concerns was that church authorities were especially prone to avarice, decadence and simony, and other 'improprieties' in distributing offices for a price to the 'ignorant, the criminal, children, unidentified persons, and those who are either detestable or manifest idiots' (II.ii.6). In this vein, Marsilius warned of the 'civil inconvenience' caused by 'corrupt' (*sacerdos perversus*) priests who can 'corrupt' (*corrumpere*) the morals of their flock (2005 [1324], II.xvii.12). Marsilius considers this a far worse danger than that of a 'corrupt prince' (*perversus princeps*) whose corruption dies with him, because priestly corruption results in 'eternal death' for those corrupted (XIII.xvii.15). In addition, corrupt church officials endangered the mystical unity of the faithful because they 'infected and...corrupted the entire mystical body of Christ' (*infecerunt...corruperunt*) (II.xxiv.2). Yet the problem of church corruption was not merely spiritual. Corrupted church officials, Marsilius argued, were likely to appoint other avaricious and criminal (*criminosum*) officials and 'men...of corrupt mind' (*corruptos*), whose perversity would expose not only the church but also 'all realms and all polities...to the danger of dissolution' (II.xxi.12). A key problem was that papal claims to supremacy (or 'plenitude of power') had been used by the church to exempt it from secular oversight. In this way, the corrupted church had 'corrupted' (*corruptis*) the morals of the faithful leading to civil strife, vice, error and dissolution of morals and good order (II.xxvi.19).

Marsilius's references to 'corruption' have a number of interesting features. First and most obviously, corruption was understood (in line with classical and Christian teachings) in terms of moral and physical degeneration; however, he used the term alongside others such as 'perversion' and 'criminality' that clearly denoted deliberate wrongdoing, and 'infection', which likened corruption to a disease with specific causes and effects, requiring specific treatments. Corruption was linked above all with his denunciations of the church, its over-inflated political claims and especially its effects on the political realm. The corruption of the church was manifested in its erroneous and self-interested teachings, in rampant sale of offices or the rendering of spiritual services in exchange for money. Importantly, those described as 'corrupt' were those least fitted for, or compromised in, exercising their authority. Above all, however, corruption represented a grave political problem in that it was closely related to civil disturbance, strife and potential political dissolution.

This representation of the problem of corruption had important implications. It implied that there were different and distinct spheres of secular and spiritual authority, and that the transgression of the boundaries between them represented a kind of corruption. Thus, corruption represented not simply a form of moral decay or disease, but a disruption of the equilibrium of the well-ordered, temperate state. Marsilius's references to corruption further implied that corruption consisted in a particular kind of transgression—namely, the control of public authority by inappropriate persons. Such misrule is to be avoided because it threatens to subvert the peace and good order of the state, undermining the advantages (*commodis*) that flow from it, including the private pursuit of wealth and sufficiency (Nederman, 2003, pp. 402–3, 406–7). While medieval thought had often considered moneymaking for its own sake to be avaricious and thereby 'corrupt' or 'corrupting', Nederman (2000a, p. 2) reminds us that medieval thinkers were well engaged with analyses of private and national wealth 'as a pursuit worthy in itself' (p. 2). More positive attitudes towards moneymaking began to develop in Europe in the wake of widespread economic changes and the development of international trade throughout the fourteenth and fifteenth centuries. Throughout the Renaissance period (c. 1400–1650), lavish consumption was employed as a demonstration of status or princely power (Jardine, 1996, pp. 327–8). Nonetheless, important doubts about the moral effects of moneymaking, and of what could be termed a 'market economy', persisted (J. R. Hale, 1993, pp. 384–5; Schama, 1987, p. 371). Importantly, early modern usage of the term 'corruption' denoted a problem that had implications not simply for the individual but also for the wider community and polity.

Machiavelli's two dimensions of corruption

Niccolò Machiavelli's (1469–1527) use of the term 'corruption' encompassed a range of distinct phenomena related by the fact that their appearance denoted degeneracy in the public, political life of the republic. Corruption could mean widespread decadence or indolence, a loss of good order and discipline among the citizens, a loss of military prowess, the predominance of faction or private interests over the common interest or the preponderance of the wealthy and powerful over the commonality. The first three and the last two phenomena are closely related, and I propose to discuss them as two dimensions of Machiavelli's understanding of corruption, first as loss of discipline or *virtù* and, second, as a preponderance of private interests over the public interest.

According to Pocock (1975), Machiavelli decisively shaped the civic-humanist ideal of the active citizen engaging in public deliberations within the *polis* by sensing that the framework of institutions that supported—indeed, enabled— such a concept of citizenship to occur had collapsed. The political world of the modern *polis*, the Italian republic of the fifteenth century (such as Florence or Venice), existed in a world of flux, indeterminacy and uncertain fortune (*fortuna*). In this environment, the idea of the active citizen needed a new foundation, a new set of orders (*ordini*) that made the pursuit of virtue (*virtù*) comprehensible. In response to this perceived need, Machiavelli provided a radically new account of the possibilities for virtue in a world where its opposite—corruption (*corruzione*)—was an ever-present possibility. Pocock (1975) contends that Machiavelli accomplished this new account by tying the mercurial concept of *virtù*, with its connotations of both individual excellence in judgment and decisiveness in action, to a notion of political virtue consisting in a collective pursuit of the health of the republic through commitment to the general good. Most importantly, he identified a citizen's militia as the vital mechanism by which individual citizens could receive training in the virtues of war (discipline, courage, fortitude) and the virtues of political stability (loyalty, obedience and love of homeland).

Republics, Machiavelli argued, could not avoid the challenges of war and conquest. All republics are brought by 'necessity' (*necessità*) to defend themselves from outside aggression and are moved by the constant 'motion' that means that things 'cannot stay steady', 'must either rise or fall' and so must be prepared to conquer (1996 [c. 1517], I.vi.22–3). Machiavelli's concept of corruption emerges in light of his analysis of the fate of republics governed by a 'mixed constitution', which was not solely produced by constitutional design, but by political contest between the forces of monarchy, aristocracy and populace (I.iii.15). The maintenance of a balance between these forces, however, is a very difficult operation, requiring the active management of public 'manners and customs' and the inculcation of *virtù*. It is in this sense that he spoke of the difficulty of re-establishing a mixed constitution in a republic that has become corrupted (*corrotto*). Here corruption is used in the context of describing the falling away of regimes from a former glory. Machiavelli's analysis here imbibes the Polybian imagery of a cycle of greatness and decline through which states pass. Conquests and imperial greatness are won by virtue; decline is brought about by the decadence that greatness facilitates, leading to an indulgence in excess and luxury or a loss of discipline among the citizens. Crucially, the danger of corruption is explicitly associated not only with those who hold public office, but also with the entire populace and the institutions of the republic (I.xvii.47). For Machiavelli, then, as Rahe (2009) has suggested, corruption and virtue were treated as *political* phenomena indicating 'the absence or presence of clientitial relations' and the either virtuous or corrupted behaviours associated with them (p. 48).

Virtue was closely associated with military service and training, and the association was emphasised in his *The art of war*. Here, Machiavelli contends that the moderns (especially the Italians, and to a lesser degree the French and Spaniards) had fallen away from their former virtues, and instead of continuing honest and wholesome had become dishonest and corrupt (1965 [1521], p. 10). The idea of corruption as a falling away from earlier virtue was a favourite theme in Machiavelli's thought. It is exemplified in a speech he puts into the mouth of an unnamed speaker who voiced the concerns of the people of Florence in 1372 in his *Florentine histories*. Motivated by 'love of their country' to complain to their government (*Signory*) through their unnamed mouthpiece, the people of Florence bewailed the 'universal corruption' that had 'infected' all Italian cities, including their own (Machiavelli, 1906 [1532], p. 167). This corruption was marked by incessant factional strife, feuds, faithlessness, avarice, luxury, indolence, deception and a general shunning of virtue in favour of whatever vice proves serviceable. What emerges from this speech is an understanding of corruption consisting of both the general phenomenon of moral decline in Italian cities and the variety of specific behaviours in which this decline is manifested and by which it has come to pass: 'truly in the cities of Italy there is to be found gathered together all that can either corrupt, or be corrupted' (p. 168). Corruption, for example, could denote greed or factionalism or indolence; but these behaviours were also corrupting, causing a weakening of public institutions and an erosion or degradation of public spirit, discipline or fortitude. In both the *Florentine histories* and *The art of war*, Machiavelli harped on the theme that contemporary Italian citizens, and especially their rulers, had renounced lives of discipline, self-sacrifice, devotion to public duty, hardship and exertion, and that such was the corruption of the age, none seemed able to deviate in the slightest from the now common indolence and to aspire to *virtù*.

Virtù has often been represented as the sum of a prince's 'manly' cunning and ruthlessness in the constant struggle to master *fortuna*; however, a fuller appreciation of *virtù* would have to include other skills, such as the emulation and inculcation of the qualities of a well-disciplined militia: order, endurance, fortitude and courage (Machiavelli, 1996 [c. 1517], II.ixx.172–3). For Machiavelli, then, one dimension of corruption centred on the loss of *virtù*; the other dimension connected the loss of *virtù* to a more modern conception of a separation of public and private interests. Towards the end of Book I of *The discourses*, Machiavelli speaks of states that are 'corrupt' (*corroto*) in the rather unusual context of not surrendering private wealth to the public account (I.lv.109–13). At first glance, this would appear to be a simple reflection on public honesty, but it also touches on a conception of the due relation between private and public realms with specific reference to finance, taxation and the influence of the wealthy.

Machiavelli developed his view in reflecting on the Germans, who, he believed, were 'honest' and displayed 'probity' by their voluntary commitment to paying their taxes and preventing any of their citizens from becoming 'gentlemen'. Gentlemen, it appears, were the chief promoters of all corruption because they lived in splendour, idleness and indulgence, possessed greater wealth and were especially dangerous when they maintained castles and retainers. Here we have a notion of 'corruption' that has two dimensions: one denoting a loss of *virtù*, the other suggesting a blurring of public and private interests weakening the 'political equality' on which the republic rested. Where corruption occurs in any part of the citizen body, it may be corrected if the entire republic has not already become too 'corrupt'. Though Machiavelli did not explicitly evoke the image of the 'body politic', he did make the analogy between the 'corruption' of the republic and physical illness, both of which will prove fatal 'unless something intervenes' (Machiavelli, 1996 [c. 1517], III.i.397–8). The autonomy of politics, then, consisted in the contest between political actors for 'glory' or supremacy within the city. The second dimension of corruption threatened the collapse of this autonomy when the public interest was supplanted by the ruler's private interests (Fontana, 2003, pp. 106–8).

It is at this point that the sting in the tail of Machiavelli's analysis of corruption, virtue and empire emerges. By means of *virtù*, leaders emerge in the quest for empire, and by means of their and the citizens' virtue republics acquire empire; however, while the liberty that is born of civil conflict in the republic delivers these great benefits, the empire that it also helps to win tempts leaders and citizens to excess and decadence, and thus to corruption. Relying on Machiavelli's account of the demise of Rome to the tyranny of Julius Caesar, Mansfield (1996) argues that corruption is 'the necessary consequence of republican virtue and, in a prince, the necessity of his nature' (p. xxxii). It is certainly true that Machiavelli traces a line that may lead from *virtù* to corruption (1996 [c. 1517], III.xxiv.269–70), but this trajectory does not seem to be inevitable. As Machiavelli's unnamed speaker put it in his *Florentine histories*, though 'great be her corruption', Florence may with 'better methods' of government and renewed purpose be 'rid' of the 'distemper that infects' the republic (Machiavelli, 1906 [1532], p. 172).

For Machiavelli, then, the problem of corruption was not simply a personal moral failing, but a political problem with systemic implications. But it would not be entirely correct to picture Machiavelli's as a functionalist analysis of corruption. As Germino (1972) has pointed out, central to Machiavelli's analysis was the idea of political humours (*umori*) corresponding with the appetitive motivations of competing social groupings (most notably, 'humouric struggle' or dynamic tension between the plebians and nobility that helped make Rome great) (pp. 67–8). As this language implies, Machiavelli sometimes spoke metaphorically of the polity as being prone to humouric imbalances or illnesses requiring medical treatment, but he tended not to use the language of the body political in any extended sense. While it would be fair to say that only part of Machiavelli's concerns about corruption related specifically to money and wealth, Pocock (1975) argues that Western political thinkers in the seventeenth century did come to share a concern over the possibilities for enhanced corruption (pp. 466–7). Their concern often related to the rise of 'new' forms of financial wealth undermining the tangible, solid and intergenerational stake in the commonwealth that landownership was thought to provide. In this new environment, Pocock argues, *fortuna* was gradually replaced with corruption as the chief danger to virtue, and the implications of this shift are most apparent in British political thought (p. 402).

Commerce and the rhetoric of corruption

While a range of European political thinkers in the early modern period thought commerce extended the possibilities for corruption, the gradually narrowing definition of corruption in this period also suggests other conceptual shifts were taking place. The changing contours of corruption can be correlated, for example, with the decline of the metaphor of the 'body politic', and the identification of new dynamics of political development focused on ensuring the financial viability and military security of sovereign states, and a political balance between newly emerging social classes. Momentum for this kind of conceptual shift built slowly throughout the late Elizabethan and Stuart reigns, during which rises in inflation and the inability of the state to levy and raise efficient taxation put pressure on state functionaries to pursue private gain through public office. This kind of concern was voiced by John Ponet (1556), for whom the good ruler seeks 'the wealthe of those he ruleth', whereas the 'evil' ruler 'spoyleth the people of their goodes' by 'making his ministers to take' them 'under the name of loanes, benevolences, contribuciones, and suche like gaye paynted wordes' (Chapter 6).

For some, the problem lay in the acquisitiveness and rapacity of human nature. Here corruption threatened when self-interest or affections overbore reason and good judgment, which was a perpetual problem because all humans were 'subiecte to affectes and all corruption' by our 'corrupte iudgements' or 'corrupte affection' (Starkey, 1973 [1540], pp. 17, 27, 39). Nonetheless, it did not necessarily follow that corruption was uniformly identified simply with the undue influence of private interests in public life. Throughout the Renaissance, patronage remained a central feature of political life at royal courts across Europe. Harding (1981) suggests that the practitioners and beneficiaries of the often subtle game of seeking and receiving patronage may have been just as keen to protect it *from* corruption as its critics were to construe it *as* corruption (p. 63). As Peck (1990) observes, contested rhetorical denunciations of patronage as corruption resulted in the concept of corruption becoming a crucial ideological weapon in parliamentary efforts to control royal revenues in seventeenth-century England (pp. 186, 203). According to Asch (1999), however, the emergence of corruption as a more clearly defined crime in European thought was a result of efforts to find a less damaging, indeed 'consensual' way to bring the sovereign to book (p. 105). The language of the 'body politic', in other words, left few options for rethinking the place of the sovereign in relation to the other members of the 'body'.[4] Recasting that relationship required a language able to separate the monarch's private person more clearly from their persona as embodiment of the 'body politic'. A narrower conception of corruption was an important tool in that quest. Adding impetus to the narrowing of the concept of corruption was the development of a new conception of the polity in which political stability was gradually divorced from citizen virtue, and tied to the effective management of the conditions favouring the development of a market economy.

The progress of these conceptual shifts can be gauged in a variety of texts from the Elizabethan and Stuart periods. Edmund Dudley's (1462–1510) *Tree of commonwealth*, for instance, was based on an alternative organic metaphor— that of the state as a tree whose 'roots' (concord, justice and peace) needed to be secured and were capable of producing 'fruits' (tranquillity, prosperity and dignity). Among the chief dangers to the 'health' of the 'tree', he argued, were simony, the '[b]eastly appetite' of covetousness and the 'venemeous core' of the fruit of prosperity, 'vaine delectacion', which 'alienate[s]...the mynd of man from god and good vertues' (Dudley, 1948 [1509], pp. 25, 26, 77). For Dudley, then, undue pecuniary interests were not spoken of as corruption, but were referred to under the conventional rubric of particular charges (such as simony) or a lack of virtue. Corruption, where it was referred to, denoted decay, 'disease' or perishability, brought on by vices such as 'vain delectation' whereby a person bestows his love 'only and intierly in corruptible and transytorie vanyitie' (pp. 94, 79). The association of undue pecuniary interest in public office with the lack of virtue, and of corruption as a loss or decay of virtue, remained in place in Britain in the sixteenth century. In a case of electoral bribery in 1571, for instance, Thomas Long was charged not with corruption, but with a 'lewd and

---

4   McLaren (1996, pp. 248-252) argues that the succession of Elizabeth I as the Protestant saviour in England raised other concerns related to the effects of a female 'head' of state . The inversion of traditional gender roles could be seen, as Knox certainly did, as corruption (Knox 1878 [1558], p. 48). Nonetheless, early modern political thought also provided avenues for representing politically influential women as virtuous opponents of corruption (Hicks, 2005).

slanderous' act (in Tanner, 1951, p. 527), while the danger of treason could be described in an official proclamation of 1601 as consisting in 'how many hearts it hath corrupted' (in Kinney, 1990, p. 326).

Nonetheless, the contours of the language of virtue and politics, pecuniary interest and corruption were changing throughout this period. In 1581, for instance, a treatise by 'W. S.' (1954 [1581]) on the impact of inflation on English society was couched in the conventional garb of the 'goode virtues' that show the '[i]mage of god in man' (p. 14). But while virtue clothed the rhetoric, the analysis suggested a new dynamic art of good government consisting in the regulation of exchange and coinage as a means of mediating between the interrelated but independent sectors of society engaged in separate economic pursuits. Nonetheless, older notions of the organic unity of the 'body politic' still made sense, as the preamble to the *Lay Subsidy Act* of 1601 shows (in Tanner, 1951, p. 612). Here the parliament could still refer to themselves as her majesty's 'faithful and obedient subjects' constituting 'one Body Politic' in which 'your Highness is the head and we the members'.[5]

Just as the image of the political community was shifting, the rhetorical appeal of corruption was also characterised by wide contours of meaning. As Noonan (1984) suggests, corruption still imbibed 'images of evil' that 'designate what destroys wholesomeness', but also pointed to specific misdemeanours such as the 'corruption of justice by bribery' (p. 322). For instance, in the impeachment in 1621 of the Lord Chancellor, Sir Francis Bacon, corruption was linked with bribery in what appears to be a consistently modern and narrow implication of the term. Interestingly, Sir Francis attempted to extenuate his guilt on the grounds that he 'was never noted for an avaricious man' and that the charges (all 23 of them) were mostly old misdemeanours that had not been continued, 'whereas those that have an habit of corruption do commonly wax worse and worse' (in Tanner, 1951, pp. 332–3). Bacon's linking of corruption with avarice and the danger of its 'infectious' spread was no more than a very distant echo of the older language of corruption as a loss of virtue.

The same echoes could be heard in the contest between King Charles I and his parliament in the 1640s, in which parliament complained of the 'corrupt and ill-affected party' advising the King who had managed to 'corrupt divers' bishops and to maintain 'pressures and corruptions wherewith your people have been grieved' (in Hughes, 1980, pp. 76–7). Corruption here meant both self-interested and extortionate financial measures and the deviation of the bishops from God's authentic word (as factions in parliament saw it). The King responded by

---

5   Here I leave aside the ambiguities associated with the legal doctrine of the 'body politic' defined by Lord Coke in *Calvin's case* in 1608, by which the monarch's private (mortal) person was separated from the public (immortal) person of the state (Thomas, 1986 [1836], p. 59).

buttressing his own claim to a divine sanction to rule by rejecting parliament's charge of 'corruptions (as you style them) in religion' (Hughes, 1980, p. 79). This exchange highlighted a connotation of the term 'corruption' derived from Aristotelian physics, in which corruption conveyed a deviation or perversion from some original state or condition. Some eight years later, in 1649, as he was about to pay for defeat in the civil war (1642–49) with his life, Charles reflected that divine sanction or no, only in resurrection could any human, even a king, triumph over corruption. Standing on the scaffold in Whitehall, he said to Dr Juxon: 'I go from a corruptible, to an incorruptible Crown; where no disturbance can be, no disturbance in the World' (King Charls his Speech made upon the Scaffold, 1649). The contours of corruption continued to shift as the very image of the 'body politic' itself was transformed by the trauma of the decapitation of the King as 'head' of the English 'body politic', and the attenuated rulership in his wake of the infamous 'Rump' Parliament (Jenner, 2002, pp. 96–102).

As the new political settlement in England was forged in the later half of the seventeenth century, corruption appeared in the efforts that political writers were making to define the role of commerce and its relationship to the distribution of power. For James Harrington (1611–77), for instance, a healthy commonwealth appears to have been one that managed to unite 'authority' or the proper ordering of laws and internal institutions and 'empire' or the control of one's enemies through popular participation in, but gentlemanly leadership of, the militia. He referred to this as 'the plastic art of government' and he suggested that 'interweaving the militia' within the commonwealth was akin to the human skeleton; it was the foundation of 'proportion or symmetry' in both body and polity (Harrington, 1977 [1656], pp. 161–70, 268–70, 299, 303, 312). Corruption referred to the process of change in both political institutions and public manners that follows from alterations to the balance between the forces of property in the republic. While stolid landownership buttressed the pursuit of virtue, Harrington and those who followed him later in the century and into the next worried about the effects of flighty and intangible commercial capital and the potential it created for the 'corruption' of the commonwealth by funding the arbitrary rule of the Crown. Nonetheless, some have claimed that Harrington's account of corruption was 'value-neutral' insofar as he argued that corruption simply meant 'change' in the political balance of forces (Barnouw, 1986, p. 63). Corruption of popular government may therefore lead to tyranny, but the corruption of oligarchical or monarchical government may lead to popular government. Corruption did not necessarily lead to chaos and decay. Nonetheless, a popular commonwealth, Harrington argued, was to be preferred because it 'bringeth the government from a more private unto a more public interest', whereas in oligarchies and monarchies, private interests (such as luxury) prevail (1977 [1656], p. 202).

An even narrower conception of political corruption can be seen in Harrington's near contemporary Thomas Hobbes (1588–1679), who was less concerned with the conditions for popular government and, indeed, considered it an anathema (Blau, 2009, p. 612). By conceptualising political legitimacy in terms of a contractual bargain between self-interested individuals seeking protection of life and property, Hobbes's thought played a pivotal role in the post-medieval rejection of the Aristotelian framework in Western political thought. Nonetheless, Hobbes's 'modernity' was still coloured by a striking use of the analogy of the body politic in his analysis of the various 'infirmities' and 'diseases' to which a commonwealth may be exposed (Hobbes, 1996 [1651], pp. 221–30). He did not, however, refer to the corruption of the body politic itself, and thus tended to use the term corruption in ways much closer to modern usage (Blau, 2009, p. 601). This is exemplified for instance in his frequent denunciation of the use of bribes to 'buy' judicial opinion or the corruption of 'counsellors' who have been 'bribed by their own interest' (Hobbes, 1996 [1651], p. 178).[6] Hence, in Chapter 26 of *Leviathan* he discusses the role and characteristics needed of judges, and speaks of the necessity that their judgments not be corrupted by reward (p. 195). For Hobbes, 'all Lawes dependeth on the Authority Soveraign' and the 'interpreters' (judges) appointed by the sovereign to apply them honestly and in line with their '[i]ntendment, or Meaning' (p. 190). Consequently, he warned of the danger of '[f]alse judgement' procured by 'corruption' of judges or witnesses (pp. 192, 212). For Hobbes, then, corruption in cases of judicial application of the law was tantamount to the vicious subversion of sovereign power, but could also refer to what Blau (2009) calls 'cognitive corruption' or the distortion of judgment by money, affection or misconstrued self-interest, all of which also subvert sovereign authority (pp. 608–12).

For a republican like Algernon Sidney (1622–83), however, the problem of corruption could not be entirely isolated from the virtue (or vice) of the sovereign. In the *Court maxims*, for instance, he posed the problem in terms of a dynamic relationship between the ruler(s), the law and the virtue of those who administer the law:

> [F]aults in the law introduce all manners of corruption into the administration of it. They who corrupted the law for corrupt ends will certainly make a corrupt use of its corruption. The effect of this is that the king does what he pleases, and the courtiers and lawyers get what they please…if there be a great defect in the law, it leaves an easy entrance for corruption in the administration…Again, if there be corruption in

---

6 Thomas Floyd described judges as the 'Phisicions of the Commonwealth' who dispense the various cures to social and political ills, and who must not be 'corruptible with giftes' (1600, pp. 86–7).

him or them who administer the law, he or they will corrupt the laws, as the depraved will darkens and corrupts the understanding. (Sidney, 1996 [c. 1665], pp. 131–3)

Sidney's language here is redolent of the ancient Greek notion of corruption as degeneration and decay, overlaid with medical connotations of disease and mortality. Indeed, the imagery becomes more explicit when he continued that corruption was a 'plague' that 'if suffered to continue' would render 'the body that was strong, healthy, and beautiful'

a carcass full of ulcers and pacrid sores. This in physics is called κακα ἕξις or *malus habitus*, which must be followed by death and dissolution; in politics it is called ἀταξία, | contrary to the εὐταξία…A people that falls into it is in the lowest degree of misery. All order is overthrown. (p. 133)

In the later *Discourses*, and in response to Filmer's notorious defence of monarchical rule, Sidney considered the chief danger of corruption lay in the sovereign becoming corrupt and corrupting the rest of the community (Sidney, 1990 [c. 1682], pp. 51, 135, 184–5, 229, 252). While his earlier imagery of corruption employed the biological metaphors of disease and decay, his *Discourses* coupled these metaphors with a strong focus on corruption as a problem of private interests dominating the public administration of the law (pp. 212–13); however, the more perceptive political theorists of the period noted that the development of commerce was transforming the nature of government and society. As they sought to make sense of these transformations, they struggled also to adapt the received language of political discourse to new realities, and the constantly changing contours of corruption were often accompanied by echoes of older organic metaphors of the 'body politic'.

Conclusion

The prospect of commerce and trade as new and influential political forces bedevilled late-seventeenth-century British political thought, in which one can detect expansive understandings of corruption alongside narrower modern understandings. In the recurrent debates between 'court' and 'country' ideologies throughout the eighteenth century, 'country' partisans might employ the rhetoric of corruption to cover a multitude of sins, ranging from threats to civic virtue from speculative capital and the encroachment of court patronage onto parliamentary independence to simple electoral maladministration (Dickinson, 1977, pp. 102–18). As Brewer (1989) has also noted, the rhetorical appeal of corruption lay in its service as an indictment of the current administration, rather than in any genuine determination to achieve wholesale moral reform (p. 74).

The charge of corruption was slowly detached from claims of moral decay and increasingly associated with specific kinds of misdemeanour in the exercise of public office. Though few went as far as Bernard Mandeville (1670–1733) in endorsing the beneficial effects of the 'slipp'rey…Perquisite' in public office, Mandeville expressed a more popular trend in dismissing the 'body politic' metaphor as 'very low' (1970 [1724], pp. 66, 72–3, 135). As even his strongest critic, Daniel Defoe (1660–1731), recognised, the development of Britain's market economy was transforming the nature of government. This would require new boundaries insulating trade and commerce against undue government interference, but also preventing unscrupulous traders from attempting to 'corrupt and procure' political power (Defoe, 1979 [1701], p. 258). Throughout the eighteenth century, free trade and good government were interpreted by European writers as distinctively European accomplishments, in contrast with the corruption, decadence and luxury of eastern societies (Whelan, 2009, p. 17; Woodfine, 2004, p. 178). Indeed, William Temple (1628–99) had previously recommended the Dutch system of government because it exempted none from the laws, it generally promoted the ablest governors and ensured that 'no great Riches…enter by Publique Payements into Private purses…to feed the prodigal Expenses of vain, extravagant, and luxurious Men' (Temple, 1932 [1690], p. 80). Rather all 'Publique Monies' were 'applied to the Safety, Greatness, or Honour of the State' in which the '[m]agistrates themselves bear an equal share in all the Burthens, they impose' (p. 80).

What writers like Defoe and Mandeville were grasping towards in very different ways were new conceptions of the polity premised on the extension of commerce and trade. Though these 'new' conceptions did not necessarily 'replace' older metaphors of the body politic, they made the application of older metaphors seem increasingly anachronistic (D. Hale, 1973, p. 70). In the terms of the 'new' language of political thought, the stability of the polity came to be seen as an artefact of governmental design decoupled from citizen virtue. As a consequence, the stable polity came to be defined in terms of meeting the requirements for a flourishing market and solvent state. Such definitions conveyed an image of a polity freed from the moral physics of decay. Polities might be well or badly designed, they may be prone to tyranny, popular disorder or poverty, but their very existence was no longer held to depend quite so much on the people's or their sovereign's emulation of virtue. In this context, corruption gradually came to be seen as a more specific problem in the execution of public authority, and its conceptual contours began to coincide more closely with the boundaries that separated private interests from public office.

Acknowledgements

This chapter is based on research supported by the Australian Research Council and Griffith University. It was originally presented in a 2004 seminar at Griffith's School of Humanities and the author would like to thank all those who participated. Thanks are also due to Mark Philp and Cary Nederman for their comments on earlier drafts and, as always, to Kathryn Seymour.

References

Aristotle (1976 [335-323 BC]). *The ethics of Aristotle: The nicomachean ethics* (J A K Thomson. Trans). London: Penguin.

Aristotle (1962 [335-323 BC]). *The politics.* (T. A. Sinclair. Trans). London: Penguin.

Asch, Ronald G. (1999). Corruption and punishment? The rise and fall of Mattäus Enzlin (1556–1613), lawyer and favourite. In J. H. Elliott & L. W. B. Brockliss (Eds), *The world of the favourite* (pp. 6–111). New Haven: Yale University Press.

Barnouw, J. (1986). American independence: revolution of the Republican ideal; a response to Pocock's construction of 'the Atlantic republican tradition'. In P. J. Korshin (Ed.), *The American revolution and eighteenth-century culture* (pp. 31–73). New York: AMS Press.

Binski, Paul. (1996). *Medieval death: ritual and representation.* Ithaca: Cornell University Press.

Blau, Adrian. (2009). Hobbes on corruption. *History of Political Thought, 30*(4), 596–616.

Brewer, John. (1989). *The sinews of power: war, money and the English state, 1688–1783.* New York: Alfred A. Knopf.

Cicero, Marcus Tullius. (1991 [44 BC]). *On duties* (M. T. Griffin & E. M. Atkins, Trans). Cambridge: Cambridge University Press.

Cicero, Marcus Tullius. (1999 [c. 51 BC]). *On the commonwealth and on the laws* (J. E. G. Zetzel, Trans.). Cambridge: Cambridge University Press.

Coleman, Janet. (1988). Property and poverty. In J. H. Burns (Ed.), *The Cambridge history of medieval political thought c. 350–1450* (pp. 107–648). Cambridge: Cambridge University Press.

Dearden, Stephen J. H. (2003). The challenge to corruption and the international business environment. In J. B. Kidd & F.-J. Richter (Eds), *Corruption and governance in Asia* (pp. 27–42). Houndmills: Palgrave.

Defoe, Daniel. (1979 [1701]). The freeholder's plea. In L. A. Curtis (Ed.), *The versatile Defoe* (pp. 151–258). London: George Prior.

Dickinson, H. T. (1977). *Liberty and property: political ideology in eighteenth-century Britain*. London: Methuen.

Doyle, William. (2004). Changing notions of public corruption, c. 1770 – c. 1850. In Emmanuel Kreike & William Chester Jordan (Eds), *Corrupt histories* (pp. 83–95). New York: University of Rochester Press.

Dudley, Edmund. (1948 [1509]). *The tree of commonwealth*. D. M. Brodie (Ed.). Cambridge: Cambridge University Press.

Euben, J. Peter. (1989). Corruption. In Terence Ball, James Farr & R. L. Hanson (Eds), *Political innovation and conceptual change* (pp. 220–46). Cambridge: Cambridge University Press.

Floyd, Thomas. (1600). *The picture of a perfit common wealth, describing as well the offices of princes and inferior magistrates over their subiects*. London: Simon Stafford (British Library 873b41).

Fontana, Benedetto. (2003). Sallust and the politics of Machiavelli. *History of Political Thought, 24*(1), 86–108.

Génaux, Maryvonne. (2002). Early modern corruption in English and French fields of vision. In Arnold J. Heidenheimer & Michael Johnston (Eds), *Political corruption: concepts and contexts* (3rd edn, pp. 107–22). New Brunswick: Transaction Publishers.

Germino, Dante. (1972). Machiavelli's thoughts on the psyche and society. In Anthony Parel (Ed.), *The political calculus; essays on Machiavelli's philosophy* (pp. 69–82). Toronto: University of Toronto Press.

Gonzalez, Jospeh M. (2005). Sleeping bodies, jubilant souls: the fate of the dead in Sweden 1400–1700. *Canadian Journal of History, 40*(2), 199–227.

Hale, David. (1973). Analogy of the body politic. In P. P. Weiner (Ed.), *Dictionary of the history of ideas* (pp. 18–70). New York: Charles Scribner's.

Hale, John R. (1993). *The civilisation of Europe in the Renaissance*. London: Harper Collins.

Harding, Robert. (1981). Corruption and the moral boundaries of patronage in the Renaissance. In G. F. Lytle & S. Orgel (Eds), *Patronage in the Renaissance* (pp. 47–64). Princeton: Princeton University Press.

Harrington, James. (1977 [1656]). *The commonwealth of Oceana*. Cambridge: Cambridge University Press.

Harvey, A. D. (1999). The body politic: anatomy of a metaphor. *Contemporary Review, 275*(1603), 85–93.

Hicks, Philip. (2005). The Roman matron in Britain: female political influence and the republican response, ca. 1750–1800. *The Journal of Modern History, 77*(1), 35–69.

Hirschman, Albert O. (1977). *The passions and the interests: political arguments for capitalism before its triumph*. Princeton: Princeton University Press.

Hobbes, Thomas. (1996 [1651]). *Leviathan*. R. Tuck (Ed.). Cambridge: Cambridge University Press.

Hughes, Ann (Ed.). (1980). *Seventeenth-century England: a changing culture. Volume I: primary sources*. London: Ward Lock Educational.

International Monetary Fund. (1997). *Good governance: the IMF's role*. Washington, DC: International Monetary Fund.

Jardine, Lisa. (1996). *Worldly goods: a new history of the Renaissance*. London: Macmillan.

Jenner, Mark S. R. (2002). The roasting of the rump: scatology and the body politic in Restoration England. *Past and Present, 177*, 96–102.

John of Salisbury. (1909). *Policratici* (Clemens C. I. Webb, Trans., Vol. I). Oxford: The Clarendon Press.

John of Salisbury. (1990 [c. 1159]). *Policraticus: of the frivolities of courtiers and the footprints of philosophers*. Cambridge: Cambridge University Press.

Kantorowicz, Ernst H. (1957). *The king's two bodies: a study in mediaeval political theology*. Princeton: Princeton University Press.

Kaufman, Peter I. (2009). Augustine and corruption. *History of Political Thought, 30*(1), 46–59.

King Charls his Speech made upon the Scaffold. (1649). Retrieved 9 July 2004 from <http://justus.anglican.org/resources/pc/charles/charles1.html>

Kinney, Arthur F. (Ed.). (1990). *Elizabethan backgrounds: historical documents of the age of Elizabeth I*. Hamden: Archon.

Knox, John. (1878 [1558]). *The first blast of the trumpet against the monstrous regiment of women*. London: Southgate.

McCall, Andrew. (1979). *The medieval underworld*. London: Book Club Associates.

McLaren, A.N. (1996). Delineating the Elizabethan body politic: Knox, Aylmer and the definition of counsel 1558-88. *History of Political Thought, XVII*(2), 224-252.

Machiavelli, Niccolò. (1906 [1532]). *Florentine histories* (N. H. Thomson, Trans., Vol. 1). London: Archibald Constable.

Machiavelli, Niccolò. (1965 [1521]). *The art of war* (E. Farneworth, Trans.). New York: Da Capo.

Machiavelli, Niccolò. (1996 [c. 1517]). *Discourses on Livy* (H. C. Mansfield & N. Tarcov, Trans). Chicago: University of Chicago Press.

Mandeville, Bernard. (1970 [1724]). *Fable of the bees and remarks*. Philip Harth (Ed.). London: Penguin.

Mansfield, Harvey C. (1996). Introduction. In Niccolò Machiavelli, *Discourses on Livy*. Chicago: University of Chicago Press.

Marsilius of Padua. (2005 [1324]). *The defender of the peace* (Annabel Brett, Trans.). Cambridge: Cambridge University Press.

Nederman, Cary J. (1988). Nature, sin and the origins of society: the Ciceronian tradition in medieval political thought. *Journal of the History of Ideas, 49*(1), 3–26.

Nederman, Cary J. (2000a). Community and the rise of commercial society: political economy and political theory in Nicholas Oresme's *De Moneta*. *History of Political Thought, XXI*(1), 1–15.

Nederman, Cary J. (2000b). The expanding body politic: Christine de Pizan and the medieval roots of political economy. Paper presented at the Au Champ Des Escriptures: IIIe Colloque International sur Christine de Pizan, Paris.

Nederman, Cary J. (2003). Community and self-Interest: Marsiglio of Padua on civil life and private advantage. *The Review of Politics, 65*(4), 395–416.

Nederman, Cary J. (2004). Body politics: the diversification of organic metaphors in the later Middle Ages. *Pensiero Politico Medievali, 2*, 59–87.

Nicholls, Colin, Daniel, Tim, Polaine, Martin, & Hatchard, John (Eds). (2006). *Corruption and misuse of public office*. Oxford: Oxford University Press.

Noonan, John Thomas. (1984). *Bribes: the intellectual history of a moral idea*. Berkeley: University of California Press.

Nye, Joseph S. (2002). Corruption and political development: a cost–benefit analysis. In Arnold J. Heidenheimer & Michael Johnston (Eds), *Political corruption: concepts and contexts* (3rd edn, pp. 281–302). New Brunswick: Transaction Publishers.

Peck, Linda Levy. (1990). *Court patronage and corruption in early Stuart England*. Boston: Unwin Hyman.

Philp, Mark. (1997). Defining political corruption. *Political Studies, 45*, 436–62.

Pizan, Christine. (1994 [1404-07]). *The book of the body politic*. (K.L. Forhan. Trans. and ed.), Cambridge: Cambridge University Press.

Pocock, J. G. A. (1975). *The Machiavellian moment: Florentine political thought and the Atlantic republican tradition*. Princeton: Princeton University Press.

Ponet, John. (1556). *A short treatise of politik power*. London: British Library (W462573).

Rahe, Paul Anthony. (2009). *Against throne and altar: Machiavelli and political theory under the English republic*. Cambridge: Cambridge University Press.

Rose-Ackerman, Susan. (1999). *Corruption and government: causes, consequences and reform*. Cambridge and New York: Cambridge University Press.

Schama, Simon. (1987). *The embarrassment of riches: an interpretation of Dutch culture in the golden age*. London: Fontana.

Shah, Anwar. (2006). Corruption and decentralized public governance. *Policy Research Working Paper WPS 3824* (pp. 1–28). Washington, DC: The World Bank.

Sidney, Algernon. (1990 [c. 1682]). *Discourses concerning government*. Indianapolis: Liberty Classics.

Sidney, Algernon. (1996 [c. 1665]). *Court maxims*. Hans W. Blom, Eco Haitsma-Mulier and Ronald Janse (Eds). Cambridge: Cambridge University Press.

Saint Augustine. (1998 [413-26AD]). *The city of God against the pagans* (R. W. Dyson, Trans.). Cambridge: Cambridge University Press.

Starkey, Thomas. (1973 [1540]). *Exhortation to unitie and obedience.* Amsterdam and New York: Theatrum Orbis Terrarum and Da Capo Press.

Swart, Koenraad W. (2002). The sale of public offices. In Arnold J. Heidenheimer & Michael Johnston (Eds), *Political corruption: concepts and contexts* (3rd edn, pp. 95–106). New Brunswick: Transaction Publishers.

Tanner, J. R. (1951). *Tudor constitutional documents AD 1485–1603 with an historical commentary* (2nd edn). Cambridge: Cambridge University Press.

Temple, William. (1932 [1690]). *Observations upon the united provinces of the Netherlands.* Cambridge: Cambridge University Press.

Thomas, John Henry. (1986 [1836]). *Systematic arrangement of Lord Coke's first institute of the laws of England* (Vol. 2). Buffalo: William S. Hein.

Von Gierke, Otto. (1958 [1900]). *Political theories of the Middle Age* (F. W. Maitland, Trans.). Boston: Beacon Press.

W. S. (1954 [1581]). *A discourse of the common weal of this realm of England.* Elizabeth Lamond (Ed.). Cambridge: Cambridge University Press.

Waquet, Jean-Claude. (1991). *Corruption: ethics and power in Florence, 1600–1770* (Linda McCall, Trans.). Cambridge: Polity.

Whelan, Frederick G. (2009). *Enlightenment, political thought and non-Western societies.* New York: Routledge.

Woodfine, Philip. (2004). The rhetoric and practice of corruption in Walpolean politics. In Emmanuel Kreike & William Chester Jordan (Eds), *Corrupt histories* (pp. 167–96). New York: University of Rochester Press.

6. Ideas of Corruption in the Eighteenth Century: The competing conceptions of Adam Ferguson and Adam Smith

Lisa Hill

Although the eighteenth century is generally conceived as the age of progress and optimism, many eighteenth-century thinkers believed the world was in its senility. Such fears focused on a concern for the dissipation of virtue and this became one of the most urgent problems of political philosophy in the eighteenth century (Pocock, 1975, p. 462). Like many of their contemporaries in the Scottish Enlightenment, Adam Ferguson (1723–1816) and Adam Smith (1723–90) were intensely interested in the development of commercialism and the accompanying social, political and material changes that were taking place in the latter half of the eighteenth century. Their resulting observations generated, arguably, the two most sophisticated early sociologies to date. But their approaches differed considerably. Although they both perceived in commercialism the potential for corruption, their aetiologies were vastly different. Ferguson, who is well recognised as a thinker absorbed with the problem of corruption, classically understood, was deeply ambivalent about progress. Though he welcomed many of its aspects as both natural and inevitable, he also expressed alarm at some of its effects on virtue and social intimacy. Drawing inspiration from classical sources, he was concerned with how much was lost in the seemingly inexorable march towards progress. By his account, community, social intimacy, intensely emotional friendships and alliances, martial vigour and civil vitality were all casualties of the commercial age.

Smith, on the other hand, is rarely associated with standard classical themes of corruption, perhaps because he was basically optimistic about the effects of commercialism. But, as I hope to show here, he also noticed that the commercial age embodied a number of corrupting pathologies. Unlike Ferguson, for Smith, these did not take the forms usually associated with the classical tradition. Smith's vision is basically modern, representing his determination to make a decisive break with the past, a past to which Ferguson remains stubbornly loyal.

One significant aspect of the thoughts of these two figures is that, together, they signpost a transitional moment in understandings of the term 'corruption'. It was during the eighteenth century that the modern conception of corruption came to overtake the classical, and by the nineteenth century this transformation had consolidated so that the term 'corruption' was rarely used in the classical sense. That the eighteenth century was a period of flux is reflected in the fact that two contemporaneous figures who were also friends could entertain vastly different understandings of the term. Ferguson represents the past in adopting a standard, classical approach to the topic, whereas Smith is moving towards a more modern, proto-liberal conception.

The disagreements between Smith and Ferguson about what 'corruption' consisted in turn on their more general attitude to progress and the commercial age. For Ferguson, corruption is understood as a progress-induced decline in civic virtue and effective political condition. Smithian corruption consists in violations of the system of natural liberty, including violations that corrupt the naturally self-governing behaviour of individual actors. In other words, corruption is instigated by obstructions to the 'natural' course of progress rather than by progress itself. In consequence, more progress is generally his solution to any of the pathologies of modernity. According to Smith, pre-commercial society generates corruption because of its tendency to discourage individual autonomy on the one hand, and interfere with the natural laws of the market on the other. Amongst these corrupting remnants of pre-commercial stages are political faction and paternalistic forms of governance, which should be purged in order to secure the commercial stage from decline.

Ferguson's approach

Like many classical authors, as well as more modern ones including Rousseau and Montesquieu, Ferguson conceives moral corruption as a problem of virtue. Loss of virtue was the cost of greatness, and he believed that political decline was more likely in prosperous empires. His declared purpose in writing the *Essay on the history of civil society* (1767) was 'to describe that remissness of spirit...that state of national debility, which is likely to end in political slavery' (Ferguson, 1996 [1767]a, p. 247).

Ferguson takes his conception of corruption from Polybius, as did Machiavelli. For Machiavelli, it represented any form of deterioration in the quality of government.[1] Ferguson agreed that corruption could affect people, not only individually but also en masse, denoting pervasive attitudinal and behavioural trends in a given polity (Shumer, 1979, p. 9). Polybius identified two possible sources of decay from natural causes: the 'external which has no fixed nature' and the 'internal' and 'self produced', which 'follows a definite order' (1979 [c. 110 BC], 6.57, p. 150). The latter, endogenous type of decay is the focus of

---

1 The term also started to become synonymous with bribery during this period. This latter, exclusively monetary meaning eventually replaced the Machiavellian meaning (Hirschman, 1977, pp. 40–1).

Ferguson's concern (Ferguson, 1996 [1767]a, p. 212). Another important source for Ferguson is Stoicism. Stoic writings focused on the cultivation of virtues of 'life conduct' to be practised by both rulers and the ruled as a method for preventing corruption and for maintaining the strength and stability of the state. Consequently, their approach to political life was always highly normative and prescriptive (Robertson, 1983, pp. 137–8). Ferguson carefully studied and adopted Stoic ideas.

Causes of degeneration

Like Polybius before him, Ferguson sought to identify the variables leading to imperial atrophy. He relates corruption to changes in conditions that work to debase civic 'spirit': specialisation, overextension and hedonism. Though many of Ferguson's insights here are prescient of much nineteenth-century sociology (Hill, 1996), his aetiology of modern corruption is linked to his views on the causes of the decline of Republican Rome, all of which could be traced, in turn, to the triumph of Epicureanism over Stoicism. Epicureanism described a godless world governed by chance, reduced morality to hedonism and taught that 'all good was private'. Devotion to its tenets resulted in prodigality and ruination (Ferguson, 1834 [1783], pp. 169–70, 305–6), while the cure lay in the teachings of Stoicism (p. 170).

Ferguson tells us that 'nations cease to be eminent' when the citizen's active nature is deprived of 'objects which served to excite (his) spirit' (Ferguson, 1996 [1767]a, p. 200). A healthy state needs a vigorous, civically virtuous and active public; without it, dissipation sets in and despotism soon follows. History teaches that nations characterised by high levels of political apathy are extremely susceptible to despotic and praetorian rule. This fear of 'military government' was a longstanding one and is constantly reiterated in all Ferguson's published works and private correspondence.

Another major cause of corruption is overextension: the growth of small-scale communities into impersonal, unwieldy cities and empires (Ferguson, 1996 [1767] a, p. 257). The tendency towards urbanisation is exacerbated by an overzealous enlargement of state territory; both trends lead to over-bureaucratisation, overcentralisation and loss of social intimacy.

The newly emerging commercial ethic was also a major source of corruption. As Ferguson saw it, the commercial imperative erodes communal sentiments, while the division of labour brings on bureaucratisation. Both tendencies limit mass engagement in civic life (1996 [1767]a, p. 178). Due to the ever-increasing refinement of task specialisation, individuals become alienated from public affairs and tend to withdraw into their private, individuated, commercial concerns. To use Ferguson's terminology, the 'separation of professions...loosen(s) the bands of political union' (pp. 206–9).

Perhaps most importantly, specialisation means professional standing armies. This tendency erodes martial and communal ardour and undermines social cohesion. The loss of martial virtue is fatal to the moral personality. Ferguson lavishly idealised the warrior-statesman of classical reports, insisting that citizens should also be soldiers (1996 [1767]a, p. 149). Lamenting the increasing 'effeminacy' of commercial cultures, he insisted on the naturalness of our belligerent tendencies, arguing that they serve a valuable function in the formation of the moral personality by 'furnish[ing] a scene for the exercise of our greatest abilities'. These qualities 'are sentiments of generosity and self-denial that animate the warrior in defence of his country' (p. 28). The use of standing armies deprives a people of their military valour (Ferguson, 1996b, pp. 142–3), their 'dignity and strength' (1756, p. 13), their enjoyment of the highest virtues and, in the end, national security itself (p. 36).

Coupled with the new spirit of commercialism, the division of labour causes 'members of a community...to lose the sense of every connection'. They have 'no common affairs to transact but those of trade', therefore 'the national spirit... cannot be exerted'. Ferguson compares commercial society unfavourably with simple or 'barbarous' nations where 'the public is a knot of friends' bound by a sense of common danger (Ferguson, 1996 [1767]a, p. 208).

Perhaps surprisingly, Ferguson rejects out of hand neither progress nor commercialism, because both are natural, inevitable and even *designed* events (see, for example, Ferguson, 1792, p. 199, 1878 [1769], pp. 90, 126). Rather, the best way to avoid impending political slavery is to offset the ill effects of progress by enhancing civic competence and awareness (Ferguson, 1996 [1767]a, p. 224; Wilkie, 1962, p. 172). In order for nations to be 'powerful and safe, they must strive to maintain the courage and cultivate the virtues of their people' (Ferguson, 1996 [1767]a, p. 61). It is not enough to simply have sound 'political establishments'; rather, the integrity of a constitution lies ultimately in the hands of the public and in its 'firm and resolute spirit' (p. 266) and determination to 'resist indignities' (p. 251). Political elites must devise the proper political arrangements by which inactive and apathetic citizens are distracted from their narrow, self-regarding concerns and enabled to redirect their attention to the public sphere (McDowell, 1983, pp. 546–7).

Citizen militias are one answer (Ferguson, 1996b, pp. 141–51) and one that Smith basically opposed (see below). Another is the encouragement of political activism and conflict but only within the context of a mixed constitution (Ferguson, 1834 [1783], p. 407, 1996 [1767]a, p. 252). Ferguson endorses the argument first set out by Polybius that the Romans maintained free constitutions 'not…by means of abstract reasoning, but rather through the lessons learned from many struggles and difficulties' and through the adoption of reforms indicated by 'the light of experience' (Polybius, 1979 [c. 110 BC], p. 311). Similarly, Machiavelli saw '[c]onflict, dissensions and even enmity' as 'the natural stuff of politics' (Shumer, 1979, p. 14).[2] According to Ferguson, although factional 'divisions…seem to endanger' the very existence of society, in fact it is faction that preserves its vitality by providing postures and roles for 'the scene that is prepared for the instruction of its members' (Ferguson, 1792, 1, p. 267). Ferguson goes so far as to endorse Plutarch's advice that legislators should deliberately encourage factional dispute.[3] So long as factional conflict is tolerated, accommodated and perhaps even encouraged, there will always be 'wise establishments' advantageous to 'Liberty and Just Government' (Ferguson, 1756, p. 2).

Smith's approach

A number of scholars have argued that Smith shares Ferguson's apparent pessimism about the corrupting tendencies of the commercial age (see, for example, Alvey, 1998; Brown, 1994; Rosenberg, 1965; Winch, 1997) and even that he perceives in 'capitalism' the seeds of its own inevitable destruction (Heilbroner, 1973; Pack, 1991). This is likely an overstatement of Smith's position, as will be shown.

Causes of corruption

Although Smith does show an interest in the link between economic growth and corruption, his conception is far from classical. In general terms, since the forms of corruption he identifies could all be described as sins against proto-liberal sensibilities, it is fair to say that he was working towards a 'modern' conception of the term. Eighteenth-century politics has been characterised as 'a racket, run by particular groups within the ruling classes largely for their own benefit' (Corrigan & Sayer, 1985, p. 89). In a sense, most proto-liberalism was, almost by definition, an implicit reaction to such corruption (understood here in its modern sense) and Smith can, with confidence, be described as a proto-liberal, due to his concerted defence of such standard liberal values as impartiality, universalism, neutrality, formal equality of opportunity and rule of law in his campaign against corruption.

---

2 A section of the *Discourses* is even entitled 'That discord between the Plebs and the Senate of Rome made this republic both free and powerful' (Machiavelli, 1998, I.4, p. 113).
3 Ferguson paraphrases Plutarch here: '(G)ood citizens should be led to dispute' (Ferguson, 1996 [1767]a, p. 63).

Yet his analysis does embody two features typical of a classical approach. The first is the broadness of his definition of corruption, which is not restricted to violations of the public interest by its servants, but which is understood as a condition capable of radiating diffusely throughout entire societies, permeating all its formal and informal institutions. Second, Smith clearly has in mind the standard classical dichotomy of the healthy versus the corrupt republic,[4] and even agrees that the former is upheld by the virtue of its members and not simply its leadership. But it is important to be aware that such virtue is no recognisable classical type and that his good republic bears little or no substantive resemblance to the classical ideal. In fact, it is a comparatively tepid model, politically speaking, relying as it does on a well-regulated leadership and a quiescent, orderly, self-governing public. While Smith is definite that virtue is the main guard against social and economic corruption, the virtues he valorises and promotes are private and commercial rather than civic, other-regarding ones: the tame, cool virtues of the 'middling' ranks. These are the virtues of prudence, justice, propriety, self-command, frugality, sobriety, vigilance, circumspection, temperance, constancy, firmness, punctuality, faithfulness, enterprise and industry (Smith, 1976, III.5.8, p. 166, VII.ii.3.15, p. 304, 1979, II.iii.36, pp. 345–6). Moreover, and in direct contrast with Ferguson, they are generated outside politics and exclusivist social units like the extended family,[5] the village, the *umma* or the feudal estate. Instead, they are forged in the impersonal, universalistic marketplace of commercial strangers.

The good polity is the natural market economy of self-regarding, lawful and mutually forbearing agents. Moral corruption does not arise from political apathy, selfishness or an inattention to the public sphere (as per classical and Fergusonian accounts) but is a product of a variety of sources that Smith regarded as outmoded remnants of a pre-commercial age—namely, institutional and legal impediments to the development of independent moral character (monopolies, poor laws, corporation laws, apprenticeship laws and regulations governing the institutions of entail and primogeniture) as well as political zealotry and factional conflict. These sources could not only corrupt individual agents but they could also threaten the prosperity and security of entire nations. Although it should be noted that Smith identifies an additional and genuinely 'modern' source of moral corruption (the division of labour), he insists that its effects are far from fatal and could be satisfactorily addressed within existing social arrangements (to be discussed further).

4   As Shumer (1979) notes: 'Corruption must be understood in relationship to its mirror-image concept, the healthy republic' (p. 8).
5   The nuclear family is, however, still seen to play a key role in the development of moral character.

Perhaps Smith's idea of corruption can be best understood in the technical dictionary sense, as a deviation from a sound or *natural* condition.[6] Smith does not really posit an ideal (sound) constitution or polity either from which societies deviated or towards which societies should gravitate. He is more interested in deviations from a state properly regulated by spontaneous *laws of nature* that he believed governed the entire universe, including societies, economies and even individual agents. There is a natural, *spontaneous* order that should not be interfered with—namely, the system of natural liberty and the market.

The system of 'natural liberty': The market as a natural, uncorrupted order

For Smith, beneath the complex of artificially imposed institutional constraints on human behaviour there exists a system of natural and spontaneous economic relations, which, when allowed to, functions harmoniously. In the system of 'natural liberty' each person is by nature the best judge of her own interest and should therefore be left unhindered to pursue it in her own way. In this manner, she is able to achieve not only her own best advantage, but that of society as well. In the spontaneous order of the market, government can rarely be more effective than when it is restrained and, for the most part, absent (Smith, 1979, IV.ix.51, pp. 687–8). Neither should monolithic private entities like the East India Company presume to interfere in the regular and self-equilibrating rhythms of this order. Smith regards interference with these spontaneous physics as a form of corruption—that is, a rebellion against nature; meddling from an assumed Archimedean perspective is extremely hurtful to 'the natural state of commerce' (Smith, 1978, [B], 306–7, p. 529).

Economic agents must be permitted the freest possible use of their bodies, minds and properties, provided that they do not themselves violate either the public interest or the system of natural liberty. Smith condemned regulations such as poor laws, corporation privileges, statutes of apprenticeship and restrictions on international trade as violations of a person's 'natural' rights (1979, IV.ix.51, p. 687). England's poor laws (and to a lesser degree its corporation laws) were the most pernicious constraint on such freedoms and were detrimental to both individual and public welfare.[7] Similarly, the laws of apprenticeship were egregious, not only because they were an impediment to the mobility of labour, but also because of their tendency to discourage industry and commercial effort (Rosenberg, 1960, p. 561; Smith, 1979, I.x.c. 14–16, pp. 139–40).

---

6   As Mark Philp (1997) notes, the term corruption is 'rooted in the sense of a thing being changed from its naturally sound condition, into something unsound, impure, debased, infected, tainted, adulterated, depraved [or] perverted' (pp. 24–5).

7   Poor laws were more pernicious than corporation laws because they disproportionately disadvantaged the poor (Smith, 1979, I.x.c.44–5, p. 152).

Other corrupting obstructions are typified by the partial and particularistic laws of entail and primogeniture, which Smith describes as 'contrary to nature, to reason, and to justice' (1978, [A], i.116, p. 48), 'founded' as they are 'upon the most absurd of all suppositions...that every successive generation of men have not an equal right to the earth, and to all that it possesses' (1979, III.ii.6, p. 384). Not only is this system of inheritance inequitable, it is also extremely maladaptive from an economic point of view due to its tendency to hinder agriculture and development (1979, III.ii.7, p. 385, III.iv.19, p. 423).

'Dependency' and the violation of natural liberty

Apart from their negative effects at the social-systems level, violations of the laws of natural liberty also have pernicious effects at the individual level on moral character. Once again, however, Smith's discussion of the corruption of moral character bears little resemblance to antique virtue discourses. His focus is on the preservation of commercial virtues such as economic independence, self-government and enterprise. Dependency, in particular, is a key source of moral corruption, and Smith roundly condemns any paternalistic and dependency-generating remnants of pre-commercial economic stages, most notably the necessary dependence associated with the feudal system of great landholders and retainers. 'Dependency' is pernicious because it breeds servility and fosters asymmetrical and therefore unhealthy and unproductive social relations (Smith, 1979, I.i.2, pp. 27, III.iv.4–7, pp. 412–15). Because of the poverty and indolence it promotes, dependency is also the source of all the 'disorder and confusions' that take place in cities. The best remedy is, of course, the expansion of 'commerce' (1978, [A], v.4–8, pp. 332–3). Because of its capacity to encourage 'independency', the growth of 'commerce and manufactures' is also 'the best police for preventing crimes' since '[n]o body will be so mad as to expose himself upon the highway, when he can make better bread in an honest and industrious manner' (1978, [B], 205, pp. 486–7).

Pre-commercial agents were limited by the fact that they had 'no other means of persuasion' by which to obtain their wants than to 'gain the favour of those whose service' was required. That meant having to resort to the debasing, inefficient and precarious method of 'servile and fawning attention' in order to 'obtain [the] good will' of others (1978, [A], vi.46–9, pp. 348–9). But in 'civilized society' agents are afforded greater independence, paradoxically, because each 'stands at all times in need of the co-operation and assistance of great multitudes'. The ability of humans to specialise and exchange the products of this specialisation makes them 'mutually beneficiall to each other' (1978, [A], vi.46–9, pp. 348–9). The dissolution of the system of great landholders decentralised dependency relations and offered greater security to individual tradespeople: now '[e]ach tradesman or artificer derives his subsistence from the employment, not of one, but of a hundred or a thousand customers.' This is a good thing because '[s/] he is not absolutely dependent upon any one of them' (1979, III.iv, p. 420). Rather than damaging the social fabric (as Adam Ferguson had suggested), specialisation generates unprecedented levels of mutuality. Associations are now increasingly voluntaristic, egalitarian and mutually beneficial—a matter of purely instrumental mutual 'good offices' (1979, I.ii.2, p. 26).

It is worth noting here that there is an initially confusing chapter of *The theory of moral sentiments* that Smith added to the sixth edition. In it, he seems to be suggesting that commercial life does, in fact, corrupt virtue. In an excursus on the apparently universal desire to emulate the rich via the pursuit of luxury status goods, Smith refers to this desire as a 'corruption' of virtue and 'our moral sentiments' as classically understood:

> This disposition to admire, and almost to worship, the rich and the powerful, and to despise, or, at least, to neglect persons of poor and mean condition…is…the great and most universal cause of the corruption of our moral sentiments. That wealth and greatness are often regarded with the respect and admiration which are due only to wisdom and virtue; and that the contempt, of which vice and folly are the only proper objects, is often most unjustly bestowed upon poverty and weakness, has been the complaint of moralists in all ages.

Smith continues by observing with dismay that in polite society, all the best virtues are 'held in the utmost contempt and derision' (1976, I.iii.3, 6, p. 63). In the normal course of events the superficial trappings of greatness are the ones that are appreciated while real virtue goes unnoticed and unvalued. In these passages, Smith seems to echo Ferguson's classically inspired idealisation of warrior cultures: 'the frivolous accomplishments of that impertinent and foolish thing called a man of fashion, are commonly more admired than the solid and masculine virtues of a warrior, a statesman, a philosopher, or a legislator.' The admiration we reserve for 'mere wealth and greatness' seems morally suspect and yet it is an empirical fact that this is how the majority of people tend to think and behave (Smith, 1976, I.iii.3, 4, p. 62). People who aspire to imitate the 'envied situation' of the rich and great 'frequently abandon the paths to virtue' by using 'fraud and falsehood…intrigue and cabal' and all manner of criminal and antisocial means to attain their goal of 'greatness' (1976, I.iii.3, 7, 8, pp. 64–5). In fact 'avarice and ambition' are the causes 'of all the tumult and bustle, all the rapine and injustice' that have ever taken place in the world (1976, I.iii.2, 8, p. 57).

At first sight it looks as though Smith is invoking a classical conception of corruption in which the pursuit of personal glory and pleasure has corrupted virtue. In this vein, Ferguson had argued that the hero of the commercial age was a dubious, even dangerous, role model capable of infecting 'all orders of men, with equal venality, servility and cowardice' (Ferguson, 1996 [1767]a, p. 241). And yet it is telling that while Smith seems to lament the corruption of moral sentiments under commercialism, in the end he does not disavow it: quite the opposite. He goes on to explain that, although the rich and great are not really worthy of the admiration they attract, the fact of the matter is that 'they almost constantly obtain it', signifying that they must be 'in some respects, the *natural* objects of it' (Smith, 1976, I.iii.3, 4, p. 62, my emphasis). Reading on, we begin to appreciate that the apparent affinity between Smith and Ferguson is only superficial, because Smith soon defends our worship of the wealthy in terms of vital social functions. First of all, our innate regard for the trappings of wealth and greatness (which fuels the work and saving motivation) is a deliberate 'deception' that has been incorporated in the human constitution for specific ends: 'It is as well that nature imposes upon us in this manner' for it *'is this deception which rouses and keeps in continual motion the industry of mankind'* (1976, V.i.7–10, pp. 181–3, my emphasis). Second, our tendency to worship the rich and powerful is 'necessary both to establish and maintain the distinction of ranks and the order of society' (1976, I.iii.1, p. 61). Third, our instinctive admiration of the rich produces the unanticipated social benefit of instilling in the masses appropriate authority values. Smith notes that the 'undistinguishing eyes' of 'the great mob of mankind' are incapable of distinguishing a wise and virtuous person from a foolish and vicious one, yet they can easily detect the presence of wealth (1976, VI.ii.1, 20, pp. 225–6). We have therefore been endowed with a reverence for those qualities immediately appreciable to even the most unsophisticated amongst us and this reverence provides a basis for leadership. Smith applauds the wisdom of nature in placing the burden of leadership, not as we might imagine, upon the shoulders of the wise and virtuous, but upon those of the rich. Smith is well aware that the rich are no more morally fit for leadership than the poor, but he does regard them as better equipped *practically* because they are generally better educated and more familiar with the trappings and protocols of authority than are the poor (1976, I.iii.2.5, p. 55).

The corruption of our moral sentiments is not really a form of corruption after all, not even in the classical corruption-of-virtue sense. What Smith really means is that it only *appears* that way. Ultimately, any disavowal of the impulse to admire prosperity and despise the failures of the poor would be counter to the decrees of 'nature' (1976, I.iii.2, 1, pp. 51–3)[8] and even the moral judgments of the impartial spectator (1976, VI.i.11, p. 215).[9] The pursuit of riches is both

---

8   It seems that it was '[p]rovidence who first divided the earth among a few lordly masters' (1976, IV.i.10, p. 185).

9   The impartial spectator allows us to see ourselves as others see us so that our self-interest never gets out of hand and our behaviour is never unsociable, thereby enabling us to maintain the sympathy, and therefore

natural and morally acceptable. All that Smith requires is that it takes place within the bounds of natural liberty, positive justice and the limits set by the impartial spectator (Smith, 1976, II.ii.1, p. 83).

The division of labour

Another topic on which Smith seems to be displaying a concern with corruption as classically understood is in his discussion of the effects of specialisation under commercial conditions.

Smith's discussion of the division of labour is noteworthy not least because it is one of the few sources of corruption he identifies as peculiar to or induced by the commercial age. Significantly, though, its maladaptive aspects are perceived neither as unnatural nor as breaches of proto-liberal values.

Smith appreciated the alienating effects of the division of labour and his comments here are genuinely prescient. The division of labour reduces the tasks of workers to one or two simple operations, and, since work is central to intellectual development, the labourer naturally loses the good part of her cognitive capacities, including natural inventiveness. Workers' physical capacities are also impaired: task separation limits the labourer's scope of duties and renders 'him' 'incapable of exerting his strength with vigour and perseverance, in any other employment than that which [s/]he has been bred'. The individual thus acquires 'greater dexterity at his own particular trade' but only at the expense of 'his intellectual, social and martial virtues' (Smith, 1979, V.i.f.50, p. 782).

The worker involved in detail labour is reduced to a kind of automaton, who is not only 'as stupid and ignorant as it is possible for a human creature to become', but is also soon bereft of any capacity to exercise her judgment or moral perception (1979, V.i.f.50, pp. 781–2). Martial virtue is a further and significant cost of specialisation. Smith was uncharacteristically animated on this point, describing the coward as a kind of 'lepe[r]' who is 'mutilated and deformed in his mind' (1979, V.i.f.60, pp. 787–8).

A pessimistic Smith?

Because of these extremely negative and apparently pessimistic observations, it has been suggested that Smith's comments on the division of labour 'constitute a major source of inspiration for the socialist critique' of capitalism (Rosenberg, 1965,

---

cooperation, of others (1976, II.ii.1, p. 83, III.5, 5, p. 165). Smith states that it is the role of the 'impartial spectator' to perpetually monitor and correct the 'strongest impulses of self-love' (1976, III.3, 38, p. 153–4, III.3, 4, p. 137, VI.iii.18, pp. 244–5).

p. 127). It has even been argued that Smith's comments should be interpreted as a sign that he anticipated the decline and eventual annihilation of the commercial regime (Heilbroner, 1973; Pack, 1991). Such claims are controvertible. To the extent that Smith's outline of the dehumanising consequences of specialisation on workers hints at the effects of fragmentation and product alienation, it is true that it does indeed foreshadow Marx's discourse on the same subject,[10] but the parallels should not be overestimated. Like Ferguson, Smith registers the drawbacks of specialisation but never recommends any devolvement in specialisation functions, believing that its attendant problems could be solved within existing social and political arrangements (see below). And unlike Marx, Smith regards specialisation as a natural development originating in our natural desire to 'truck, barter and exchange' (Smith, 1979, I.ii.2, p. 26) and in our inventive, progressive faculties.

Further, Smith sees the mind-numbing effects of the division of labour as of relatively low importance in the grand scheme of things. At a more general social level, the entire system of commercialism and specialised labour generates great levels of liberty and independence for all members of society, including the working poor. It also delivers better security and is the source of almost all of the progress and prosperity of the commercial age (see, for example, 1979, I.i.10–11, pp. 22–4). This is significant because for Smith, the happy society is the prosperous, materially abundant society (1976, I.iii.2, 1, p. 51, III.5, 7, p. 166, 1979, I.V.iii.36, p. 96). He generally takes the view that whatever makes a country rich—and the division of labour does this better than anything else—enriches the poor as well and is therefore, in the long view, to their benefit (1978, [B], 212–13, pp. 489–90, Early draft of *The wealth of nations*, 5–6, in Smith, 1978, pp. 563–4). Thus, on balance, and despite any ill effects, the division of labour yields more, rather than less, human happiness all round.

From Smith's point of view the main problems with the division of labour are not the loss of civic virtue or the imminent collapse of commercialism itself, but its entirely ameliorable consequences for public order and personal comportment. To this end, he advocated the establishment of a compulsory and publicly funded school system to inculcate patterns of civility suitable for market-society subjects (1979, V.i.i.5–6, p. 815, V.i.f.57, p. 786, V.i.f.54, p. 785). An educated people are 'more respectable' and orderly because they are more inclined to acknowledge the authority of their 'lawful superiors'. They are also 'more capable of seeing through the interested complaints of faction and sedition' (1979, V.i.f.61, p. 788) and therefore less easily roused to political tumult.

---

10   As first noticed by David Kettler (1965, pp. 8–9).

Faction

Another aspect of Smith's approach to corruption, and one that further distances him from classical (and Fergusonian) approaches, is his attitude to political conflict in general and to political factions in particular. Contrary to Ferguson's view, faction fighting neither enhances civic virtue nor in any way preserves just government (Smith, 1976, III.3.33, p. 151). Factions have a tendency to 'deceive and impose upon the Public' and to 'oppress' rather than serve government (Smith, 1987 [1785], p. 286). Dispute between political factions 'distract[s] the nation' and corrupts the 'moral sentiments' (1976, III.3.43, p. 155–6).[11] The behaviour of factions is generally 'atrocious', violent and unjust (1976, III.3.25, p. 231, V.iii.12, p. 242), and they invariably exacerbate sectarian conflict (1979, V.i.g.7, pp. 791–2). Smith disparaged all forms of conflict and social disharmony, insisting that '[t]he peace and order of society, is of more importance than even the relief of the miserable' (1979, V.i.ii.1, 20, p. 226, VI.ii.2, 12, p. 231). Contrary to Ferguson's enthusiastic promotion of mass activism and political turbulence, Smith wanted to see a dampening, a professionalisation and institutionalisation, of political spirit. Once a sound constitution has been put in place,[12] politics seems to have been reducible to two main functions: the rational administration of populations, and the management of the practical exigencies of security, both economic and military.[13]

The differences between Smith and Ferguson on the issue of conflict underline their more general differences in terms of traditions. Smith signals his allegiance to progress and modernity when he draws upon the *doux commerce* thesis popularised by Montesquieu. In this view, progress and commercialism have a positive, softening effect on manners. With the new politeness and civility comes also an aversion to war and all other forms of conflict. Smith regards emotions such as hatred, resentment, revenge and anger as 'unsocial' passions that 'poison...the happiness of a good mind' (1976, I.ii.3.7, p. 37). As such, they needed to be reined in and kept within the bounds of civility and justice. Smith disliked all forms of conflict including war (Hill, 2009). Ferguson, on the other hand, tended to idealise war, perceiving it as an opportunity to exercise the classical martial virtues and to enhance social cohesion. Even as Smith was celebrating the pacifying effects of progress and commerce, Ferguson was still writing nostalgically of those '[s]mall and simple tribes' whose conflicts with out-groups were 'animated with the most implacable hatred' (Ferguson, 1996 [1767]a, p. 25).

---

11 Hume agreed (see 1987 [1774], p. 171).

12 Such a constitution would be characterised by features such as the separation of powers (1979, V.i.b.25, pp. 722–3).

13 'As reported by Dugald Stewart from a document no longer in existence in his *Account of the Life and Writings of Adam Smith* in his *Collected Works*, ed. Sir William Hamilton, 1858, Vol. X, p. 68' (Winch, 1978, p. 4, n. 2).

Concluding remarks

Whereas Ferguson's aetiology of corruption fits fairly readily within corruption traditions, Smith's approach is more modern. Contrary to Ferguson's account, Smith did not think that hedonism (Epicureanism), privatisation, civic quiescence and the breakdown of exclusivist social categories were the problem. In fact, they might even be the *solutions* to the potentially corrupt state.

Ferguson tended to look to the past for remedies to the problems of modernity. He hoped to reconstitute national identity, social intimacy and civic virtue through a kind of cultural atavism, coupled with such practical measures as citizen militias and political institutions for the safe discharge of factional conflict. But Smith regards these strategies as remnants of a pre-commercial age that ought to be purged in order to *prevent* corruption. Similarly, while Ferguson observes with dismay the increasing depersonalisation, dispassion and impartiality of the commercialising state, Smith embraces such developments with enthusiasm.

Though Smith was keenly aware of 'the disadvantages of a commercial spirit', he seems more convinced that commercialisation is natural, inevitable and basically positive. His views are ultimately those of an early liberal and classical political economist, so corruption is seen as a deviation from a natural (broadly liberal) state. Ferguson, by contrast, though in many respects a friend to progress, is reluctant to abandon a civic-humanist diagnostic tradition that stressed the value of personalism, particularism, community, martial virtue and intense forms of interdependence.

Acknowledgements

The author wishes to thank the Australian Research Council whose generous funding for DP0770499 made the completion of this chapter possible. She also thanks her research assistant, Kelly McKinley, for her able assistance.

References

Alvey, James. (1998). Adam Smith's three strikes against commercial society. *International Journal of Social Economics, 25*(9), 1425–41.

Brown, Vivienne. (1994). *Adam Smith's discourse*. London: Routledge.

Corrigan, Philip, & Sayer, Derek. (1985). From theatre to machine: old corruption. In Philip Corrigan & Derek Sayer (Eds), *The great arch: English state formation as cultural revolution* (pp. 87–113). Oxford: Basil Blackwell.

Ferguson, Adam. (1756). *Reflections previous to the establishment of a militia.* London: R. & J. Dodsley.

Ferguson, Adam. (1792). *Principles of moral and political science: being chiefly a retrospect of lectures delivered in the College of Edinburgh.* London and Edinburgh: A. Strahan & T. Cadell, and W. Creech.

Ferguson, Adam. (1834 [1783]). *The history of the progress and termination of the Roman republic.* London: Jones & Company.

Ferguson, Adam. (1878 [1769]). *Institutes of moral philosophy.* New York: Garland Publishing Company.

Ferguson, Adam. (1996 [1767]a). *An essay on the history of civil society.* Fania Oz-Salzberger (Ed.). Cambridge: Cambridge University Press.

Ferguson, Adam. (1996b). Separation of departments. In Yasuo Amoh Kyoto (Ed.), *Collection of essays* (pp. 141–51). Kyoto: Rinsen Book Company.

Heilbroner, Robert. (1973). The paradox of progress: decline and decay in *The Wealth of Nations*. *Journal of the History of Ideas, 34*, 243–62.

Hill, Lisa. (1996). Anticipations of nineteenth and twentieth century social thought in the work of Adam Ferguson. *European Journal of Sociology, 37*(1), 203–28.

Hill, Lisa. (2009). Adam Smith on war (and peace). In Ian Hall & Lisa Hill (Eds), *British international thinkers from Hobbes to Namier* (pp. 71–89). New York: Palgrave Macmillan.

Hirschman, Albert O. (1977). *The passions and the interests: political arguments for capitalism before its triumph.* Princeton: Princeton University Press.

Hume, David. (1987 [1774]). Letter 141 from Hume to Smith, St Andrew's Square, 13 February 1774. In E. C. Mossner & I. S. Ross (Eds), *The correspondence of Adam Smith*. Oxford: Oxford University Press.

Kettler, David. (1965). *The social and political thought of Adam Ferguson.* Indiana: Ohio State University Press.

McDowell, Gary L. (1983). Commerce, virtue and politics: Adam Ferguson's constitutionalism. *Review of Politics, 45*(4), 536–52.

Machiavelli, Niccolò. (1998). *The discourses*. Edited and with an introduction by Bernard Crick. Suffolk: Penguin.

Pack, Spencer J. (1991). *Capitalism as a moral system: Adam Smith's critique of the free market economy*. Aldershot: Edward Elgar.

Philp, Mark. (1997). Defining political corruption. In P. Heywood (Ed.), *Political corruption* (pp. 20–46). Oxford: Blackwell.

Pocock, J. G. A. (1975). *The Machiavellian moment: Florentine political thought and the Atlantic republican tradition*. Princeton: Princeton University Press.

Polybius. (1979 [c. 110 BC]). *The rise of the Roman Empire* (Ian Scott-Kilvert, Trans.). Selected and with an introduction by F. W. Walbank. London: Penguin.

Robertson, John. (1983). The Scottish Enlightenment at the limits of the civic tradition. In I. Hont & M. Ignatieff (Eds), *Wealth and virtue: the shaping of political economy in the Scottish Enlightenment*. Cambridge: Cambridge University Press.

Rosenberg, Nathan. (1960). Some institutional aspects of *The Wealth of Nations*. *Journal of Political Economy, 69*, 557–70.

Rosenberg, Nathan. (1965). Adam Smith on the division of labour: two views or one? *Economica, 33*, 127–39.

Shumer, Sara M. (1979). Machiavelli: republican politics and its corruption. *Political Theory, 7*(1), 5–34.

Smith, Adam. (1976). *The theory of moral sentiments*. D. D. Raphael and A. L. MacFie (Eds). Oxford: Clarendon Press.

Smith, Adam. (1978). *Lectures on jurisprudence*. R. L. Meek, D. D. Raphael and L. G. Stein (Eds). Oxford: Oxford University Press.

Smith, Adam. (1979). *An inquiry into the nature and causes of the wealth of nations*. R. H. Campbell and A. S. Skinner (Eds). Oxford: Clarendon Press.

Smith, Adam. (1987 [1785]). Letter 248 addressed to Le Duc de la Rochefoucauld, Edinburgh, 1 November 1785. In E. C. Mossner & I. S. Ross (Eds), *The correspondence of Adam Smith*. Oxford: Oxford University Press.

Wilkie, Jean. (1962). The historical thought of Adam Ferguson. Unpublished doctoral dissertation. Washington, DC: The Catholic University of America.

Winch, Donald. (1978). *Adam Smith's politics*. Cambridge: Cambridge University Press.

Winch, Donald. (1997). Adam Smith's problem and ours. *Scottish Journal of Political Economy, 44*, 384–402.

7. Corruption, Development, Chaos and Social Disorganisation: Sociological reflections on corruption and its social basis

John Clammer

Corruption is now widely understood to be one of the main distorters of effective development intervention, leading to the illegal misappropriation of aid, inefficiencies and crime in local and national bureaucracies, the failure of poverty-alleviation schemes to reach the very poorest, and general lack of access to primary health care, education, housing and clean water. High levels of corruption can distort the operation of social justice and the fair distribution of resources. Corruption is also often seen as a 'local' problem—as a form of crime that requires ethical, legal or managerial mechanisms to prevent, contain or eradicate it, or as a failure of individual morality or traditional norms when vulnerable people are placed in a position of temptation.

This chapter will advance the thesis that corruption is, in fact, a systemic problem in which whole social systems are implicated, and which is generated in large part by dysfunctions in systems themselves. In standard sociological parlance, the notion of social organisation implies the smooth running of a given social system. 'Social disorganisation' is therefore seen as its opposite or as the degeneration of a functional system. This term is, of course, relative and often substantially ideological. For example, the 'social harmony' ascribed to Singapore and North Korea perhaps represents control more than functionality. Yet we can identify with reasonable accuracy situations in which social breakdown or non-functionality is evident through its negative impact on the quality of life, particularly of the non-powerful, non-privileged or excluded members of a given society, and the expression of this non-functionality in rising levels of crime, violence and corruption (Jones-Finer & Nellis, 1998).

This chapter should therefore be read as an exercise in social theory, not as an empirical analysis of corruption in specific cases. It is an attempt to broaden the scope and range of reference of organisational sociology in order to include within its ambit issues of development and social change, alongside its traditional preoccupation with the internal structure of organisations, particularly businesses and bureaucracies.

The problems listed at the beginning of this chapter can reasonably be seen as examples of social disorganisation. This claim rests on the assumption that the desirable outcome of any social system is that, within reasonable limits, it satisfies the material, psychological and spiritual needs of the majority of its population without the unreasonable diversion of public resources to a minority.

In other words, a 'functional' system is not one in a state of functionalist or Parsonian 'equilibrium', which is, in fact, a rare if ever actually encountered empirical situation. A 'functional' system is one that allows a reasonably secure normal human social life to flourish and also extends the range of that life beyond the satisfaction of basic needs into areas of cultural creativity, psychic security and leisure—a point validly promoted by the now largely abandoned 'basic human needs' theory of development priorities developed in the 1980s (for example, Dube, 1984).

If societies are understood in this way then corruption is arguably not just an epiphenomenon of forms of social organisation that are manageable by better policing, moral education or institutional adaptation. Rather, corruption is a key to understanding the nature of social disorganisation in much more fundamental theoretical and empirical sociological ways, because corruption itself emerges largely from that disorganisation. The question then becomes how to think about that disorganisation in fresh ways that will both advance our understanding of the endemic occurrence of corruption and point beyond limited solutions to more systemic ones.

In this chapter I will attempt this task in four ways. First, I relate the analysis of corruption more fully than has been done before to some important aspects of contemporary social theory and to current anthropological theories of culture. Second, I explore corruption through the prism of chaos theory as a potentially creative way of investigating social disorganisation. Third, I relate corruption to systemic changes in the world system, in particular to the spread of what might be termed 'capitalist morality', the consequences of economic globalisation and its consumerist 'ethic'. Fourth, I argue that in failed or authoritarian states, there is a deliberate attack on—or progressive dissolution of—civil society and the forms of social solidarity on which it is based, and a corresponding attack on indigenous forms of morality (see also Clammer, 2004). This argument applies equally to states that have been undermined by the penetration of capitalist social relations and the economic crises caused by globalised finance, in South-East Asia and Mexico in the 1990s, and from 2001 in Argentina.

Although corruption has probably been a feature of human societies in every historical period, we must also face the possibility that there are distinctively modern forms and indeed forms created by modernity itself. Even as Zygmunt Bauman (1999) has argued that modernity reached its climax in the Holocaust, not emancipation or enlightenment, so too it might be argued that modernity has eventuated in forms of social disorganisation quite unforeseen by its architects. Such disorganisation has included escalating levels of violence, corruption and ecological degradation and the non-arrival of the 'development' that much of the world has been eagerly expecting. Or rather, the form that 'development' has taken has brought in its wake these unexpected consequences—and especially its current manifestation as globalisation, with all its multiple levels and ambiguities (Hay & Marsh, 2000) and its impact on identities, concepts of citizenship and patterns of migration and settlement (Hudson & Slaughter, 2007). In a kind of inversion of Norbert Elias's (2000) theory of the 'civilising process', I will argue that corruption is not accidental or contingent but an endemic and intrinsic part of the social forms created out of the macroscopic forces of modernisation and globalisation, and their highly unequal spread and penetration.

Corruption and social process

The study of corruption, rather like the parallel study of criminology, shows up the ragged edges of sociological explanation. There are several reasons for this. Corruption and its endemic nature and distribution suggest a less than pleasant view of human nature, one in fact more congenial to Hobbes than to Rousseau. Corruption calls seriously into doubt functionalist theories of human society and similar versions based on assumptions of equilibrium. Corruption suggests the need for a much more chaotic modelling of social reality than is psychologically attractive to most sociologists. It poses awkward questions for discourses of rights, social ethics, the place of values in development, democratisation and the possibility of so-called post-development as an image and model of the future (Rahnema & Bawtree, 2003). The analysis of corruption also suggests that a new vocabulary might be needed in legal and political anthropology. We need to recognise that the systematic ignoring and distortion of both legal mechanisms and informal or 'cultural' ones by corrupt practices and procedures bring into question some fundamental assumptions. These assumptions are of 'order and continuity in everyday life' and that mechanisms of social control and dispute resolution other than law are somehow more efficient and humane (Roberts, 1979).

To make this claim is not to discount the role of culture. Many practices that might now be regarded as corrupt in the context of modernist assumptions about the nature of the state and the behaviour of public servants would, in the past, have been seen as parts of gift exchange or the natural and civilised lubrication of social relationships (see, for example, Yan, 1996). Indeed, a common problem is the normative discontinuity between the practical coexistence of 'traditional' and modernist social norms in the same social and political spaces, with a corresponding lack of clarity about the appropriate application of acceptable rules. The fundamental problem with a culturalist approach to corruption is, however, that it tends, as with older conceptions of culture generally, to take a somewhat essentialist approach to both the possession and the practice of culture. Paradoxically, this approach to corruption is occurring at the same time as many anthropologists are abandoning the concept of 'culture' because of its diffuseness and the impossibility of coherently defining it. Several authors have remarked that 'culture' is a strategic device not an essence—in short, that 'culture' is political (Fox & King, 2002).

Scholars increasingly see culture as something negotiated, fluid and constantly in the condition of being constructed and deconstructed. This perspective comes much closer to a chaos model of social organisation than to older holistic and functionalist ones; however, the solution to the shortcomings of a culturalist approach is neither a total abandonment of the appreciation of cultural factors in corrupt behaviour nor the wholesale adoption of an economic approach. Rather, what is required is a new form of systems approach. This approach would combine these elements with, and into, a more accurate model of the nature of social processes. It would take account of the current context of contemporary globalised modernity and would recognise this modernity's impact on identity, subjectivities and social relations (for example, Giddens, 1991).

The possibility and desirability of attributing ethical responsibility to individuals are a given in what follows, and should not be taken as an argument against personal honesty and authenticity. My argument is, in fact, an attempt to demonstrate the complexity of the social context in which ethical decisions are taken and the extent to which those decisions are deeply influenced by the dissolution of norms.

Much corrupt behaviour on the part of individuals represents what Jean Baudrillard (2001 [1979]) would perhaps call 'seduction'—that is, not only the rational calculation of economic advantage in a situation where one thinks one will not get caught, but also, more importantly, the manipulation of values by socioeconomic institutions that systematically manufacture anomie. While Durkheim (1952 [1897]) saw anomie as a highly negative symptom of the collapse of organic and integrative values in society, one could now argue that globalised capitalist society is a huge machine for the manufacture of just that very anomie.

In fact, without naming it as such, many of the currently prominent analyses of contemporary society and culture point to exactly this conclusion. Amongst these are: from a German standpoint, Ulrich Beck's 'risk society' (1992); from a French perspective, Michel Maffesoli's vision of the collapse of the social structures of consumerist societies into neo-tribalism (1996); or from a British perspective, Anthony Giddens' theory of selfhood in late capitalist society (1991).

Psychological factors play a role in corruption. For example, people can enter into corrupt transactions because of the personal power that they confer, to manage their insecurities or to enhance their sense of self. But just as Durkheim was concerned to rescue sociology from psychology, so my concern is to delineate a new systems approach in which the very elements of those systems—while essential to the overall structure—are inherently unstable. This paradox of unstable stability now needs stating, explaining and applying to a theory of corruption.

Unstable systems and the theory of corruption

In introducing a collection of essays on corruption, Peter Larmour and Nick Wolanin (2001) note that 'the recent scandals surrounding the Olympic games show how reliance on the virtues of "good people", such as former athletes, is insufficient unless good systems are also in place' (p. xiv). The revelations of systematic prisoner abuse in Iraq by US military personnel, and the tragically large number of accounts of abuse in hospitals, old-age homes, schools and other contexts, drive home this point.

Situation—or location within a system, structure or organisation—as much as culture, moral weakness or personality, plays the major role in determining when and if corrupt behaviour will occur, assuming that opportunities exist. Although various organisational theories of corruption and its prevention exist (such as the so-called 'managerial' approach), what tends to be missing is an understanding of the interactive nature of subsystems with each other.

Assuming that opportunities for corruption exist in all societies, a corrupt outcome is more probable in situations of weak organisational culture, an inefficient or corrupt police force or a cowed press or one with little tradition of investigative journalism. Corrupt behaviour is likely to occur at the point where these three subsystems meet—at the point of negative synergy, as it were. In turn, these subsystems will be embedded in larger political cultures and norms of economic activity.

This proposition has significant implications for organisational sociology. A key implication is that organisational sociology should greatly expand its agenda beyond the analysis of 'normal' institutions to include dysfunctional ones. The analysis needs to incorporate fully the fact that dysfunctional events and processes constantly occur even in the most apparently 'normal' ones.

The situation is intensified when the managerial or organisational system is subverted from the top—where the system itself is dysfunctional or corrupt, or simply lacks efficiency or the ability to implement the initiatives that it might itself generate. Such is the case in the so-called 'failed states' of central Africa, where, even if a government exists on paper, it either cannot carry out its mandate or is itself the centre of corruption (Kahl, 2006). A parallel situation can be found in Latin American states that have or are experiencing high levels of internal violence. Examples are Argentina or Chile under their recent military regimes, and contemporary Colombia, Mexico and Brazil, where much of the violence is led by the drug trade or by the extremities of social inequality and mal-development (Scheper-Hughes, 1992). Even more extreme cases can be found in those zones or states where civil war or separatism is rampant (for example, Sudan or Chechnya), or where external forces destroy a previously existing sociopolitical order with no viable plan for re-establishing order (for example, Afghanistan and Iraq), or where multilateral aid agencies impose a set of pro-market policies on a socioeconomic order ill equipped to deal with, implement or even understand them (as with International Monetary Fund intervention in Indonesia in the wake of the 1997 Southeast Asian economic crisis, or a little earlier as in Argentina and Mexico).

A theory of organisational disintegration or systems meltdown is consequently necessary. It would be nice to agree fully with Larmour and Wolanin (2001) that 'organisational integrity means being able to drill down into any part of an organisation, to any depth, and see evidence of the guiding ethics, whatever they might be' (p. xxiii). A problem arises, however, when the drilling reveals corruption at every level, encouraged by the culture of the top seeping into lower levels, where poverty and insecurity of health, food, shelter and even of life are the constant daily reality, and/or where incomes are low, erratic and unpredictable.

The nexus between corruption and these forms of violence is, I argue, a key issue. Furthermore, today all organisational cultures, whether we personally approve of them or not, are embedded in the bigger totality of globalisation and certain discourses of 'development'. It is to globalisation and understandings of development that we must also look for a deeper explanation of the endemic nature of corruption and its failure to diminish, despite decades of so-called development.

Corruption, violence and globalisation

There is well-documented evidence that the past three decades of development have raised the living standards of some, promoted the spread of consumerism amongst the wealthy and the corresponding emergence of new class factions, and greatly accelerated certain social trends such as urbanisation. At the same time, in many parts of the world and in particular in Africa, development has dismally failed to eradicate poverty, promote social and gender equity and increase real political participation. It has also brought in its wake unprecedented environmental degradation, climate change, resource depletion, destruction of indigenous cultures, and risk and instability (W. Sachs, 1995). Rampant crime, like corruption, seems to accompany mal-development, together with the perception and experience of high levels of inequality and unfairness, as in Brazil or in Argentina after its IMF-sponsored economic crisis. Although bringing about real increases in income in some cases, development has also promoted greater inequality in the distribution of those incomes both between and within nations (J. D. Sachs, 2009). These failures can be illustrated in many ways, with examples multiplied almost to infinity. Certainly development has promoted growth but, at best, the record is mixed and ambiguous, as apparent advances on one front mirror retreats on others. The failure of development is the root of corruption.

Parallel with material growth has gone what Ulrich Beck (1992) has aptly called the 'risk society': rising uncertainty and lack of knowledge or verifiable information about the complex environments that people must now navigate to survive daily life, and the job insecurity that comes with what is quaintly termed 'flexible accumulation'.

The notion that corruption arises when opportunity meets lack of ethics needs serious qualification. Although corruption may indeed be a perennial social problem, it can take new forms. A precise understanding of those forms is necessary to its management and control. In fact, we find three major factors in the contemporary 'corruption environment': mal-development that produces new or increasing patterns of inequality and the parallel recognition of social injustice on the part of its victims; violence and the intense psychological risks, pressures and uncertainties that such a life context generates; and capitalist-led neo-liberal globalisation. I have covered mal-development in my discussion above and now turn to violence, globalisation and neo-liberalism.

Violence

Violence is frequently left out of discussions of corruption. But it is now a feature of or indeed part of the very fabric of everyday life, not only in conflict situations (Iraq, Afghanistan) or in many supposedly post-conflict ones (Kosovo, the Congo), but also in many so-called 'normal' societies (Colombia, Mexico, Brazil, the United States, and so on). Violence is particularly common in societies experiencing rapid political and economic transformations.

Kay Warren and collaborators argue that 'heterogeneous formations of violence' have become part of the normal chaos of post–Cold War society (Greenhouse, et al., 2002; Warren, 1994). While they focus on Latin American, African and South Asian situations, the phenomena they describe are also present throughout Central Asia, the Balkans, Ireland, the Basque country and parts of the former Soviet Union. Warren's view builds on the now classic statement by Hannah Arendt (1970) that public life is being progressively colonised by violence and that we have witnessed, both domestically and internationally, the erosion of the rule of law. In this analysis, violence is the result of the complex interaction of colonial histories, new forms of identity politics (especially ethnic and ethno-nationalist forms), population displacement, land pressure, demographic growth, globalisation, neo-liberal economic policies, regional and state politics (and now presumably international ones, too) and the unintended by-products of well-meaning humanitarian and other forms of intervention.

The invasion of public life by violence has appeared in state terrorism (for example, the death squads of Argentina and Chile during their most recent military dictatorships), insurgency and counterinsurgency, peasant rebellions, the militarisation of society and the blurring of the boundaries between civilians and the military, and the loss of trust within one's own social group as well as between groups. There is a loss of solidarity, as violence unmakes both morality and community, and as boundaries and allegiances become fluid. Predatory violence and new cycles of opportunism, uncertainty, improvisation and involution replace 'traditional' or 'normal' patterns of social interaction. This process is clearly seen in the humanitarian disasters that accompany civil war, ethnic and tribal conflict and natural disasters where there is a breakdown of social organisation (Eade & Williams, 1998). When the 'public secret' of 'acceptable' levels of violence becomes normalcy, the fabric of life is fundamentally transformed (Warren, 1994, p. 7). Chronic violence flourishes when states are weak and as allegiances, social networks and levels of trust are also weakened—just as violence also flourishes when the state is over-strong and has provoked opposition to itself.

In either condition, corruption is a by-product of—or rather is built into—the system itself. Corruption is both the means by which things routinely get done and the mechanism through which those with less power but in high-risk life contexts will attempt to protect themselves. In such conditions (as in Suharto's Indonesia), corruption becomes normal. It may even be regulated by informal but quite binding 'rules' of distribution, amounts, frequency and so forth— closely paralleling the mechanisms of the gift economies that anthropologists love to study, and in many cases replacing or displacing these mechanisms. An example is the Chinese notion of *guanxi*, which is in reality a point of contact between the economy of the gift and the economy of corruption (Gold, et al., 2002).

Also interesting is that there appears to be a convergence of forms of violence and crime across cultures. This convergence suggests that globalisation can take some unexpected and sinister forms.

Globalisation and neo-liberalism

In their list of factors influencing the rise of modern forms of violence, Greenhouse et al. name both globalisation and neo-liberalism (2002). I think that they are correct. Here we are getting closer to the root conditions of both violence and contemporary forms of corruption, and indeed of the nexus between them. Globalisation and 'development' go hand in hand and are, in a sense, expressions both of one another and of the underlying economic philosophy of neo-liberalism.

Many detailed critiques have been made of globalisation and the social impact of neo-liberalism as espoused by multilateral agencies (in particular the IMF, the World Trade Organisation and World Bank) and the politico-economic elites of many if not most modern nation-states, including some that are theoretically socialist (Greider, 1998). Market-led (or market-driven) globalisation promotes new forms of inequality, labour migration and new conditions of work (Scrase, et al., 2003). It also has a moral impact and implications for human rights and citizenship (Brysk & Shafir, 2004). Globalisation engenders 'market cultures', as Hefner (1998) and colleagues show in an analysis that specifically exposes the connection between morality and capitalism in East and South-East Asia.

A 'market culture' in this sense is not simply a neutral ethnographic description of the operation of capitalism. The notion of 'culture' points to how capitalism transforms social relations, brings into existence new social strata, monetises what were formerly gift or cooperative rather than commoditised relationships, introduces new values (including the alien idea that time is money) and fundamentally reframes morality. Although most capitalists or advertising people might not like to name it as such, this morality is based on greed, acquisitiveness, unequal distribution of rewards (in the form of wages or of profits), the high evaluation of material success and possessions, and individualism.

While these same societies often continue to uphold traditional religious values and attempt to curb the worst excesses through law enforcement and managerial means, in reality a serious divergence exists between these mechanisms of control and actual praxis. To preach restraint in an environment in which to get rich is glorious is almost certainly to be preaching to the deaf, or at best to people who may compartmentalise ethics into those pertaining to the private sphere where traditional values still at least theoretically prevail, and the marketplace where they most certainly do not.

In this light, we may see market-driven globalisation at two levels or from two perspectives. On the one hand, market mechanisms create a system for the intensification of international and domestic inequalities. On the other hand, these mechanisms reshape values in the direction of hedonism, greed and competition. Market-driven globalisation is a transformative force quite on par with the historical impact of any of the great world religions. It may even exceed them, since it appears that in many respects it is the capitalist morality that prevails, even in areas where in principle commodification should not apply, as in the art world (Hughes, 1990, pp. 3–28).

In its contemporary manifestations, corruption is a product of growing inequalities, capitalist morality and endemic conflict and violence. Globalisation is the root cause—and so are the policies of the multilateral trade and aid organisations whose own neo-liberal ideology is a contributing factor. As Zoe Pearson (2001) has pointed out, their foot-dragging over identifying and addressing issues of corruption until very recently is because 'these institutions have long been linked with corrupt behaviour associated with their schemes and projects' (p. 38).

I wish to go a step further and argue that not only do individual projects generate corrupt behaviour but also the very form of development that is promoted. Thus, in the case of individual schemes, corruption should be seen as a symptom of the underlying disease (compare with Elliott, 1997). Likewise, it is commonly argued that corruption negatively affects sound governance, the outcome of elections, administrative efficiency, the deployment of government resources and the generally smooth running of the political process (see, for example, Nye, 2002). Although true, this argument assumes that corruption is an epiphenomenon of otherwise workable political structures and institutions. In a developed, democratised situation, this argument is credible. But here I am advancing a stronger case for recognising structural corruption of and within politico-social systems, and especially in the context of weak or failed states, authoritarian regimes with their corresponding lack of public transparency, and situations of endemic conflict and violence—situations where the government fails to work in the interests of the people and where there is also a meltdown of social solidarity and the normal bonds of kinship, trust and friendship. Clearly, these apparently 'extreme' situations are not present in all cases where corruption is endemic. Nevertheless, currently and in the recent past the linkage is very common. (We could add Liberia, Sierra Leone, Ethiopia, Nicaragua, much of Burma and many other cases to earlier examples.)

Even in more politically stable contexts, high crime levels, AIDS/HIV, poverty, chronic economic uncertainty, ethnic and religious conflict, environmental stress, hyper-urbanisation and familial disorganisation can underlie the apparent political stability, which is a kind of optical illusion.

All societies—developing or 'developed'—are framed by globalisation and its impact on ethical practices via marketisation and consumerism. Although I do not in any way deny the validity of more 'local' approaches to the analysis of corruption, and the consequent formulation of locally appropriate policy and anti-corruption strategies, I am here arguing for a 'strong' approach that situates such local solutions within their larger, and indeed global, structural determinants.

Structure and chaos

When social scientists use the word 'structure', as many often do, it clearly implies order and stability. I suggest that the current international order, and the results of its impact on the domestic spheres on which it constantly impinges, is in fact essentially chaotic.

Corruption must consequently be seen not only in a transnational frame (linked to globalisation, development, marketisation, the operations of multilateral agencies and international business) but also as a by-product of chaotic systems. Although corruption in situations of violence is a clear example of this chaos, we are facing instances of a wider systemic malaise in which structural violence is endemic. And violence at any level is always chaotic.

Rather than being the guardians of rights, governments themselves often prove to be the sources of structural instability. Although many states are signatories to the UN-sponsored international convention on human rights, in practice they do not observe it. Others refuse to become signatories to universally beneficial treaties—for example, the Kyoto Protocol or the UN charter on the rights of migrant workers. Wars are prosecuted without UN sanction and without regard to the Geneva Conventions on the rights of prisoners of war, at the same time as states seek to exempt their own war criminals from prosecution by the International Court. Heads of state routinely enrich themselves with the assistance of a small number of wealthy developed countries and their less-than-transparent banking systems.

Transnational crime itself is facilitated by the nature of globalisation and its economic structures and contributes to further undermining state sovereignty (Lupsha, 1996). Transnational crime feeds off the chaotic nature of the system of which it is now an integral part. Transnational crime is not simply an epiphenomenon of an otherwise functional system that requires policing or managerial remedies.

If a 'network' approach is to be taken (Warburton, 2001), a clearly necessary supplement is to recognise the transnational nature of these networks, in which even local transactions are modified or informed by globalised considerations. These networks are themselves unstable—that is, chaotic—especially in situations where trust is problematic. Warburton claims that 'the market is merely a simplified representation of complex networks of social exchange and social action' in which the 'general population is so used to participating in the buying and selling of material goods that the layers of social exchange that underpin such transactions are invisible and instinctive' (p. 229). On the contrary, the 'market' is a strategy, a manipulative mechanism that is far from neutral and is a prime generator of chaos, not its solution.

It is axiomatic in chaos theory that small changes in initial conditions can result in large and qualitative changes in behaviour, and that formally the same behaviour exhibits different characteristics depending on its location within the total system. Thus, local behaviour differs from global behaviour, although the two are linked or mirror each other in highly complex and often indirect ways. It is exactly in these complex interconnections (rather than in 'networks' in conventional social science terms) that the dynamic nature of a system or pattern of behaviour—in this case, corruption—resides. Or to put it differently: 'chaotic and near chaotic systems bridged the gap between macro-scales and micro-scales. Chaos was the creation of information' (Gleick, 1988, p. 260).

These perspectives suggest at least two things.

First, corruption can be seen as the product of a chaotic (cyclical, unplanned, unpredictable, risk-filled) socioeconomic system in which the very behaviour allegedly condemned by the system is in fact not only generated by it but also is its mirror and shadow counterpart. In other words, corruption is generated by the system itself and, as such, is an integral part of it. Hence corruption cannot disappear unless the system itself does, because corruption is not so much parasitic on the system as a reflection of the very system itself. Managerial solutions, better policing and ethical exhortation are thus all bound to fail in the long run, or at best to be bandaid solutions to local eruptions of a much more fundamental underlying disease.

Second, corruption is a system of information and, in many ways, can be analysed in exactly the same terms as any other information flow—in terms of access to knowledge, resources and technology; relationships between 'senders' and 'receivers'; the sociological characteristics of the 'audience'; the redundancy and miscommunications that occur in any transmission of information; 'translation' problems and so forth.

This perspective also suggests to sociologists the parallels between the analysis of corruption and that of social movements. Both corruption and social movements are systems of communication and mobilisation. Both require—corruption in a perverse way—a 'morality' (for social movements from this perspective, see Jasper, 1997).

In assessing the possible applications of chaos theory to the social sciences, Frederick Turner (1997) has the following to say:

> Likewise, in the area of social policy, the attempt to change established nonlinear systems by the use of socioeconomic laws is turning out to be disappointing. After the principled application of a trillion dollars, the 'cycle of poverty' remains untouched in the country's urban areas; indeed, it has gained strength. We may have been trying to push a string. The new nonlinear science would suggest that the answer, if there is one, may lie in a totally unexpected direction—in the emergence, perhaps, of some artistic or religious or cultural attractor that will suddenly form the basis of a new kind of market of exchange and a new dimension of interdependence. Since the application of money, which is stored and abstracted negative obligation, has proven to exacerbate the problem, or at least to leave it untouched, perhaps the problem has something to do with the direction of the flow of obligation, or of a difference between the perception of its flow and its actual flow, or with an attempt to constrain its flow in one direction or another when it should find its own way, or in a misinterpretation of the meaning of money, or with the use of obligation—money—as a tool in the first place. (pp. xviii–xix)

This view, as Turner goes on to suggest, implies both the limits of policy studies and the hollowness of much 'management science' when inappropriately applied to development situations and to the analysis of complex and dynamic social systems. It leads him to recommend that less attention be paid to 'fixing' problems and more to the general cultivation of virtue in the population. I think this recommendation is correct, although the task is difficult when, at many levels, the larger socioeconomic system itself works precisely against the cultivation of that virtue.

It is axiomatic in chaos theory that, over time, dynamic systems tend towards increased—not diminished—complexity. Sociologically, this axiom means that a system of behaviours such as corruption will not tend to diminish when certain 'needs' have been 'satisfied' by those behaviours. On the contrary, the system will breed more needs and corruption will ramify and spread to permeate more levels of the given society. The one major systems theorist in sociology who has really noted this, Niklas Luhmann (1990), summarises this insight as follows:

> Autopoietic systems, then, are not only self-organizing systems, they also produce and eventually change their own structures; their self-reference applies to the production of other components as well. This is the decisive conceptual innovation. It adds a turbocharger to the already powerful engine of self-referential machines. Even elements, that is, last components (individuals) that are, at least for the system itself, undecomposable, are produced by the system itself. Thus, everything that is used as a unit by the system is produced by the system itself. This applies to elements, processes, boundaries and other structures and, last but not least, to the unity of the system itself. Autopoietic systems, then, are sovereign with respect to the constitution of identities and differences. (p. 3)

Complexity, then, is not just an expression of the number of parts in a system. It is a modelling of the variety of their interactions and how they can align into many possible configurations, including ones not necessarily 'predictable' from the initial conditions. In this sense, corruption is a 'self-organising' system that is nested within the larger externalities of globalisation, development and marketisation.

Complexity theory then becomes a powerful tool for linking the micro and macro levels in a non-deterministic fashion that has practical and policy outcomes. This approach is linked to other 'non-necessitarian' trends in contemporary social theory (Unger, 2001). Corruption becomes a pattern of behaviour and opportunity, not to be understood in a reductionist fashion as the outcome of certain fixed variables, but as an emergent system. As Thomas Smith (1997) phrases it: 'A complex adaptive system is a system in which interactions give rise dynamically to emergent phenomena that are resilient in the face of perturbations' (p. 55). Methodological individualism proves to be a weak framework for the explanation or understanding of corruption (amongst many other things) because it suppresses the systems dimension of social interaction and also fails to explain how an emergent phenomenon can persist even in the face of quite extreme measures to control or eradicate it. From a complexity theory point of view, what is necessary is the detailed analysis of individual dynamic social systems in which corruption occurs—just as physicists analyse discrete aspects of material reality to reveal their behaviour as chaotic systems. Issues of prediction, control and public policy do not disappear. But they are reframed in a way that points towards fresh solutions, provided that those solutions themselves are understood in a less deterministic and much more modest manner (Elliott & Kiel, 1997) and point towards a sophisticated understanding of the actual mechanisms of social change (Senge, et al., 2005).

The very nature of the prevailing global system—and the acquisitiveness and undermining of communities that it produces with its compulsive consumerism—promotes social exclusion and rising levels of social inequality and poverty, including new forms hitherto not seen. It undermines democracy and contributes to environmental degradation, and creates the conditions for a globalised criminal economy (Bauman, 2004). The route to change must be radically changing the system, no longer in the direction of old-style socialism but in line with what we now know about human aspirations, the operation of complex systems and the mechanisms of social change (Capra, 2003; Harvey, 2002; Korten, 1999; Theobald, 1999). Corruption must be seen in the context of a systems approach and its eradication as a function of systems change, not of piecemeal and ultimately ineffective 'solutions'. Much the same can be said about 'development' in general and the perennial problem of why the best-intentioned policies often do not work (Black, 1999).

Concluding remarks

I believe that the approach just sketched connects the analysis of corruption to much wider issues in social theory, policy studies and development theory. Far from being a peripheral issue, the study of corruption is a critical means for uncovering much more extensive social processes, their 'breakdown' and the apparent insolubility of many of the social problems that beset contemporary societies, both 'developed' and 'developing'. Furthermore, corruption proves to be the interface, or certainly one of the main ones, between ethics and social theory. This little explored intersection is of the greatest significance. It is one of the major silences of the social disciplines, few bridges having been built here between philosophy and the social sciences (Smart, 1999).

The view presented in this chapter could be seen as pessimistic. If the outcome of dynamic systems is unpredictable, policy interventions become fruitless; however, this conclusion should not be drawn. Rather, this chapter points to the high levels of uncertainty and non-predictability in all the social sciences, including economics. In so doing, it suggests the necessity of fresh methodological and theoretical approaches that more realistically address the actual nature of the world and thereby bring together social theory and policy studies in creative new synergies.

Of course, the chapter can also be read as a critique of liberal concepts of politics, which have never successfully resolved the tensions between their desire for a non-corrupt politics and their encouragement of the pursuit of self-interest. These tensions are seen here from a rather different perspective: better institutions can be part of the solution only if those institutions can successfully analyse how they themselves are caught up in larger dynamic processes of which they are often unaware. If capitalism is the economic system generated by or in elective affinity with liberalism then globalisation, the alienating effects of capitalism and liberalism with its theories of human agency lie at the root of modernist modes of corruption (Gray, 2002).

Indeed, exploring the nexus between corruption and modernity has been at the heart of my argument. Corruption has been read here not as an unfortunate deviation from an otherwise smoothly functioning socioeconomic system, but as a product of that system itself.

Within the socio-logic of market capitalism, corruption is an 'enterprise' amongst others. It is generated by the very forces that have brought about 'modernisation', 'development' and their latter-day expression: globalisation. Corruption is often distinguished from 'legitimate' enterprises—for example, the manufacture and export of weapons or dumping in the Third World pharmaceutical products that are not considered safe enough for consumption in wealthy countries. Legal fictions and conventions—not the actual social morality of these activities—create these disguises.

Corruption is more salient in transitional economies, either those on their way from socialism to marketisation or 'developing' economies in which the cash economy is still a new experience. Few guidelines link the older patterns of solidarity to the experience of 'everything solid melting into air' and the adoption of a morality that is attractive because it is 'modern'. Then corruption indeed appears.

While the moral sources of corruption remain as perennial as they have been throughout history, morality itself needs to be situated in the context of the contemporary forces of marketisation, modernity and globalisation. Without this siting, the nature of corruption and its potential solutions will remain forever elusive.

References

Arendt, Hannah. (1970). *On violence*. New York: Harcourt, Brace, Jovanovich.

Baudrillard, Jean. (2001 [1979]). *Seduction* (Brian Singer, Trans.). Montreal: CTheory Books.

Bauman, Zygmunt. (1999). *Modernity and the Holocaust*. Cambridge: Polity Press.

Bauman, Zygmunt. (2004). *Wasted lives: modernity and its outcasts*. Cambridge: Polity Press.

Beck, Ulrich. (1992). *Risk society: towards a new modernity*. London: Sage.

Black, Jan Knippers. (1999). *Development in theory and practice: paradigms and paradoxes* (2nd edn). Boulder: Westview Press.

Brysk, Alison, & Shafir, Gershon (Eds). (2004). *People out of place: globalization, human rights, and the citizenship gap*. New York and London: Routledge.

Capra, Fritjof. (2003). *The hidden connections: a science for sustainable living*. London: Flamingo.

Clammer, John. (2004). Crisis, states and the sociology of Southeast Asia: constructing and deconstructing 1997. *Copenhagen Journal of Asian Studies, 20*, 10–31.

Dube, S. C. (1984). *Development perspectives for the 1980s*. Kuala Lumpur: Pelanduk Publications for the United Nations Asian and Pacific Development Centre.

Durkheim, Emile. (1952 [1897]). *Suicide: a study in sociology* (J. A. Spaulding & G. Simpson, Trans). London: Routledge & Kegan Paul.

Eade, Deborah, & Williams, Suzanne. (1998). *The Oxfam handbook of development and relief*. Oxford: Oxfam.

Elias, Norbert. (2000). *The civilizing process: sociogenetic and psychogenetic investigations* (revised edn). Oxford: Blackwell.

Elliott, Euel, & Kiel, L. Douglas. (1997). Nonlinear dynamics, complexity and public policy: use, misuse and applicability. In Raymond A. Eve, Sara Horsfall & Mary E. Lee (Eds), *Chaos, complexity and sociology* (pp. 64–78). London: Sage.

Elliott, Kimberly Ann (Ed.). (1997). *Corruption and the global economy*. Washington, DC: Institute for International Economics.

Fox, Richard G., & King, Barbara J. (Eds). (2002). *Anthropology beyond culture*. Oxford and New York: Berg.

Giddens, Anthony. (1991). *Modernity and self-identity: self and society in the late modern age*. Stanford: Stanford University Press.

Gleick, James. (1988). *Chaos: making a new science*. New York: Penguin.

Gold, Thomas, Guthrie, Doug, & Wank, David (Eds). (2002). *Social connections in China: institutions, culture and the changing nature of guanxi*. Cambridge: Cambridge University Press.

Gray, John. (2002). *False dawn: the delusions of global capitalism*. London and New York: Granta and The New Press.

Greenhouse, Carol J., Mertz, Elizabeth, & Warren, Kay B. (2002). *Ethnography in unstable places: everyday life in contexts of dramatic political change*. Durham: Duke University Press.

Greider, William (1998). *One world, ready or not: the manic logic of global capitalism*. Chicago: Simon & Schuster.

Harvey, David. (2002). *Spaces of hope*. Edinburgh: Edinburgh University Press.

Hay, Colin, & Marsh, David (Eds). (2000). *Demystifying globalization*. London and New York: Macmillan and St Martin's Press.

Hefner, Robert W. (Ed.). (1998). *Market cultures: society and morality in the new Asian capitalisms*. Boulder: Westview Press.

Hudson, Wayne, & Slaughter, Steven (Eds). (2007). *Globalization and citizenship: the transnational challenge*. London and New York: Routledge.

Hughes, Robert. (1990). *Nothing if not critical: selected essays on art and artists*. New York and London: Penguin.

Jasper, James M. (1997). *The art of moral protest: culture, biography and creativity in social movements*. Chicago: University of Chicago Press.

Jones-Finer, Catherine, & Nellis, Mike (Eds). (1998). *Crime and social exclusion*. Oxford: Blackwell.

Kahl, Colin H. (2006). *States, scarcity and civil strife in the developing world*. Princeton: Princeton University Press.

Korten, David C. (1999). *The post-corporate world: life after capitalism*. West Hartford and Singapore: Kumarian Press and Alkem.

Larmour, Peter, & Wolanin, Nick. (2001). Introduction. In Peter Larmour & Nick Wolanin (Eds), *Corruption and anti-corruption* (pp. xi–xiii). Canberra: Asia Pacific Press.

Luhmann, Niklas. (1990). The cognitive program of constructivism and a reality that remains unknown. In Wolfgang Krohn, Günther Küppers & Helga Nowotny (Eds), *Selforganization: portrait of a scientific revolution*. Dordrecht: Kluwer.

Lupsha, Peter A. (1996). Transnational organized crimes versus the nation state. *Transnational Organized Crime, 2*(1), 21–48.

Maffesoli, Michael. (1996). *The time of the tribes: the decline of individualism in mass society*. London: Sage.

Nye, Joseph S. (2002). Corruption and political development: a cost–benefit analysis. In Arnold J. Heidenheimer & Michael Johnston (Eds), *Political corruption: concepts and contexts* (3rd edn, pp. 281–302). New Brunswick: Transaction Publishers.

Pearson, Zoe. (2001). An international human rights approach to corruption. In Peter Larmour & Nick Wolanin (Eds), *Corruption and anti-corruption* (pp. 30–61). Canberra: Asia Pacific Press.

Rahnema, Majid, & Bawtree, Victoria (Eds). (2003). *The post-development reader*. London and New Jersey: Zed Books.

Roberts, Simon A. (1979). *Order and dispute: an introduction to legal anthropology*. Harmondsworth: Penguin.

Sachs, Jeffrey D. (2009). *Common wealth: economics for a crowded planet*. New York and London: Penguin.

Sachs, Wolfgang (Ed.). (1995). *The development dictionary: a guide to knowledge and power*. London and New Jersey: Zed Books.

Scheper-Hughes, Nancy. (1992). *Death without weeping: the violence of everyday life in Brazil*. Berkeley: University of California Press.

Scrase, John C., Todd, Timothy J., Holden, Joseph M., & Baum, Scott (Eds). (2003). *Globalization, culture and inequality in Asia*. Melbourne: Trans Pacific Press.

Senge, Peter M., Scharmer, C. Otto, Jaworski, Joseph, & Flowers, Betty Sue. (2005). *Presence: an exploration of deep change in people, organizations, and society*. New York: Currency Doubleday.

Smart, Barry. (1999). *Facing modernity: ambivalence, reflexivity and morality*. London and Thousand Oaks: Sage.

Smith, Thomas S. (1997). Nonlinear dynamics and the micro–macro bridge. In Raymond A. Eve, Sara Horsfall & Mary E. Lee (Eds), *Chaos, complexity and sociology* (pp. 52–63). London: Sage.

Theobald, Robert. (1999). *We DO have future choices: strategies for fundamentally changing the 21st century*. Lismore: Southern Cross University Press.

Turner, Frederick. (1997). Chaos and social science. In Raymond A. Eve, Sara Horsfall & Mary E. Lee (Eds), *Chaos, complexity and sociology* (pp. xi–xxxii). London and Thousand Oaks: Sage.

Unger, Roberto Mangabeira. (2001). *False necessity: anti-necessitarian social theory in the service of radical democracy*. London: Verso.

Warburton, John. (2001). Corruption as a social process: from dyads to networks. In Peter Larmour & Nick Wolanin (Eds.), *Corruption and anti-corruption* (pp. 221–37). Canberra: Asia Pacific Press.

Warren, Kay (Ed.). (1994). *The violence within: cultural and political opposition in divided nations*. Boulder: Westview Press.

Yan, Yunxiang. (1996). *The flow of gifts: reciprocity and social networks in a Chinese village*. Stanford: Stanford University Press.

8. Professionalising Corruption? Investigating professional ethics for politicians

John Uhr

In this chapter, I try to open up a new perspective on professional ethics as applied to elected politicians by exploring two questions. First, given that the main goal is to improve the state of political ethics, is a professional-ethics model the best way to proceed? I answer with a very qualified 'yes', arguing that democracy needs real ethics, not the empty formalism sometimes found in professional-ethics schemes. My answer draws on J. M. Coetzee's novel *Elizabeth Costello* (2003, pp. 284–7), a fascinating recent account of the limits of professional ethics.[1]

Second, how can real ethics affect real politics to strengthen democratic practices of self-government? My answer distinguishes between two overlapping policy preoccupations: one interested in external accountability to combat unethical politics, particularly political corruption; and another interested in internal responsibility to promote ethical politics, especially ethical political leadership. Here my attempt is to take the 'ethics' in 'political ethics' seriously, in order to contribute to the debate over ethical politics—not simply political ethics.

What passes as political ethics is itself a political issue, best determined through political processes that give the public opportunities to weigh up contending views about the prudence and good sense of questionable political conduct—the view endorsed by the Canadian Senate Ethics Officer (2009–10, p. 12). Open, deliberative processes can allow politicians to account for and justify the public value of suspect conduct—before other politicians and before the public. Prudence is more valuable than prescription, although prescribed structures of public deliberation can bring prudence to the fore if used responsibly by politicians. Ultimately, that is a question for the public to judge.

I am sketching a regulative ideal rather than a regulatory mechanism. The ideal trusts politicians to reward decent and honourable conduct and to punish unethical conduct. How they do that is best for them to judge, according to the constitutional conventions of each political system. My preference for deliberative structures is consistent with many of the checks and balances

---

1   Parts of the novel were published in Coetzee (1999, pp. 15–69) along with several responses (pp. 73 ff). For further discussion, see Leist & Singer (2010).

common to liberal constitutionalism; and even if the regulative ideal is never matched in political practice, at least it gives politicians a fair sense of the standards of political ethics that we as a democratic political community might want of them.

The issue of responsibilities

My argument is in two parts. The first part reduces the prominence of 'professional' in the style of professional ethics we might expect of politicians. The aim here is to clear a space for what I am tempted to call 'real ethics' by reducing the domination of professional or role ethics. The second part builds on this proposal. It widens the scope of the political in political ethics to include recognition, and even encouragement, of decent political ethics and aims to balance the prevailing focus on indecent or corrupt political ethics.

And what might encourage ethical political decency? Drawing on principles of deliberative democracy, including those examined in my *Deliberative democracy in Australia* (Uhr, 1998), my answer is that public political deliberation can encourage political decency. How can public deliberation strengthen political decency? By allowing all parties to governance relationships to have their say on the state of their official responsibilities, thereby providing the public—should it be in a position to listen—with opportunities to review standards of political responsibility.

Much turns on these two concepts of 'responsibility' and 'relationship', clarified below. The two parts of my argument work together to support my contention that democracy has more to gain by trusting politicians to take greater (but not by any means total) responsibility for regulating their own ethics than by distrusting politicians and subjecting them to regulation, primarily through external anti-corruption commissions.

The term 'politicians' covers a diverse class of public actors. My scheme presumes that this very diversity can encourage a proactive system of checks and balances where non-executive politicians (including legislators, backbenchers and the opposition) use the publicity of deliberative processes to keep those with greater political power (such as heads of government or cabinet ministers) 'responsible' in the conduct of their official relationships (ministers with civil servants, for example). The hope is that structures of public deliberation would enable politicians with 'professional' capacities to be trusted to regulate much of their own public conduct.

The case against professional ethics faces two prominent claims, amongst many others. Most basically, there is the theoretical claim that the full nature of ethical conduct cannot be reduced to the forms appropriate to professional conduct, despite the welcome public benefits of properly managed professional conduct. Ever since Bradley (1962 [1876]) explored the ethic of 'my station and its duties', the ethics of office or role have won at best only qualified praise—even from Bradley himself, who was more interested in social than vocational roles. Yet many aspects of his approach escaped the attention of his early critics like Sidgwick (1967, pp. 284–7). Second, there is the practical claim that forms of self-regulation typical of professional ethics are plagued by practical defects deriving from the capture of the regulatory system by the professions. Contaminating private interests too often weaken the promised public benefits. If we take these two claims into account, political occupations provide one of the hardest test cases for advocates of professional ethics, who face considerable odds in persuading critics that either or both of these two counterclaims can be overcome.

While I acknowledge the force of the general case against professional ethics, I want to sketch the principles of a version of professional self-regulation that is suitable to democratic politics. One test of professionalism is the capacity for self-regulation of official conduct. I favour models of political ethics that include opportunities for politicians to take greater responsibility to regulate their own conduct. But this preference is unrelated to any political professionalism. The reverse is more likely: politics being a public rather than simply a professional activity, decisions about what constitutes appropriate political conduct are matters for public debate. Politicians can help or hinder that process but they should not be excluded from it for fear about conflicts of interest. Conflicts of interest can and do arise, and abuse of office has to be regulated. But there can be conflicts of *responsibility* as well as conflicts of *interest*, where competing ethics of political responsibility clash.

The most dramatic example from recent Australian experience comes from President George W. Bush's 2003 visit to the Australian Parliament, where his address was interrupted by the two Greens senators who later refused to vacate the chamber when so directed by the presiding officer. The government successfully moved to exclude the two Greens senators from the next day's joint session with the Chinese President. Both incidents—the senators' conduct in interrupting President Bush and the government's excluding them from the subsequent parliamentary meeting with the Chinese President—ignited considerable public debate over who should have the political power to determine how elected representatives conduct themselves when engaged in parliamentary business. At one extreme was support for the right of every elected representative to make their own decision on when and where to speak out on issues of public concern—including, if they are prepared to stand by their judgment, interrupting an address to the national parliament by the US

President. At the other extreme was support for the decision of the Howard Government that there should be no repeat of any such allegedly irresponsible conduct—particularly at a time when Australia was about to sign an important energy contract with China.

These extremes reflect contrasting norms of political responsibility, with no hint that either is tainted by suspicion of illegality or corruption. But the lively community debate over these contrasting ethical postures tells us much about the neglected end of political ethics: democratic communities are surprisingly keen to talk through the political ethics of self-government when confronted with contrasting examples of responsible ethical judgment by politicians. My point is not to award ethical points for exemplary decency to either position but to call attention to the larger issue of process: democratic political ethics are tested through public deliberation over the responsibilities of debatable political conduct. This deliberation occurs in relation to contrasting models of political decency, no less than in relation to models of corruption. Frequently this does not involve any issue of self-interested abuse of office but rather is a clash of ethical expectations about the proper use of political office or about standards of political decency. Debate over failures by politicians to do the right thing (such as failure to listen in silence to a visiting head of government or failure to allow elected representatives their right to join other parliamentarians in a meeting with a visiting head of government) can be just as central to public life as debate over alleged criminal misconduct by politicians.

Ethics or corruption?

My point of departure is that it is misleading to treat political ethics solely with the analytical tools used to deal with political corruption. Large parts of the 'ethics' in political ethics go un-investigated when the methods of corruption analysis dominate the scene. To exaggerate for effect: 'ethics' itself is corrupted when the focus is on the negative effects of corrupt conduct with little or no interest in the positive effects of ethical conduct. For those who like big concepts: this analytical 'corruption' limits our access to the phenomenology— or full range of characteristic conduct—captured by the category of 'political ethics'. Missing from most accounts are the phenomena at the ethical end of political ethics. One useful example of neglected practice is the investigation of types of exemplary public conduct in the Cooper and Wright reader *Exemplary public administrators* (1992).

Importing a distinction I defend at greater length in *Terms of trust* (Uhr, 2005, particularly pp. 197–204), I distinguish studies of political ethics from studies of political corruption by reference to the public conduct they seek to explain. Put crudely: corruption analysis explains how different forms of external accountability (that is, external to the politicians concerned) impede political corruption, and ethics analysis explains how different forms of internal responsibility (that is, internal to the politicians concerned) promote political ethics. Those familiar with the old Friedrich–Finer debate in US public administration will recognise this distinction as derivative from that influential exchange over the contest of the two values of accountability and responsibility—values that are distinguishable even if in practice they are inseparable.

The topic of 'political ethics' covers two poles of conduct: the unethical pole with the tension between corruption and its detection through public accountability; and the ethical pole with the tension between ethics and its discovery through personal responsibility. I want to distinguish the study of political ethics from the study of political corruption—the latter usually understood as a form of criminal misconduct best regulated by non-politicians. Investigation of political ethics gets at other forms of abuse of office: conduct that is not illegal but not necessarily right or decent. I argue that democratic standards of ethical political conduct are matters for political debate and determination, ideally (nice word!) managed politically through processes of political argument and public deliberation.

The issue of relationships

My take on professional political ethics will focus on the ethics of official relationships. Ethically responsible conduct by democratic politicians is largely about their management of official relationships. Other approaches deal with conflicts of interest or with outright corruption. My worry is that many aspects of what we might call 'constitutional morality' go unnoticed in these approaches. Of particular concern is the lack of scholarly attention to the ethical responsibility politicians have for managing relationships amongst the various institutions of government. To the extent that politicians have 'professional' duties, I think these duties derive from their share in the collective responsibility for the appropriate public use of political power. As I describe a little later, different political offices will have different types of responsibilities, depending on the specific powers at their disposal (legislative, executive, head of government, member of cabinet, senior advisor, civil service, military service, and so on). As responsibilities change, so do the specific institutional relationships necessary to give effect to the public powers in question. The ethics of institutional relationships might be less tidy than the ethics of personal power, but they are the building blocks of any 'profession' of public responsibility suitable to a democratic society (Uhr, 2010a).

To simplify: ethical responsibility is tested in judgments about the management of political relationships. My suggested distinction between political ethics and ethical politics can help keep the focus on ethical relationships. By 'political ethics', I am referring to the political conventions for managing disputes over ethical conduct through rules and regulations over the fine lines between private interest and public duty. This is what is usually meant by ethical regulation of political conduct, the aim being to reduce the incidence of private use of public office. The conventional approach moves along a path of distrust and is based on assumptions that politicians generally cannot be trusted with the responsibility of regulating their own ethical conduct. Relevant policy prescriptions include peer investigation but increasingly focus on external regulation of political conduct by ethics or integrity commissions and the like. By contrast, 'ethical politics' builds on trust rather distrust, conferring a kind of professional autonomy on politicians to manage their own power relationships through a framework with considerable self-regulation. Here the aim is not the negative one of reducing the incidence of the vices associated with the private use of public office but the more positive one of stimulating the virtues associated with praiseworthy political management of official relationships of power.

Politicians cannot be expected *not* to be political. It makes good policy sense to take precautions against unethical forms of political conduct. The path of distrust leads to greater and greater public accountability of politicians, with many external accountability agencies holding the line against formal breaches of ethical rules and expectations. But it also makes good policy sense to try to promote higher forms of ethical political conduct, beyond simple compliance with the rules. This alternative path of trust opens up possibilities for more substantial ethical responsibility, in the quite traditional sense represented by the political virtue of prudence as the driver of ethical responsibility in public life. In its most expansive sense, being ethical for politicians means acting prudently—taking prudence to mean the political virtue of practical wisdom so necessary for the sound management of official relationships. Actions speak louder than words, and political actions that build relationships can be more effective in promoting ethical politics than any number of fine words in a formal code of conduct. For example, the prudent decision by former UK Prime Minister Tony Blair to appear before the House of Commons Liaison Committee twice a year had probably greater potential power to improve the tone for British parliamentary conduct (should both sides in this relationship be willing) than any set of revisions to the Commons' code of conduct.

Now I admit that it stretches belief to suggest that the use and abuse of political prudence lend themselves to professional self-regulation. Prudence thus understood is not only the exercise of judgment but it is the exercise of political judgment in managing official relationships. Matters of judgment attract debate over the use and abuse of discretion; and matters of political judgment attract debate over the use and abuse of political deliberation by parties to the decisions in dispute. But this very recognition of prudential deliberation through open political debate highlights the nature of the professional standard invoked when speaking of professional ethics for democratic politicians. The model of professionalism here is not that of the single provider responsible for professional services but that of an assembly sharing responsibility for the provision of professional services. That, at least, is the ideal.

But is politics a profession?

But does the ideal match our realities? The case for treating politicians as a profession deserving the public trust associated with self-regulatory professional responsibilities seems far-fetched, at least initially. Across the democratic world, politicians universally lack the public confidence of professionals like health professionals, legal professionals, teachers, many police forces and the military. This lack of public confidence reflects widespread suspicion that politicians lack the capacity for responsible self-regulation of their professional conduct.

For all I know, this suspicion might be well founded. After all, politics is an occupation open to all comers with no easily discernable professional training that might qualify would-be politicians for political practice. The best-known case for treating 'politics as a vocation'—that presented by Max Weber—certainly had an ethical theme, and related writings by Weber highlight the importance of supervised experience and career training in the development of political leaders (Weber, 1994 [1919]). But remember the nature of this ethical theme: politics can be treated as 'a vocation' because of the distinctive calling seen in the practice of truly great political leaders who are prepared to live *for* and not simply *off* politics. These exceptional public figures not only break the rules but also break the mould of conventional political ethics. They take personal responsibility for their own political conduct and are prepared to be judged by the consequences of their own decisions. By taking responsibility, they are not simply 'taking charge' but also, in democratic systems, preparing to face up to a wider public reckoning of their political ethics.

Weber's approach is less an argument for professionalism and more one for exceptionalism: political ethics are exceptions to the normal ethical rules. This argument is one of the most influential in favour of a kind of ethical autonomy for politics. But it is an argument that seems to concede too much autonomy, sheltering irresponsible schemers beneath the scaffolding intended for responsible leaders. Weber's ethic is compatible with the 'dirty hands' ethic, which, certainly in the time since Weber, has been reformulated to justify everything from the grand exceptionalism of a 'capital M' Machiavellian leader to the corrupt conduct of many 'small m' machiavellian schemers. What holds for leaders does not necessarily hold for schemers. This schemer-stealth is a classic example of what gives professional ethics a bad name. Norms of appropriateness devised to apply to distinct and distinguished practitioners are seized on by indistinct and undistinguished competitors. The danger is that any public benefit accruing to professional claims of ethical exceptionalism will be jeopardised by the private benefits of the professional pretenders. Most professional associations granted self-regulatory powers strive to justify their due diligence in policing their own professional ethics. Once again, politics is exceptional, in that there are so few examples to reassure a suspicious public that politicians deserve to be granted authority to regulate their own affairs. Periodic stories of corruption are enough to drive out the high hopes for ethically responsible politics.

The dismal record of political self-regulation is one important practical count against political professionalism. Another is the deeper theoretical reservation about the ethical integrity of professional or role ethics. One of the most striking examples of the critique of professional ethics in public life comes from the novel *Elizabeth Costello* (2003) by the 2003 Nobel Prize winner for literature, J. M. Coetzee. His novel contains a dramatic illustration of the merits and pitfalls of professional or role ethics. Within limits, I support a professional approach to the regulation of politicians' ethical conduct, one that confers considerable responsibility on elected or representative politicians to take the initiative in managing the resolution of conflict over alleged breaches of appropriate standards of ethical conduct. The relevance of Coetzee's novel is that it helps clarify what I mean by 'within limits'.

The novel draws attention to the limits of attempts to reduce ethics to role compliance, and implicitly to the dangers of professions' claims of ethical exceptionalism. At the end of the day, being ethical means doing the right thing, regardless of what one's profession deems to be right according to the professional role. In the case of politicians, being ethical is more than simply not breaching the rules of official conduct or even obtaining formal clearance from an ethics committee of one's peers. Weber, to his credit, knew this and made the test of ethical responsibility a demanding version of consequentialism: having the courage to stand firm, taking personal responsibility for non-compliance with the unconditional obligations of conventional orthodoxies and being prepared to justify the public benefits of one's deviation from conventional norms.

Rethinking the ethical in professional ethics

The novel *Elizabeth Costello* is subtitled 'Eight lessons', with the eight substantive chapters each tackling a particular 'lesson'. Elizabeth Costello is an imaginary Australian writer, who, in her older years, becomes the invited celebrity at many literary and academic conferences. She knows that her celebrity reflects her early work, not her present writing, and that these invitations cannot last. In some ways, the end of these invitations would be a blessed relief, as she would be released from the obligation of having to explain herself and her work—a task she finds increasingly difficult as she ages and weighs the merits of her earlier work, and becomes increasingly aware of the better work that she has never completed. Much of the novel deals with this tension between the public persona of 'the author' and the private character of the writer who is more and more detached from her prominent role as celebrity author. Tired of making public statements, Elizabeth Costello retreats into a private world where she permits greater honesty about her self and her talents as a writer and person.

The topic of professional ethics appears in the last lesson, entitled 'At the gate', when Elizabeth is called on to account for her moral beliefs, encountering her final act of public scrutiny 'at the gate' of heaven—Coetzee never uses this traditional term for the resting place of the good (compare with Funk & Palm, 2010, pp. 193–225). In fact, it is probable that Coetzee is not writing about the afterlife of Elizabeth Costello at all, but is letting the reader see how she anticipates this prospect well before her death. The publication of yet another Elizabeth Costello story after the publication of the novel supports this interpretation (Coetzee, 2004, 2005, chs 13–20, especially pp. 27–30). Not that Coetzee makes things easy for readers. What Coetzee says of Philip Roth applies equally to himself: readers must struggle with the author's 'long-running practice of complicating the line of transmission along which the story reaches the reader and putting in question the mediator's angle on it', such that readers are bound to be 'dominated by uncertainty about how far the narrator is to be believed' (2010).

Back, then, to Elizabeth's imaginary anticipation of her final rite of passage. Arriving at the gates by bus (we are not alone even in this, the final journey), Elizabeth asks permission to pass through the closed gate separating heaven from the world of the still-restless souls. But the authorities ('the guardians') tell her that before she can enter, she 'must make a statement' (p. 193). Will this posturing never end, she thinks; why can't I simply pass through the gate and put paid to my earthly debt? Handed a blank piece of paper, Elizabeth is told that the required statement is to be a statement of 'what you believe' (p. 194). As the burden of this 'trial' begins to dawn on her, Elizabeth realises that 'before she will be found good' she must do what she can to provide evidence of her goodness in her beliefs.

Can her beliefs carry this burden? Elizabeth protests that as a writer, 'it is not my profession to believe, just to write. Not my business. I do imitations, as Aristotle would have said' (p. 194). Then she begins a slippery process of plea-bargaining: 'I can do an imitation of belief, if you like' (p. 194). She gets no encouragement. She later regrets 'this tendency to flare up' (p. 203), which reflects her conviction that she is typically misunderstood and that she deserves better. She is a true professional and wants to be appreciated as a model of a professional writer. Generally, she resists inquiries into her inner world of personal interest and deflects attention back to the external world of her professional capacity.

Now taking an even more radical turn, Elizabeth writes a statement of belief to challenge the rule about statements of belief. Understanding herself as a writer who trades in fictions, she records that she maintains beliefs 'only provisionally: fixed beliefs will stand in my way' (p. 195). So on these grounds—which she calls 'professional, vocational'—Elizabeth requests 'exemption from a rule' requiring every petitioner to 'hold one or more beliefs' (p. 195). Her strategy is unsuccessful. The guardian figure tries to encourage her with an incentive. He allows her a brief glimpse of the brilliant light through the open gate; then, in a 'surprisingly personal' gesture, he acts out of keeping with his own professional role and pats her on the arm, inviting her to 'try harder' (p. 196). Forgetting herself or her place, Elizabeth tries to behave smarter rather than harder. She begins to joke with the guard, but to no avail. Humour works no better than serious pleas for exemption, so she accepts that she had better return to the task at hand and prepare the required statement of beliefs.

Elizabeth takes stock of her situation and returns to this, the most difficult act of writing she has ever attempted. Eventually, she completes the statement to her satisfaction and her day in court arrives. Elizabeth is called before the court of nine 'male and elderly' judges to present her statement (p. 198). She begins reading her statement, explaining why writers have no beliefs. Her thesis is simple: 'my calling: dictation secretary' (p. 199). Later she identifies this as 'a secretary's way of life', their special vocation being to record but not to judge the worth of what they hear (p. 204). Claiming that as a writer it is not her role 'to interrogate' or 'to judge' the beliefs of those about whom she writes, Elizabeth says that 'what I write is what I hear', not what people might want to hear (p. 199). As a 'good secretary', the writer 'should have no beliefs (p. 200). It is 'inappropriate to the function' (p. 200). Her rather compelling argument is that personal beliefs act as obstacles to writers, resisting their capacity to hear properly what others say and believe.

The response is not long coming. Says one judge: 'Without beliefs we are not human' (p. 200). Elizabeth's response is that her 'sense of duty' follows her 'function', with the result that 'I have beliefs but I do not believe in them' (p. 200). The next response is quick and acute: what effect, the judge asks, does this 'lack of belief' have on 'your humanity?' (p. 201). Elizabeth protests that her own humanity is of no consequence, claiming that her 'own emptiness' is outweighed by her contribution as a writer to the humanity of her readers (p. 201). For 'professional reasons', Elizabeth cannot afford to believe: she 'cannot afford to take myself too seriously' (p. 201). She begins to appreciate that this must sound as though she is treating the court proceedings with contempt.

At this point a judicial voice asks: 'And what of the Tasmanians?' (p. 202). What might appear an obtuse aside is in fact a confronting move intended to tease out whether this Australian writer really has 'no beliefs to guide her' in thinking about the miserable fate of the Indigenous Tasmanians—exterminated, Elizabeth now recognises to herself, by 'her countrymen, her ancestors' (pp. 201–2). A judge asks why Elizabeth presents herself 'not in your own person but as a special case, a special destiny, a writer' (p. 203). Forcefully, the judge asks if being a professional secretary means that one makes no judgments and is therefore 'bankrupt of conscience?' (p. 204). Elizabeth now knows that she is 'cornered', beaten down by what appears to be 'a contest of rhetoric' rather than a real interrogation into truth (p. 204). Weighed under by too many 'heady abstractions', Elizabeth departs the hearing with a severe headache, knowing that she has lost her case (p. 205).

Eventually she gets a second chance. She is now aware that her problem is that she 'cannot afford to believe' because in her 'line of work one has to suspend belief' (p. 213). Despite this, Elizabeth gets her second hearing, this time before a new panel of judges, smaller than the first one and now including a female judge. She takes advice from another petitioner and presents a case illustrating her passion rather than her beliefs. It is a riveting performance, an exemplary apologia of her life history, presented 'not as a writer but as an old woman… telling you what I remember' (p. 217). Passing over her remarkable presentation about her memories of her childhood in rural Victoria and her relish for the natural environment, I simply note that the judges are confused. Is Elizabeth replacing her former plea with its absence of beliefs with a new one based on explicit beliefs? Or are her recollections of her passionate life evidence of a very human belief in life? Elizabeth's desperately truthful answers to their many questions are attempts to defend the integrity of both of her two formal statements of belief. But this is of little avail, finally provoking the judges to 'howl with laughter' at this picture of strained personal integrity (p. 221).

Elizabeth recognises that 'the special fidelities' of her vocation will not allow her win this final rite of passage (p. 224; compare with Lodge, 2003; Wood, 2003).

Coetzee does not allow us to see any further into Elizabeth Costello's final saga. As I suggested, the saga may well be all in Elizabeth's mind, a kind of mental rehearsal for the real thing. But given Coetzee's artistry, the power of her passion is no less real for the readers of *Elizabeth Costello*. The lesson ends where it began, with Elizabeth restlessly wondering just what it takes to get through the gates to the peace on the other side. Elizabeth ponders her new knowledge of the cost of her own loyalties to her vocation, appreciating that fidelity is 'the word on which all hinges' (p. 224). At least she has learnt that her pride in her professionalism does not, in the end, count for much in the eyes of her gatekeepers. The advice to try the path of passion is useful because it brings out more of her own personal beliefs, even if Elizabeth is ill prepared to explain their meaning. Her tendency to slip back into her professional mode of non-evaluative recording probably shows that the early passion has faded, at a cost only now beginning to be appreciated in the afterlife of this gifted writer.

Where does this leave us? Elizabeth Costello presents herself very much as an individual but for our limited purposes, which do less than justice to Coetzee's own purposes, she can stand as an example of a professional type: indeed, the type of a professional. Professions do differ and not all have the same degree of impersonality that the writer Costello thinks appropriate to her calling. But this studious impersonality with its restraints on partiality of judgment in the business of storytelling causes us to wonder about the parallels with other professions. In general, the ethics of professionalism are variations on this theme of impersonality. Professional ethics tell practitioners to carry out their duties informed by their professional, as distinct from their personal, judgments about the responsible course of conduct in the circumstances. This point highlights rather than minimises the role of discretionary judgment in professional practice, but according to a demanding model of discretion with little or no place for personal value judgment. For good reasons, practice is never as tidy as this impersonal model: the best professionals tend to be good human beings as well as good professional practitioners. In the context of his novel, Coetzee invites us to ask if the judges are so blind that they cannot see that Elizabeth Costello is a good person as well as a good writer. Perhaps they are the models of professional limitation, so blinded by their adherence to form that they fail to give Elizabeth her due justice.

Rethinking the political in political ethics

I move now from my reorientation to ethics to my reorientation to politics. The first move attempted to widen the scope of appropriate ethical conduct to include the positive pole of the decent as well as the negative pole of the dishonest. Of course, broadening the category of researchable conduct does nothing to increase the incidence of decent conduct. Broadening the category simply opens up the possibility of fresh research into debates over decency to balance the prevailing preoccupation with debates over dishonesty. Decency typically begins with compliance with the rules, but there is plenty of scope for debate over the supra-legal expectations of appropriate political conduct. To my mind, this is as much a political as an ethical question—in fact, an ethico-political question.

The second move reinforces the turn from political ethics generally to ethical politics more specifically. If democracy is the basic political norm under consideration then the study of ethical politics is going to involve investigation of a democratic ethic of shared responsibility for self-government. What orientation to 'the political' would be compatible with this new research impetus? My suggestion is drawn from theories of deliberative democracy because of their attention to the importance of norms of responsible political argument in structuring democratic politics. To say that decency or ethical responsibility amongst politicians is an ethico-political question is to say that standards of appropriate conduct are, in a democracy, ideally determined through responsible public deliberation over the forms and substance of ethical politics. This proposition allows for a considerable contribution by politicians, through open and accountable systems of self-regulation of suspect or debated instances of political conduct. While the standards of appropriate conduct might be thought to belong to the democracy itself, responsibility for detailed management of claims and counterclaims over suspect conduct rests with serving politicians, in keeping with their public responsibilities as representatives of the political community.

What are the institutional implications of this preliminary conclusion? To me, the most important principle is that 'professional political ethics' makes sense only if we recognise the *collective* character of political professionalism. Think of this, if you want, as a version of the 'many hands' thesis: that political responsibility is shared responsibility—between electors and the elected, between executive and legislative officials, between political branches and the judiciary, between cabinet ministers and the bureaucracy, between insiders and outsiders, and so on. In keeping with the many hands thesis, politicians can evade ethical responsibility by claiming that others took a greater role in instances of debatable conduct. But there is another dimension to this collective arrangement sometimes neglected in the many hands literature. It is the other side of the evasion story: political ethics is not so much about individual conduct as about shared responsibility for the conduct of relationships. If we put to one side the conventional approach to criminal misconduct through abuse of office, there is still plenty to investigate in the legal-but-questionable conduct by politicians in the use and abuse of relationships of public power. Westminster-derived parliamentary systems provide many examples: in the ways that prime ministers dominate relationships with cabinets, ministers dominate relationships with civil servants, ministerial consultants dominate relationships with both ministers and civil servants, higher civil servants dominate relationships with lower civil servants, who in turn dominate service providers, who in turn dominate consumers of public services. I emphasise 'domination' to bring out the incompatibility of these sort of power relationships with democratic norms. This recital of dominating relationships is a caricature but it conveys the message: political ethics is about many things, not least the conduct of those official relationships amongst public institutions that 'constitute' the political and policy process. The study of political ethics deals with the state of relationships amongst the many political offices sharing political power, including the basic organising offices of citizen and government. Thus, political ethics includes the study of the norms that constitute democracy as evident in the political management of governance relationships.

A final institutional consequence to note here is that political relationships are relationships of mutuality. Political ethics cannot be gauged solely through investigation into one party to the relationship. Indeed, whole webs of relationships influence the political conduct of individual political actors. The institutional implication is that political ethics should include the study of the conduct of public processes and not just the study of the conduct of individual actors. To give but one illustration: parliamentary systems typically have codes of ministerial conduct, occasionally even including independent advisors on ethics and integrity. Within limits, these codes of conduct can help clarify expected standards of official conduct by ministers. But in almost all instances, the codes are creatures of the political executive, illustrating a very circumscribed relationship within the holders of executive power. When push comes to shove, the professed standards of high responsibility are overridden by the operational norms of executive convenience.

The Australian story is one of prime ministerial discretion to interpret ministerial conduct in the light of the political interests of the serving government. The relationship does not include the wider body of elected representatives, despite the constitutional rhetoric of responsible parliamentary government. Elsewhere I have argued that parliament has only itself to blame because it has failed to deal itself in by establishing or instituting a relationship with ministers whereby they agree to honour parliamentary as distinct from ministerial standards of public conduct (Uhr, 2010b, pp. 124–9). This failure also means that parliament has failed in its relationship with electors by not living up to its responsibilities as an accountability agency that protects the public interest in open and honest government.

Ethics by example

I can try to bring this together with an Australian example: the so-called 'children overboard' affair in the lead-up to the 2001 national election. This example balances my earlier use of Coetzee's novel with an account of Australian lapses in political decency that reads all too much like a novel. If only the events described were fictional.

There is a growing academic literature on the political and administrative ethics surrounding these events, most of which suggests that the re-election of the Howard Government came at the price of unprecedented damage to the government's reputation for public integrity. The government won the election and, not surprisingly, defended its integrity in terms of having earned the public mandate to retain the responsibilities of executive power. It defended its ethical credentials by pointing to the balance between its right to use the responsibilities of governmental power as it saw fit (acknowledging that this right is subject to the limits of the law) and its proven public accountability as evidenced by its electoral victory. From the government's point of view, no law was broken during its tenure in office and the people had spoken, giving fresh legitimacy to the governing Coalition. In this simplified account, the Howard Government's take on ethics in government was a classic attempt to justify the discretionary use of its powers by reference to the renewal of public trust in it, as granted by electors at the election.

Mandates are tricky things, and that same election also returned a solid non-government majority in the Senate, which contested the right of any government to claim a mandate to govern. The Senate select committee that inquired into 'the certain maritime incident' reported adversely on the Howard Government's ethical performance (Select Committee on a Certain Maritime Incident, 2002). A subsequent Senate committee built on this initial inquiry and reported on the need for new legislation to bring greater accountability to bear on governments' use and abuse of the hidden power of ministerial staff (Finance and Public Administration References Committee, 2003). Both reports contain detailed examinations of government ministers' suspect conduct in abusing their powers over the Public Service and the responsibilities stipulated in the ministerial code of conduct not to deceive the public, and their obligation to correct any misleading public information, even in cases where there has been no deliberate intention to deceive.

The best investigative account of the 'children overboard' and related incidents is Marr and Wilkinson's *Dark Victory* (2003; compare with Weller, 2002). The book is a war story of sorts, detailing the armed resistance marshalled by the Australian Government against a perceived threat to the security of the country's sovereignty in the months leading up to a general election. It is also a political thriller, documenting the struggle within the government over deployment of military forces and the daring risk-management of the government's most astute political advisers, which won out against the traditional caution and risk-averseness of the professional military, particularly the Navy, which was committed as much to due process as to results.

The story begins in August 2001 with a Norwegian vessel, the *Tampa*, going to the rescue of 438 'illegals'—mainly Afghans fleeing the Taliban government—on a sinking Indonesian vessel. They had been collected together in Indonesia by people smugglers intent on ferrying them to Australia. The Navy was instrumental in preventing the *Tampa* from docking at the Australian Territory of Christmas Island, and eventually shipping them to Nauru. Then in early October, the Navy rescued a further 223 people from another boat known as the 'SIEV 4'. The Howard Government portrayed both incidents as an attack, not just on Australian territory, but on sovereign Australian values. In the latter case, the 'SIEV 4 illegals' were not only unwelcome 'queue jumpers' but also untrustworthy and uncivilised manipulators of Australian assistance, even to the point—it was claimed—of throwing children overboard to get Australian authorities to accede to their demands for rescue and access to Australian care and custody. The claims were attributed to navy officials. Initially, these claims appeared correct, but the government made no mention of subsequent contrary defence 'doubts' or 'uncertainties' when the story wore thin.

These events dovetailed with John Howard's own personal experience in Washington on 9/11 when visiting the Bush Government. Less than a month later, as the 'war on terror' began, Howard called the 2001 election. The supposed attacks by 'boat people' became an election theme.

Marr and Wilkinson suggest that the 2001 electoral victory was marked by a stain of darkness: the Howard Government's deceit of the public by manipulating the truth about the significance of the increase in asylum-seekers during 2001, which culminated in the contortions of the 'children overboard' affair that helped consolidate electoral support for the government. The issue is, however, not really whether the government lied to voters but how it had already committed itself to playing the race card in the battle for public support. Howard's advisers may have been flattered to find how closely Marr and Wilkinson trace their skilful reinforcement of public sentiment about Australian vulnerability and the need for decisive leadership.

Marr and Wilkinson's story holds that the Howard Government's victory in 2001 is a case study in 'international best practice' political management, with Howard deserving recognition as Australia's master of the political art of misinformation. The 'v for victory' is overshadowed by the 'w for wedge', with Howard portrayed not in terms of international leadership but as a world leader of wedge politics: getting between political opponents and their natural supporters. Marr and Wilkinson do not hide their own personal views about the nastiness of the dark arts of deception practised by the Howard Government, epitomised by the singular achievement of retiring Defence Minister Peter Reith as the wizard of weasel words, as gifted in consolidating public support as he was in fracturing the confidence of the Labor Opposition.

Marr and Wilkinson are reporters, with no inclination to preach about solutions. The strength of the book is the authors' ability to mine the record, including through the use of freedom-of-information requests for defence evidence, and to relate the surface of daily events during the second half of 2001 to a deeper source of partisan calculation. If the devil is in the detail then their book is an account of the devil's workshop, showing a government tempting a people with the fear of terrorism. The authors' extensive use of the public record, particularly that generated by the Senate inquiry, is also supplemented by quite extensive interviews with most of the key players, to build up a richly layered picture of contemporary Australian governance. A strength of this account is the use of the court records relating to the Federal Court challenges against the government's alleged unlawful naval detention of asylum-seekers. Marr and Wilkinson show that there rarely is a 'whole of government' view on such basic things as legal duties, with important differences of professional opinion across defence, attorney-general's and central agencies.

For those who care little about the authors' advocacy of the rights of the refugees, *Dark Victory* still delivers fresh evidence about the norms of power in Australian government. The book profiles prominent figures, beginning with the Norwegian captain Arne Rinnan, then Commander Norman Banks of *HMAS Adelaide*, joined by close studies of the Howard ministry activists such as Philip Ruddock and Reith, followed by portraits of power illustrating the style of many bureaucratic chiefs. The book is a gallery of public managers, proving the point that systems are held in place by individuals, each with a distinctive sense of their professional role. Some of these officials participated in interviews with the authors and, in the case of Chris Barrie in particular, we are offered many quotes that help explain his delicate situation as Chief of the Defence Forces, acting as something of a powerboard with multiple leads connecting various military, bureaucratic and political agencies. Reading this book, one might conclude that no one person can play that role and expect to do justice to the interests of all concerned. There are bound to be power surges and blockages.

The bureaucracy deserves all the adverse attention Marr and Wilkinson give it. The Department of Immigration in particular comes in for an unsympathetic portrait. Attorney-General's gets a more flattering picture, more in tune with the authors' commitment to the high watermark of international obligations. The Department of Prime Minister and Cabinet is crucial but seems reduced here to two or three individuals, as though only they mattered. Defence features through the detailed and supportive account of the Navy's stubborn professionalism, to the point of getting up the nose of government loyalists. The civilian arm of defence gets off very lightly, as though Minister Reith knew how to manage well enough on his own. The great Canberra debate over ministerial staff and their accountability obligations passes without trace, implying that the Senate inquiry was chasing the tail of the wrong dog. The report of the Senate committee fails to get a mention, although the record of hearings is used frequently to good effect. All this is to say that *Dark Victory* is less about the weaknesses of defence intelligence about 'children overboard' and, in a backhanded compliment, more about the strengths of the Howard Government's strategy of 'truth overboard'. *Dark Victory* goes to the rescue of many truths left in the wake of the victorious Howard ship of state.

Conclusion

The above example illustrates my focus on professional relationships. It also illustrates my interest in political conduct that is, paradoxically, as corrupting as it is legal. Although this Australian practice is broadly consistent with current regulatory expectations, it falls far short of the regulative ideal I began with. The story is significant because it highlights the suspect ethical quality of so many political relationships within the Australian Government—including relationships of accountability. I have no magic box of regulatory mechanisms that can transform Australian or similar systems. Intent on bringing politicians closer to the task of self-regulation, I have contrasted prevailing tendencies with a regulative ideal. For all practical purposes, the prevailing tendencies are winning.

The 'children overboard' story does not turn on mundane conflicts of interest but on conflicts of constitutional responsibility, taking constitutional to refer not to the black letter of the law but to the norms of the different political offices 'constituting' a democracy. It is a classic example of the contestability of political ethics, testing in unprecedented ways the decency of many political relationships by politicians whose personal decency is not the question. It is a good example because it shows how political corruption advances under the cover of many disguises, including the disguise of 'politics as usual' (Uhr, 2001, particularly pp. 723–6). Putting Australian developments to one side, I conclude with some general lessons arising from this attempt to apply a professional ethics framework to democratic political ethics.

Most forms of professional or role ethics apply group norms to recognised individual practitioners of the profession in question. Politics is different, not only because the professional skill is unrelated to any specialised training and any associated professional academy, but also because the practice in question is fundamentally a shared or collective practice. This is so particularly in democratic regimes that quite properly pride themselves on participative public decision making and typically privilege the constitutional power of an elected assembly, even to the point of protecting the participation rights of non-government or opposition members. The collective nature of political professionalism extends beyond power-sharing within the ranks of elected representatives to include relationships between politicians and related professionals in public administration.

In this approach, professional political ethics refers to the widely distributed responsibility for determining appropriate standards relevant to these relationships of shared power and, in addition, to the collective resolution of disputed instances of unethical conduct. Particulars of responsible ethical conduct vary according to the nature of the political office under discussion: the precise ethical responsibilities varying with the power relationships managed by different political offices. This range of official responsibilities is itself subject to any formal constitutional constraints—a matter for the collective determination of the assembled professional politicians, acting under public oversight.

Thus, professional political ethics as used here refers to the collective determination of appropriate political conduct, which will be more ethically responsible when structured around due processes of fair and open political deliberation, in place of 'politics as usual'. Most existing systems of political ethics try to overcome the defects of 'politics as usual' by conferring special power on small groups of politicians comprising dedicated 'ethics' or 'privileges' committees with responsibility for investigating and adjudicating ethics infringements, judged against 'the rules' or codes of official conduct. My idealised model differs because it is a relationship-centred rather than a rule-centred approach. My approach is inevitably more uncertain and unpredictable than narrower forms of professionalism based on compliance with 'the rules'. But this very openness reflects, I think, the true nature of political ethics as a matter of political judgment—with disputes managed through collective political deliberation over appropriate relationships of power: representatives relating to their own offices and relating to other public offices sharing public power.

The implications of this focus on collective professionalism are considerable, including not least a surprising role for the public as the court of ultimate appeal. Democratic politics rests on the relationship between the professionals and the people; and the ethical quality of democratic politics depends in no small part on the ethics of the relationship between the people and their political representatives. Democracy can be thought to hold 'the people' in some sort of 'professional' regard, in that they have the responsibility (the final say) over the system of self-regulation we call democratic self-government.

Acknowledgements

My thanks to Patrick Dobel, Andrew Lister and Andrew Sabl for helpful comments on drafts of an earlier version of this paper (Uhr, 2006), reprinted here with revisions with the kind permission of the publisher. (See Uhr, 2010b, for another version of this argument.)

References

Bradley, F. H. (1962 [1876]). My station and its duties. In Richard Wollheim (Ed.), *Ethical studies* (2nd edn, pp. 160–213). Oxford: Clarendon Press.

Canadian Senate Ethics Officer. (2009–10). *Annual report*. Ottawa.

Coetzee, J. M. (1999). *The lives of animals*. Princeton: Princeton University Press.

Coetzee, J. M. (2003). *Elizabeth Costello*. New York: Knopf.

Coetzee, J. M. (2004). As a woman grows older. *The New York Review of Books*, 15 January, 13–20.

Coetzee, J. M. (2005). *Slow man*. New York: Knopf.

Coetzee, J. M. (2010). On the moral brink. *The New York Review of Books*, 28 October.

Cooper, Terry L., & Wright, N. Dale (Eds). (1992). *Exemplary public administrators: character and leadership in government*. San Francisco: Jossey-Bass.

Finance and Public Administration References Committee. (2003). Staff employed under the *Members of Parliament (Staff) Act 1984*. Canberra: The Senate.

Funk, Michael, & Palm, Ralph. (2010). Irony and belief in *Elizabeth Costello*. In Anton Leist & Peter Singer (Eds), *J M Coetzee and ethics* (pp. 337–56). New York: Columbia University Press.

Leist, Anton, & Singer, Peter (Eds). (2010). *J M Coetzee and ethics: philosophical perspectives on literature*. New York: Columbia University Press.

Lodge, David (2003). Disturbing the peace. *The New York Review of Books*, 20 November.

Marr, David, & Wilkinson, Marian. (2003). *Dark victory*. Sydney: Allen & Unwin.

Select Committee on a Certain Maritime Incident. (2002). *Report*. Canberra: The Senate.

Sidgwick, Henry. (1967). *History of ethics*. London: Macmillan.

Uhr, John. (1998). *Deliberative democracy in Australia*. Cambridge: Cambridge University Press.

Uhr, John. (2001). Public service ethics in Australia. In Terry L. Cooper (Ed.), *Handbook of administrative ethics* (2nd edn, pp. 719–40). New York: Marcel Dekker.

Uhr, John. (2005). *Terms of trust: arguments over ethics in Australian government*. Sydney: UNSW Press.

Uhr, John. (2006). Professional ethics for politicians. In Denis Saint-Martin & Fred Thompson (Eds), *Public ethics and governance* (pp. 207–25). Oxford: JAI Press.

Uhr, John. (2010a). Be careful what you wish for. In Jonathan Boston, Andrew Bradstock & David Eng (Eds), *Public policy: why ethics matters* (pp. 79–97). Canberra: ANU E Press.

Uhr, John. (2010b). Modernised modes of government ethics. In Rainer Koch, Peter Conrad & Wolfgang H. Lorig (Eds), *New public service* (pp. 329–44). Wiesbaden: Gabler Verlag.

Weber, Max. (1994 [1919]). The profession and vocation of politics. In Peter Lassman & Roland Spiers (Eds), *Max Weber: political writings* (pp. 309–69). Cambridge: Cambridge University Press.

Weller, Patrick. (2002). *Don't tell the prime minister*. Melbourne: Scribe Books.

Wood, James. (2003). A frog's life. *London Review of Books, 25*(20), 23 October.

9. Corruption and the Concept of Culture: Evidence from the Pacific Islands

Peter Larmour

Ideas about culture

Ideas about 'culture' have often been used to explain or excuse acts of corruption. Gift-giving, it is sometimes said, is 'part of our culture', and outsiders should not confuse it with bribery or corruption. Such a relativistic approach has been strongly criticised by academic writers on corruption such as Syed Alatas in his classic *Sociology of corruption* (1968), and by activists like Transparency International (TI).

Alatas sees cultural relativism as another kind of Western naivety and condescension towards non-Western societies. The West, he argues, imagines the latter societies as incapable of telling right from wrong, a notion that Alatas thoroughly disproves in the course of his study by providing copious evidence of concern about abuse of public office from different historical periods dating back to ancient Rome, and different cultural traditions (Muslim and Chinese). Leaders violating norms knew those local norms existed. Cultural practices are used for the purposes of corruption rather than being the cause of corruption (Alatas, 1968, pp. 96–7).

More recently, TI has taken a robust stand against what it calls the 'myth' or 'excuse' of culture. Its influential *Source book 2000* quotes one of the organisation's founding fathers, Olusegun Obasanjo, who went on to be elected President of Nigeria (Pope, 2000). Talking of the distinction between gifts and bribes, Obasanjo said:

> I shudder at how an integral aspect of our culture could be taken as the basis for rationalising otherwise despicable behaviour. In the African concept of appreciation and hospitality, the gift is usually a token. It is not demanded. The value is usually in the spirit rather than in the material worth. It is usually done in the open, and never in secret. Where it is excessive, it becomes an embarrassment and it is returned. If anything, corruption has perverted and destroyed this aspect of our culture. (p. 8)

Nevertheless, ideas linking culture with corruption won't go away easily. TI is an international organisation; whatever universalistic beliefs it holds, in practice it has to defer to claims of national and cultural difference. Meanwhile, ideas about culture have become increasingly influential in the social sciences, particularly in the field of cultural studies.

This chapter suggests how concepts of culture in general—and gift-giving in particular—may still be useful in understanding corruption and the problems associated with controlling it. It draws for empirical evidence on a series of reports on national integrity systems (NIS) in the Pacific Islands. The reports follow a standard template provided by TI, which asked about the existence and performance of various aspects of each country's 'national integrity system': the executive, the legislature, the auditor-general, civil society, and so on (Larmour & Barcham, 2006). The authors of the reports were also asked to comment generally on the corruption situation in each country. For 12 of the 14 reports, the authors were specifically asked to comment on the role played by culture; the two remaining authors discussed culture without being prompted.

The Pacific Islands consist of 14 small countries, ranging in population from 1600 to six million, with a median of about 100 000 inhabitants. The region is typically divided into three main 'culture areas': Micronesia to the north-west; Melanesia to the south-west; and Polynesia to the east (see Table 9.1). All but two of these 14 countries are parliamentary democracies. The two exceptions are Tonga, where the government is still responsible to a hereditary monarch rather than the legislature, and Fiji, which has been ruled by a military government since a coup in December 2006.

The region has also been important for Western study of anthropology, providing evidence for Marcel Mauss's classic study *The gift* (2002 [1950]) and other key texts in the discipline. In each country, arguments about the role of custom and tradition are an important part of everyday life and politics, including discussions about corruption.

Local cultural values show little sign of going away under pressures of colonialism or (now) globalisation. Marshall Sahlins has analysed the way Pacific Islanders use introduced materials to amplify their indigenous ways of life rather than abandon them, although he concedes they may eventually do the latter (1999). Chris Gregory talked about the 'efflorescence' of traditional culture on contact with Western goods that allowed people to have bigger funerals, wider circuits of exchange, more costly political campaigns and more remittances than ever before (1982). The upsurge of anxiety about corruption may reflect this upsurge in the volume and visibility of traditional practices, amplified by cash and new technology.

Table 9.1 Pacific Islands Population and Political Status

Name	Population (mid-2011 estimate)	Political status
Melanesia		
Fiji Islands	851 745	Independent 1970
Papua New Guinea	6 888 297	Independent 1975
Solomon Islands	553 254	Independent 1979
Vanuatu	251 784	Independent 1980
Micronesia		
Federated States of Micronesia	102 360	Free association with the United States
Kiribati	102 697	Independent 1979
Marshall Islands	54 999	Free association with the United States
Nauru	10 185	Independent 1968
Palau	20 643	Free association with the United States
Polynesia		
Cook Islands	15 576	Free association with New Zealand
Niue	1446	Free association with New Zealand
Sāmoa	183 617	Independent 1962
Tonga	103 682	Never colonised
Tuvalu	11 206	Independent 1978

Source: Secretariat of the Pacific Community (2012). Population estimates and projections for several years. *Pocket statistical summary 2011*. Nouméa: Secretariat of the Pacific Community.

Each country in the region is dependent to some degree on foreign aid, loans from international development banks and, in Fiji's case, concessionary access to the European Union for its sugar exports. These donors, banks and international organisations have become increasingly vocal about 'good governance' and increasingly willing to insist that Pacific Island governments meet the standards they set as a condition for their grants, loans and concessions. Island leaders, in turn, are tempted to resort to ideas about 'culture' to explain why those external standards should not apply to them (Larmour, 1997).

The concept of culture

'Culture', according to Raymond Williams, is 'one of the two or three most complicated words in the English language' (1983, p. 87). In his influential book *Keywords*, he distinguished three broad usages. The first refers to a process of intellectual, spiritual and aesthetic development, which is related to the idea of civilisation. The second focuses on particular ways of life. This focus was adopted by mainstream anthropology, which entails consideration of both the practical and material aspects of a way of life and the signifying and symbolic ones (Kuper, 1999). The third usage is applied more narrowly to artistic and intellectual endeavours, notably theatre, dance, music and film.

The first (developmental) usage seems relevant to the way corruption has been interpreted by development banks and aid donors since the 1990s. For example, Daniel Kaufmann's statistical work for the World Bank finds corruption linked to development (Kaufmann, et al., 1999).

Williams' second usage seems most relevant to the perspective that something regarded as corrupt in one particular culture or subculture might not be regarded as corrupt in another, which raises the issue of 'cultural relativism'.

The third usage, to do with the expressive arts, is particularly relevant to the Pacific Islands. Collective performances cost money and other resources. Participation in cultural events is part of a leader's role and is hard to distinguish from the politics of alliances and democratic electioneering. The TI Sāmoa report, for example, talks about 'pressure to contribute to cultural functions' (So'o, et al., 2004, p. 5).

A recent update of Williams' *Keywords* warns that 'there is now a good deal of hesitancy over the value of the word culture' (Bennett, et al., 2005, p. 63; but see Sahlins, 1999). The authors note the gradual triumph of Williams' second anthropological meaning (culture as a way of life), often accompanied by rejection of the idea that these ways of life might be fixed, uncontested from within or clearly distinct, as colonial governments in the Pacific Islands are said to have made them.

Two dominant approaches to social science—Marxism and rational choice theory—have tended to deal with 'culture' indirectly. Marxism tended to treat it as an effect of more fundamental economic processes, while rational choice theories try to grasp it through individual attitudes and dispositions. Writing in a Marxist tradition in the 1960s, Colin Leys famously wondered 'what is the problem about corruption?' while explaining how corruption is at the foundation of what US society considers prestigious 'old money' (1965).

The inventor of TI's influential Corruption Perceptions Index, Johann Lambsdorff, has reviewed what he calls empirical research into the cultural determinants of corruption (Lambsdorff, 1999). His analysis tends to focus on individual attitudes and dispositions. He cites a survey conducted by La Porta et al. (1999) that found that trust has a significant negative impact on corruption (Lambsdorff, 1999, p. 12). The same survey also found some positive correlation between corruption and membership of a hierarchical religion (Catholic, Orthodox or Muslim) and, it seems, a negative correlation with Protestantism. Lambsdorff concludes his discussion of cultural determinants by stating that '[c]ulture can only explain a certain fraction of the level of corruption and there remains sufficient room for improvements of a country's integrity. Moreover, cultural attitudes can also be a reflection of the organisational patterns that led to their formation' (p. 13).

Believing that 'culture matters', Thompson et al. propose that 'the trouble with taking explicit account of culture is that explanation tends to go out of the window' (2006, p. 322). They identify three typical misuses of the concept that seem relevant to understanding corruption. *First*, culture can be invoked as an 'uncaused cause' when someone is said to have acted corruptly 'because his culture told him to' (p. 322). But this explanation does not address the prior question of what caused the culture to be like that. *Second*, culture is invoked as 'an explanation of last resort' (p. 322). That is, having exhausted other explanations for corruption—political, economic, ethical, and so forth—we turn to culture as a kind of residual category, or noise. *Third*, culture is invoked as a 'veto on comparison' (p. 323). You can't compare, for example, corruption in Australia with corruption in China because each can only be understood in its own terms. Some statements about culture in the Pacific have the same blocking and checking character. To say 'corruption is part of a culture' is not unlike saying 'back off: this is none of your business'.

Culture in the NIS Pacific reports

Each of the TI NIS reports makes general points about culture and corruption, and typically describes the connection between the two in terms of tensions, contradictions or dilemmas in relationships.

The Solomon Islands report remarks that some village people would regard impartial treatment from an official to whom they were related as 'culturally unacceptable', even insulting, but those familiar with relatives in professional positions do not think this (Roughan, 2004, p. 9). The Fiji report talks of a cultural 'dilemma', in which the official role of public servants is interwoven with and often compromised by their traditional obligations (Singh & Dakunivosa, 2001, p. 9). In Nauru, 'it may be that tradition and culture also causes corruption' (Kun, et al., 2004, p. 10). The reports on Tonga and Vanuatu both use the metaphor of hiding 'behind the culture' (James & Tufui, 2004, p. 5; Newton Cain & Jowitt, 2004, p. 23). The Vanuatu report stresses that 'Melanesian culture does not cause corruption—it does not condone behaviour that benefits an individual at the expense of the community. Instead there is a mismatch between introduced notions of corruption and local culture' (p. 12).

The PNG report says that 'it can be argued that there are certain attributes of the culture which seem to be more compatible with corruption' but is quick to add that 'does not mean that PNG has a corrupt culture' (Mellam & Aloi, 2003, p. 12). In a similarly circuitous way, the Sāmoa report says that '[a]lthough Sāmoan culture does not necessarily teach corrupt behaviour, the propensity to use public resources and misuse entrusted power have sometimes been associated with the pressure to contribute to cultural functions' (So'o, et al., 2004, p. 5).

Two reports use the positive words 'caring' and 'sharing' in describing local cultural values. The PNG report says that 'sharing and caring is synonymous with leadership in Melanesian culture' and that the traditional responsibilities of a leader include 'mobilisation and distribution of wealth' (Mellam & Aloi, 2003, p. 11). The Nauru report describes Nauruans as 'by culture a sharing and caring people' (Kun, et al., 2004, p. 11). Similarly, the Fiji report refers to 'the friendly forgiving nature and extreme tolerance inherent in the culture' (Singh & Dakunivosa, 2001, p. 12).

The Tuvalu report lists important traditional values as: 'reciprocity, status, gift giving, family ties, and community links' (Taafaki, 2004, p. 4). Kiribati culture is characterised as egalitarian (Mackenzie, 2004, p. 4). In the Cook Islands, by contrast, 'the political and social hierarchy ensures that people obey their superiors and political bosses' (Ingram & Urle, 2004, p. 28).

Traditional cultures are sometimes depicted as in tension with those introduced from the West. In the Marshall Islands, 'many feel as though Marshallese culture heritage has been overridden by American ideologies and materialism' (Pollock, 2004, p. 12). In describing the operations of a Westminster-based parliament, the Tuvalu report sees an unresolved tension between the 'confrontational style of debating in the Westminster system' and the 'Tuvaluan search for agreement, consensus, value for respect and cooperation' (Taafaki, 2004, p. 6). The result is an ineffective opposition and cabinet members who tend 'to dominate the discussions' in the parliament (p. 6). The authors believe 'the "laid-back" attitude of members in general in discharging their over-sighting and legislative role over public finances is a cause for great concern' (p. 6).

Some reports identify differences within countries. The PNG report points to the country's cultural diversity and notes, for example, that parts of Milne Bay and New Ireland are exceptions to the report's claim that 'traditional political systems have little impact on PNG's political configurations' (Mellam & Aloi,

2003, p. 9). The document on the Federated States of Micronesia (FSM) also found strong cultural differences between states and different levels of corruption between them, with Chuuk being regarded as the most corrupt (Hill, 2004, p. 8).

Culture is not always regarded as a factor mitigating or softening accusations of corruption. Particularly in Kiribati, local councils of elders deploy 'the force of culture as the informal anti-corruption system' (Mackenzie, 2004, p. 19). Similarly, village councils in Sāmoa (called *fono*) deploy sometimes draconian punishments as part of the 'traditional integrity system' (So'o, et al., 2004, pp. 6, 26, 66). Corruption can bear heavily on the consciences of political leaders in Palau: 'strong traditional awareness of right and wrong brings its own pressures, as some suicides of middle-aged men may have resulted from the heavy conscience burden resulting from involvement in corrupt practices that generated quiet, but powerful scorn' (Shuster, 2004, p. 8).

The template required for country reports has forced NIS authors to treat culture as something of a residual category, which was literally added to the TI questionnaire's central focus. They tend to treat culture as an 'uncaused cause', one of the three usages of the concept identified by Thompson et al. (2006, p. 322); however, some reports offer the country's 'smallness' as one explanation for their cultural characteristics (see Larmour & Barcham, 2006). For example, Tonga's smallness leads to a 'lack of anonymity' that prevents people from lodging complaints (James & Tufui, 2004, p. 43). Tuvalu is described as 'a small, closely-knit society where family connections and reciprocity provide the basis of social relations', with the result that 'notions of impartiality and independence can be blurred' (Taafaki, 2004, p. 4). In Sāmoa, 'almost all organisations' contain 'people in decision-making capacities who are related or would know someone the decision they are making would affect' (So'o, et al., 2004, p. 12).

The reports also use culture in two more specific senses.

First, culture is seen as something attached to particular institutions—for example, a so-called 'civil service culture'. This interpretation corresponds with Williams' second usage: culture as a way of life in relatively closed and total institutions like the police or the civil service. Similarly, the Solomon Islands report talks of a public service 'ethos of procedure', which (the report argues) was the object of 'active subversion' by politicians like Solomon Mamaloni (Roughan, 2004, p. 10). The Tuvalu report also suggests that civil servants' reluctance to be frank with ministers might reflect a 'cultural problem' (Taafaki, 2004, p. 9).

Second, culture is seen as something pervasive and entrenched, such as a 'culture of corruption' in the forestry industry in Solomon Islands, a 'culture of permissiveness' in Solomon Islands (Roughan, 2004, pp.10, 28) or a 'culture of welfare' in Marshall Islands (Pollock, 2004, p. 10). The Fiji report quotes the Ombudsman's remark about a 'culture of silence' that inhibits complaints (Singh & Dakunivosa, 2001, p. 21). Here the socialised aspect of culture is emphasised, inviting questions about how that culture is learned or could be unlearned. Cultural practices also raised professional problems for a designated 'Cultural Officer' in Kiribati (Mackenzie, 2004, p. 9), where the job presumably dealt with organising dancing and cultural shows—Williams' third sense.

Gifts and bribes

The first section of this chapter presented an excerpt of the TI sourcebook where Obasanjo argues that it is simple to distinguish a gift from a bribe (Pope, 2000). In an interview with the authors of that country's NIS study, Sāmoa's Prime Minister argued that '[w]hat determines an acceptable gift is 5 per cent policy/ law and 95 per cent common sense'. For example, 'a bottle of whisky or ten *tala* (US$3.60) would be regarded as an acceptable gift, while a gift of say 3,000 *tala* (US$1,080) would certainly be regarded as unacceptable and there would be seen as a bribe' (So'o, et al., 2004, p. 10).

The Sāmoa report explains that 'gift giving has always been a means of obtaining and maintaining political support in Sāmoa's traditional society' (So'o, et al., 2004, p. 5). The report talks of 'the quality and quantity' of gift-giving as driving the recipient to follow the donor's wishes: 'It is quite normal for a customer to give the employee who is serving him/her during normal duty hours a small amount of money' (p. 10). Similarly, in Tonga, relations of respect 'require the presentation of a gift when making a request of another person, especially a social superior'. Here, 'educated people are now aware that in certain situations such gifts can be construed as bribery' although 'the point at which a traditional gift becomes a bribe is hazy' (James & Tufui, 2004, pp. 5, 10, 25). Churches also engage in fundraising through 'annual public displays of free gifting' (p. 22). According to Hill, in FSM 'under the cover of tradition' politicians may make 'strategic donations to leaders and customary chiefs, sometimes in relation to a wedding or funeral' (2004, p. 5).

In *The gift*, Mauss uses anthropological evidence from Melanesia and Polynesia (as well as North America and India) to understand social systems based on systematic and repeated exchanges between collectivities—clans, tribes and families—which often act through chiefs, rather than exchanges between individuals. The most extended form is the famous Kula Ring in what is now Papua New Guinea, where various prestigious forms of shell money are given and received in expeditions around a ring of islands—bracelets moving from west to east and necklaces from east to west (Mauss, 2002 [1950], pp. 27–39).

In fact, the most intense form of gift-giving was not in the Pacific Islands but in the north-west of what is now US territory. In 'potlatch', chiefs engage in intensely competitive gift-giving. Prestige and honour depend on how much one gives and on repayment with interest of gifts received. At the extreme, valuable goods are publicly destroyed to demonstrate one's wealth and humble one's rivals. The point—as Mary Douglas argues in her foreword to her edition of *The gift*—is that there is no such thing as a free gift (1990). Gifts create obligations, which is the point of giving them and also a reason one might refuse them. They may look voluntary but in practice are compulsory if one is to survive with honour intact. A milder Western version might be birthday presents.

Mauss sums up the three obligations that underpin a gift economy as follows.

- *The obligation to give.* Leaders are always obliged to invite their friends, share their food and so on.
- *The obligation to accept.* Refusal offends, even if it means an added burden.
- *The obligation to reciprocate, often with interest.* Objects must be passed on, not hoarded. A gift of one blanket must be reciprocated with two (Mauss, 2002 [1950], pp. 50–5). For economists, Mauss estimates rates of interest of '30–100 per cent per year' in potlatch (p. 53).

Some features of this 'war of property' between competing chiefs seem to be continued and reproduced in election campaigns throughout the Pacific region. In Sāmoa, politicians are expected to provide gifts such as school fees to voters and 'in the form of food, fine mats and money' (So'o, et al., 2004, pp. 16, 21). In Niue candidates make 'donations' (Talagi, 2004, p. 5). More generally, in the Marshall Islands 'chiefs and elites are expected to offer services and gifts when available' (Pollock, 2004, p. 11). Ministers also give gifts between elections—for example, when a minister visits an outer island in Tuvalu, local people might offer a feast and, in return, expect one of their 'pet projects' to be funded or shipping schedules to be altered in their favour (Taafaki, 2004, p. 14).

These gifts are not token, spiritual or undemanded, to use Obasanjo's characterisation of the African gift. The politician who has to make such gifts often feels they are excessive, although the reports contain no examples of gifts deemed so excessive that the recipient returned them. In Nauru gifts are a 'legitimate part of the electoral process' (Kun, et al., 2004, p. 10). They may involve traditional items, like the fine mats in Sāmoa, or non-traditional things, like 'fairy lights, a stereo system and a small car' in the Marshall Islands (Pollock, 2004, p. 11).

The third obligation of gift-giving is to pass it on, which is an understudied aspect of corruption. It tends to be assumed that corrupt payments are wasted or consumed (or sent overseas to buy real estate or hidden away in a Swiss bank).

Clearly, conspicuous waste is part of the north-west American potlatch culture; however, money exchanged may also be usefully invested. A logging company bribes a politician who builds a road, albeit 'in the wrong place' according to planners. Or the politician pays the school fees of the child who later goes to university. We do not yet know enough about the grey or black economy in the Pacific Islands.

The potlatch aspect is especially obvious in gift-giving beyond government. Thus, the Tonga report worries about public ceremonies of 'free gifting' to churches 'despite active policies inveighing against it' (James & Tufui, 2004, p. 50), and the Tuvalu report is concerned about competition between villages over the size of gifts to retiring church ministers (Taafaki, 2004, p. 22).

Points of entry for cultural factors

'Culture' can be quite broad and therefore not particularly helpful as a means of understanding notions of corruption. The academic study of public policy often has recourse to the idea of a 'policy cycle' in which problems move through a process of identification, definition, legislation and implementation. Adopting a similar approach helps identify how cultural factors manifest themselves in the Pacific Islands.

In a general public suspicion of corruption

Writing about South Asia, Gunnar Myrdal talked of the 'folklore of corruption' (1968). The Sāmoan report describes a 'public perception' that is not based on particular evidence (So'o, et al., 2004, p. 11). Rather, perception results from the government's 'secure grip on power' and its track record in the 1990s, which included constitutional amendments to increase the size of cabinet and reduce the Auditor-General's term of office, and the assassination of a minister named in the auditor's reports (p. 11). This suspicion was hard to shake off.

Similarly, the Solomon Islands report uses the phrase 'insidious tolerance' to describe a situation where 'people express suspicion of corrupt activity at the slightest indication, but at the same time are willing to accept inaction concerning that suspicion' (Roughan, 2004, p. 9).

The culture here may be *a culture of suspicion*, which may be exaggerated or well founded. Its opposite might be the 'trust' that is given such importance by writers on social capital.

In identifying particular people or behaviour as corrupt

This is the point at which people consider whether a particular action or inaction is corrupt. It should be noted that it may also be decided that this line of action is bad for reasons other than because it is corrupt. The decision that something is corrupt might appear to be an isolated occurrence but is in fact a social event. The decision involves language, and in practice is likely to involve discussion with colleagues, friends, family or some kind of internal dialogue that reproduces these interactions. The process of consideration may refer to what others have done before or would do. It may invoke role models, childhood injunctions and the lessons to be learned from folktales, literature or film.

In Vanuatu and Nauru, for example, it seems that only the givers—not the receivers—of bribes are seen as acting corruptly. In Vanuatu: 'in the popular perception, ordinary people who receive bribes are not "corrupt". Chiefs who tell individuals how to vote after receiving bribes or goods for their villages are sometimes perceived as corrupt, but not always. The person offering the bribe is, however, acting corruptly' (Newton Cain & Jowitt, 2004, p. 10).

Similarly in Nauru, people encouraging or benefiting from corruption tend not to be regarded as corrupt. Where people are paid to vote one way or another, 'the blame attaches to the person who offers the temptation rather than the person who accepts it' (Kun, et al., 2004, p. 9).

In the seriousness with which corruption is taken

An important part of any anti-corruption policy is to assess how serious corruption is, but this is complicated by the fact that assessments vary. Non-governmental organisations (NGOs) now imbue any discussion of corruption with a deadly earnestness, but corruption may be taken less seriously by recipients than by donors. Epeli Hau'ofa created several tales around the fun of fooling donors in an imaginary Pacific Island country very like Tonga (1994).

Some assessment of seriousness is necessary for any practical action, which has costs in fractured social relationships and police time. It is easy for an agency or campaign to get bogged down in trivial examples and miss more serious manifestations.

According to the country reports, in FSM people don't think that misappropriated money has been 'taken out of the pockets of citizens' (Hill, 2004, p. 12). In Nauru, carelessness may have been higher when people thought 'resources were in abundance' (Kun, et al., 2004, p. 11). In Vanuatu, 'grassroots' people see the activities of law and government as 'irrelevant to their everyday life' and they therefore do not 'place any burden of expectation on their leaders' (Newton Cain

& Jowitt, 2004, p. 5). They become concerned only when they see their own money is at stake, as in the case of the 1998 riots in Vanuatu, which followed a report by the Ombudsman revealing that although 33 000 people were members of the National Provident Fund, there were only 784 applications for housing loans, of which only 150 were successful. The majority of the beneficiaries 'were Ministers, members of parliament, Vanuatu Provident Fund Board members and staff, UMP party supporters (the UMP was the dominant party in Government at the time), political appointees and families of these groups' (Newton Cain & Jowitt, 2004, p. 14). Many of the favoured groups had loans approved without even submitting applications, while many other applications were never considered (p. 14).

In the willingness to criticise and report corruption

The Cook Islands report talks of 'fear of reprisal': 'people would rather live with the consequences of corrupt politicians than face losing their jobs' (Ingram & Urle, 2004, p. 12). In Palau, 'people find it difficult to correct or discipline or even report that a friend, relative or co-worker is behaving in a corrupt manner…Quiet and subtle scorn' are preferred to overt rebuke, and 'indirectness is a virtue' (Shuster, 2004, pp. 8–9). In Tonga, people won't report others to avoid 'shame to the family involved, damage to the social fabric, and the breaking of relationships' (James & Tufui, 2004, p. 10). In FSM, 'it is very improper to question or openly criticise others or cause someone to lose face' (Hill, 2004, p. 11).

In the Solomon Islands, there has been 'lack of public or institutional pressure to redress blatant corruption acts' (Roughan, 2004, p. 11). The report points to 'a marked unwillingness of leading individuals' in the relevant institutions (p. 11). The Fiji report argues that in small societies with strong cultural ties 'everyone knowing each other makes the act of ignoring illegal practices easier than "blowing the whistle"' (Singh & Dakunivosa, 2001, p. 9).

The Cook Islands report talks of 'the traditional practice of respect for elders and leaders that leads to reluctance to question their actions' (Ingram & Urle, 2004, pp. 5, 12). In FSM there is 'reluctance to openly criticise others, particularly chiefs' (Hill, 2004, p. 8). The Nauru report follows the same line, and states that 'traditionally, Nauruans do not question the actions and behaviour of their chiefs out of respect or fear or both' (Kun, et al., 2004, p. 12). The 'welfare and cohesion of the extended family' are held more dearly than the putative cost to the country (p. 12). In Vanuatu, 'tradition discourages the criticism of leaders' (Newton Cain & Jowitt, 2004, p. 5).

In FSM, 'traditional deference', for example, might make a customs officer 'unlikely to closely question or search a chief arriving in the country from abroad' (Hill, 2004, p. 12). It was also suggested, however, that people were reluctant to report corruption less from fear of reprisal than from the expectation that they will 'get their chance' to benefit corruptly next (p. 12).

In reaching authoritative decisions about corruption

The report on Tonga found that people can 'hide behind the culture' because there were no authoritative guidelines to 'distinguish between cultural practice and corruption' (James & Tufui, 2004, p. 5). The report suggested that a planned code of conduct for public servants might improve the situation (p. 5). Courts in Kiribati have been particularly engaged in drawing lines between appropriate and inappropriate gift-giving, and are required to take custom into account in deciding cases (Mackenzie, 2004, p. 6). In 1997, following a series of cases involving ministers and campaigns (see Larmour, 1997), the Kiribati electoral ordinance was amended as follows: 'any person making a customary offering to a Maneaba [meeting house] referred to in I-Kiribati as "Mweaka", "Moanei" or "Ririwete", with the sole intention of showing respect for the customs and traditions of Kiribati, shall not be guilty of bribery' (Mackenzie, 2004, p. 9).

The Kiribati courts have also become involved in distinguishing between 'respect for customs and tradition' and 'intention to influence voters' (p. 9). For example, the custom of *bubuti* makes it 'acceptable for someone lacking in [certain] resources to make a specific request to another who is better endowed' (Mackenzie, 2004, p. 9, quoting Chief Justice Williams, 15 October 2003). Such requests had been made in the form of a fine demanded of a candidate visiting a *Maneaba*, and had involved gifts like a chainsaw or a video set. In the case before the High Court, it was decided that the issue depended on the intention of the giver and that the gifts 'were made because of custom. The candidates had no choice' (Mackenzie, 2004, p. 9).

In a similar case in Tuvalu—where a candidate had provided chiefs with food and drink prior to a by-election, and chiefs had promised their villagers' votes in return—the High Court found the feasting to be in accordance with custom rather than 'corrupt practices' (Taafaki, 2004, p. 15).

In enforcing existing laws against corruption

Most countries in the region have laws prohibiting bribery and other instances of corruption. The laws are often part of the criminal code, which police are responsible for enforcing; however, police can exercise a great deal of discretion in deciding whether to investigate and—later—prosecute alleged offences. While police may be corrupt themselves, the complaints in the NIS studies tended to focus on matters of competence and professionalism, rather than police corruption. In FSM, however, police were reported as failing to implement the law against relatives, and in Papua New Guinea police performance was 'watered down by lack of capacity, political influence and regionalism' (Hill, 2004, p. 14; Mellam & Aloi, 2003, p. 27).

In punishing corruption

The Cook Islands report notes in relation to a recent successful prosecution for secret commissions that 'public attitudes are often sympathetic' to the person found guilty (Ingram & Urle, 2004, p. 12). People often said things like 'we feel sorry for his children', 'how much did the community lose from his criminal actions?' and 'the community did not suffer any loss' (p. 12). There were no obvious victims, so principles of restorative justice might have suggested leniency.

In Nauru, people who are the subject of headlines or gossip 'continue to be re-elected' (Kun, et al., 2004, p. 9). In Papua New Guinea it was reported that 'it is very unlikely for disgraced ministers to be re-elected', two notable exceptions being the dismissal of two ministers in 1991 (Ted Diro) and 1992 (Melchior Pep) and their re-election (respectively) in 1997 and 2002 (Mellam & Aloi, 2003, pp. 32–3). In FSM, 'a willingness to ignore or forget transgressions by leaders' was reported (Hill, 2004, p. 8). In Vanuatu, people who have been damned in Ombudsman Commission reports 'continue to get elected' (Newton Cain & Jowitt, 2004, p. 10). And in Nauru, every time a new president is elected, there is a batch of presidential pardons (Kun, et al., 2004, p. 18).

In Kiribati, however, it was reported that a decline in cultural sanctions such as ostracism of those involved in theft was contributing to the rise of petty corruption among junior officials (Mackenzie, 2004, p. 10).

Other issues in the relationship between culture and corruption

Cultural arguments can be excessively deterministic, treating people as 'dopes' who are just following orders. Corruption often presents itself as a dilemma between two ethical claims—for example, between the claims of office and family.

Some of the calculation involves rehearsing how a person will explain or justify what they did if there is a complaint about corruption, with cultural concerns determining the actual factors that people take into account and how they are weighed.

In this vein, Barbara Reid studied how Sāmoans and Europeans in New Zealand judged a series of vignettes of common ethical dilemmas. Looking for differences in ethical style, she identified reasoning processes, justifications and implicit ethics (1990). Generally, she found that people from different cultures were equally principled in their moral reasoning but differences arose in the contexts in which particular principles were applied. Differences existed among Sāmoans according to their differential acculturation within New Zealand society and to a 'lack of consensus in Sāmoan culture' about how certain moral problems should be solved. Finally—and here is the crunch—'cultural differences in moral reasoning are due to a contrast between a socio-centric world view on the part of Sāmoans and the more ego-centric world view of Europeans' (Reid, 1990, p. 53). Other things being equal, Sāmoans tended to give greater weight to the social consequences of actions, while Europeans tended to give greater weight to individual consequences.

So far we have been treating 'cultures' as specific to particular countries (Sāmoa, Tonga, and so on) but as similar within national boundaries. In fact, most countries are multicultural—and the Pacific Islands are no exception. Suspicions and accusations of corruption can occur along social frontiers and can be said to mark differences between 'us' and 'them'. Evers and Mehmet propose that accusations of corruption in South-East Asia arise from a distinct division of labour between 'trading minorities' (such as the Chinese) and indigenous cultures, which value caring and sharing, redistribution and honour over profit (1994). The latter faced a 'trader's dilemma': how to prosper economically while preserving respected subsistence-based traditions.

The dilemma was resolved, say Evers and Mehmet, by partnering with ethically suspect traders, who 'did the dirty work'. According to the country reports, similar divisions of labour seem to have been taking place between Chinese, Vietnamese and other Asian minorities and indigenous leaders in many parts of the Pacific. Similarly, the contrast between supposedly competitive Indo-Fijians and 'caring and sharing' indigenous Fijians is often belied by business alliances between them. In these cross-cultural situations, corruption can be interpreted broadly as an undignified pursuit of profit, which is best done at arm's length through ethically and ethnically distinct intermediaries. In Mauss's terms, the honour gained in the gift economy needs to be insulated from contaminating investment in the money economy. A tight system of exchange and indebtedness underlies the apparently voluntary friendship of an indigenous leader and their adviser(s) because they desperately need one another.

The Cook Islands report refers to dubious foreigners—a New Zealander 'investor' in this case—with financial connections to politicians who protect him from scrutiny by the Immigration Department (Ingram & Urle, 2004, p. 9). The Solomon Islands report connects the arrival of Asian logging companies with a sharp increase in the level of corruption, including a 1994 leadership code case in which a logging company allegedly bribed two ministers to defect from the government (Roughan, 2004, p. 29). The Marshall Islands report blames 'Asian business procedures' for increases in corruption, particularly in the fishing industry (Pollock, 2004, p. 11).

Another form of corruption linked to multiculturalism is 'affirmative action' programs designed to advance indigenous people but which often become a focus for individualised corruption. For example, the Fiji report worries that 'it has been difficult to determine the extent of nepotism and cronyism in the backdrop of existing policies on affirmative action' and that 'if nepotism and cronyism are not quickly identified and addressed, they could easily become part of the system in the closely knit society as exists in Fiji' (Singh & Dakunivosa, 2001, p. 7).

Most of the NIS reports equate local culture with tradition; however, the Vanuatu report points to modern as well as traditional culture (Newton Cain & Jowitt, 2004, pp. 11, 26, 62). The Solomon Islands report mentions the growing influence of young people—and the perceived social problems this generates (Roughan, 2004, p. 7).

A distinction between popular and elite culture parallels the distinction in the corruption literature between petty and grand corruption. Petty corruption consists of small, routine payments made to poorly paid junior officials simply to do their job. It is often illegal, but may be accepted as necessary by both sides in the transaction. Grand corruption consists of larger, more secretive payments made to ministers and senior officials to secure such things as contracts.

Sociologists and anthropologists are pursuing a new strand of qualitative study on corruption, which helps refine and elaborate this distinction. They are interested in popular and informal understandings of corruption, the differences between the law and popular opinion on what counts as corruption, and how much corruption matters to whom. Alena Ledeneva, a sociologist writing about the former Soviet Union, analyses a system of low-level exchanges of favours (*blat*) through which people work around bureaucratic difficulties and mobilise relatives and acquaintances to 'get by' (1998). Elisabeth Harrison (2004) relates corruption to the responsible exercise of official discretion by field officers in Africa, while Akhil Gupta (1995) looks sympathetically at the role of middlemen between clients and bureaucrats in India.

Petty or popular corruption seems less widespread in the Pacific Islands compared with other parts of the developing world. The reports found it in only three or four countries, although it may be growing. The PNG report remarked on the practice of making small payments 'to speed up enquiries and service delivery'

(Mellam & Aloi, 2003, p. 15). The use of belittling euphemisms to describe these payments—'six packs' of beer or 'bus fares'—seemed to suggest ethical uneasiness. The Fiji report found what it called 'kickbacks' being demanded for all sorts of licensing: passports, work permits and drivers' licences (Singh & Dakunivosa, 2001, p. 6). In Sāmoa, giving small gifts to government employees for services rendered was 'normal', as noted above (So'o, et al., 2004, p. 47). The Tonga report quotes a government minister saying that 'departmental heads often augment the salaries of their low-paid staff from their own pockets in order to encourage them to come to work, work on time, or carry out their functions efficiently' (James & Tufui, 2004, p. 35).

The anthropological and sociological research cited above is sympathetic to popular forms of corruption, which are seen as necessary for 'getting by'. In contrast, grand corruption is often characterised as a crime of the powerful against 'the people', who are typically cast as innocent victims.

Ordinary people, however, may also be participants in and beneficiaries of grander forms of corruption. Writing about the Pacific Islands, Ron Crocombe argues that '[p]eople do not approve of corruption in principle, nor generally in practice, unless they benefit from it. Even then they may condone it, or rationalise it on other terms, rather than approve of it' (2001, p. 516).

That's probably true everywhere. Politicians often hold this jaundiced view of people, at least as voters and constituents. For example, the PNG MP Dame Carol Kidu wrote to a PNG newspaper defending colleagues under the Ombudsman's scrutiny for expenditures in their constituencies and describing the pressures that constituents place on MPs:

> Because aspects of the bureaucratic machinery are dysfunctional, people who should be going to the bureaucracy instead go to the politician for water, roads, clinics, school fees and endless needs that should not be seen as MPs' functions. Some people are desperate and some are demanding, threatening and aggressive (my staff have sometimes faced weapons and even rape threats).

> There is a popular perception that politicians become rich. But how many ex-politicians (or serving politicians) are rich? Many are struggling to survive because their businesses were destroyed by politics or they gave away most of what they earned as a politician—not as bribes but because they feel a Melanesian obligation and compassion for the situation many people are in. (2006)[1]

---

1   I am grateful to Bill Standish for bringing this letter to my attention.

Popular corruption intersects with other popular scams, gambling and get-rich-quick schemes that operate on a grander scale than petty corruption. The Solomon Islands report mentions 'fraudulent schemes' that have been rife in the region, with varying degrees of legality and sanction by regulators (Roughan, 2004, p. 9). Such schemes range from chain letters to the pyramid investment scheme known as 'U Visitract', in which the widely respected PNG Ombudsman was found to be personally involved, and consequently resigned. The perpetrators—such as Noel Misingu in Papua New Guinea—can even become folk heroes.

It is often hard to draw lines between these popular schemes, the dubious projects that attract ministers and national get-rich-quick schemes that get domestic legal sanction—for example, the tax havens in Vanuatu, Cook Islands and Nauru. Among such dubious schemes, the Tuvalu report frets about official attempts to market Tuvalu's Internet domain name, 'dot tv', in the United States (Taafaki, 2004, p. 8).

When popular culture is indifferent (as in Vanuatu) or sympathetic to some forms of corruption, it raises questions for a standard aid donor strategy of relying on an angry population to induce reluctant politicians to grasp the 'political will' to attack corruption. As we have seen, popular grumbling about 'corruption' is relatively common, and anger against elites can be easily mobilised. But, in fact, popular opinion often seems to be ambivalent. It is against corruption but approves of politicians who provide support for local or personal events and of timber companies who promise development. And in Papua New Guinea, according to Kidu, this ambivalence is heightened by popular fatigue with politicians and the increasing failure of the government to deliver.

Elite culture is the opposite of popular culture. In its anti-corruption strategies, TI's style is deliberately elitist. It works through coalition building, seminars and quiet lobbying, rather than demonstrations in the street. Williams' first sense of the word 'culture', referring to a process of spiritual and aesthetic development, was closely linked to ideas about 'civilisation'. Here the sociologist Norbert Elias's (1998) arguments about a 'civilizing process' seem to be relevant to discussions about corruption in several ways (Larmour, 2006). Elias was writing about the development of European states, noting that the successful monopolisation of power was accompanied by a social and even psychological process of elite 'self-restraint' whereby warriors became courtiers. Bodily functions became hidden behind screens. Violence became stylised, and hidden. This civilising process was not directed, but emerged, and it could easily go into reverse (as in Nazi Germany). It happened to have taken place in Europe, China and other places, but could take place in any part of the world. In the Pacific, the centralisation and monopolisation of power by the Hawaiian monarchy, and the parallel growth of an elaborate court politics, are good examples of civilising processes. Some chiefly virtues seem to be of the restrained and dignified kind that Elias identifies. Its dark side lies in the violence that is displaced offstage onto serfs and commoners, and in wars against other chiefs.

The current international turn against corruption involves and seeks a shift in values within elites. Often it is an intergenerational shift, as the sons and daughters of the first generation of nationalist leaders turn against corruption (and join the local branch of TI). Corruption is now something about which elites are becoming faintly ashamed. It is felt to be something 'we used to do in the past'. If we do it now it is done secretly, shamefully and is screened from the public gaze. If Elias is correct, these elite values—and the social constraint towards self-restraint—may become generalised throughout society. Corruption may become less visible, but it won't necessarily go away. It should be noted that Elias also points to the link between self-restraint and state-building. If states 'fail', there is no guarantee that the civilising process will not go into reverse with elites resuming their outwardly rapacious ways.

Conclusions

Despite attacks on cultural relativism, and the universalistic doctrines of TI and the international community, ideas about culture still seem useful in understanding how people recognise and respond to what is judged to be corrupt behaviour. These reflections on culture do not deny the ethical basis of judgments about corruption. Rather, they show how ethical meanings develop and change, how people give different weight to different factors in weighing up what is the right thing to do, and to how they may displace onto others the ethical load of doing business. Anti-corruption practices need to adapt to this more nuanced picture of how different people decide to behave.

Acknowledgements

I am grateful for comments on an earlier draft of this paper to Geoff White, Raymond Apthorpe, Manu Barcham and Ashwin Raj. Any faults remain my own. A version of this chapter was published in the journal *Crime Law and Social Change* (Larmour, 2008) and in a recent monograph on the subject of corruption in the Pacific (2012).

References

Alatas, Syed Hussein. (1968). *The sociology of corruption: the nature, function, causes and prevention of corruption*. Singapore: D. Moore Press.

Bennett, Tony, Grossberg, Lawrence, & Morris, Meaghan (Eds). (2005). *New keywords: a revised vocabulary of culture*. Malden and Oxford: Blackwell.

Crocombe, Ron (2001). *The South Pacific* (3rd edn). Suva: University of the South Pacific.

Douglas, Mary. (1990). Foreword. In Marcel Mauss (Ed.), *The gift: the form and reason for exchange in archaic societies* (2nd edn, pp. ix–xxiii). Abingdon: Routledge.

Elias, Norbert. (1998). *On civilization, power and knowledge: selected writings*. Stephen Mennel & Johan Goudsblom (Eds). Chicago and London: University of Chicago Press.

Evers, Hans-Dieter, & Mehmet, Ozay. (1994). The management of risk: informal trade in Indonesia. *World Development, 22*(1), 1–9.

Gregory, Chris A. (1982). *Gifts and commodities*. London: Academic Press.

Gupta, Akhil. (1995). Blurred boundaries: the discourse of corruption, the culture of politics, and the imagined state. *American Ethnologist, 22*(2), 375–402.

Harrison, Elizabeth. (2004). The 'cancer of corruption'. In Italo Pardo (Ed.), *Between morality and law: corruption, anthropology and comparative society* (pp. 135–54). Aldershot: Ashgate.

Hau'ofa, Epeli. (1994). *Tales of the Tikongs*. Honolulu: University of Hawai'i Press.

Hill, Edward R. (2004). *Federated States of Micronesia national integrity systems: country study report*. Blackburn South: Transparency International Australia.

Ingram, Takiora, & Urle, Mathilda. (2004). *Cook Islands national integrity systems: country study report*. Blackburn South: Transparency International Australia.

James, Kerry, & Tufui, Taniela. (2004). *Tonga national integrity systems: country study report*. Blackburn South: Transparency International Australia.

Kaufmann, Daniel, Kraay, Art, & Zoido-Loban, Pablo. (1999). Governance matters. *Policy Research Working Paper Series 2196*.

Kidu, Carol. (2006). Letter to the editor. *The National*, 7 March.

Kun, Ruben, Togomae, Whitlam, & Kun, Roland. (2004). *Nauru national integrity systems: country study report*. Blackburn South: Transparency International Australia.

Kuper, Adam (1999). *Culture: the anthropologists' account*. Cambridge: Harvard University Press.

Lambsdorff, Johann Graf. (1999). Corruption in empirical research—a review. Paper presented at the 9th International Anti-Corruption Conference, 10–15 December, Durban, South Africa.

La Porta, R., Lopez-de-Silanes, F., Shleifer, A., & Vishny, R. W. (1999). The quality of government. *Journal of Law, Economics and Organization, 15*(1), pp. 222–79.

Larmour, Peter. (1997). Corruption and governance in the South Pacific. *Pacific Studies, 20*(3), 1–17.

Larmour, Peter. (2006). Civilizing techniques: Transparency International and the spread of anti-corruption. In Len Seabrooke & Brett Bowden (Eds), *Global standards of market civilisation* (pp. 97–106). London: Routledge.

Larmour, Peter. (2008). Corruption and the concept of 'culture': evidence from the Pacific Islands. *Crime, Law and Social Change, 49*, 222–39.

Larmour, Peter. (2012). *Interpreting corruption: culture and politics in the Pacific Islands—topics in the contemporary Pacific*. Honolulu: University of Hawai'i Press.

Larmour, Peter, & Barcham, Manuhuia. (2006). National integrity systems in small Pacific Island states. *Public Administration and Development, 26*, 176–84.

Ledeneva, Alena. (1998). *Russia's economy of favours: 'blat', networking and informal exchange*. Cambridge: Cambridge University Press.

Leys, Colin. (1965). What is the problem about corruption? *Journal of Modern African Studies, 3*(2), 215–30.

Mackenzie, Ueantabo Neemia. (2004). *Kiribati national integrity systems: country study report*. Blackburn South: Transparency International Australia.

Mauss, Marcel. (2002 [1950]). *The gift: the form and reason for exchange in archaic societies* (W. D. Halls, Trans., 2nd edn). Abingdon: Routledge.

Mellam, Albert, & Aloi, Daniel. (2003). *Papua New Guinea national integrity systems: country study report*. Blackburn South: Transparency International Australia.

Myrdal, Gunnar. (1968). *Asian drama: an inquiry into the poverty of nations*. New York: Atheneum.

Newton Cain, Tess, & Jowitt, Anita. (2004). Vanuatu national integrity systems: country study report. Blackburn South: Transparency International Australia.

Pollock, Nancy J. (2004). *Republic of the Marshall Islands national integrity systems: country study report*. Blackburn South: Transparency International Australia

Pope, Jeremy. (2000). *TI source book 2000. Confronting corruption: the elements of a national integrity system*. Berlin and London: Transparency International.

Reid, Barbara. (1990). Weighing up the factors: moral reasoning and culture change in a Samoan community. *Ethos, 18*(1), 48–71.

Roughan, Paul. (2004). *Solomon Islands national integrity systems: country study report*. Blackburn South: Transparency International Australia.

Sahlins, Marshall. (1999). Two or three things I know about culture. *Journal of the Royal Anthropological Institute, 5*(3), 399–421.

Secretariat of the Pacific Community. (2012). Population estimates and projections for several years. *Pocket statistical summary 2011*. Nouméa: Secretariat of the Pacific Community.

Shuster, Donald R. (2004). *Republic of Palau national integrity systems: country study report*. Blackburn South: Transparency International Australia.

Singh, H. P., & Dakunivosa, Mosese. (2001). *Fiji national integrity systems: country study report*. Blackburn South: Transparency International Australia.

So'o, Le'apai L. Asofou, Sinclair, Ruta-Fiti, Va'a, Unasa L. F., & Lāmeta, Sonny. (2004). *Sāmoa national integrity systems: country study report*. Blackburn South: Transparency International Australia.

Taafaki, Tauaasa. (2004). *Tuvalu national integrity systems: country study report*. Blackburn South: Transparency International Australia.

Talagi, Mary. (2004). *Niue national integrity systems: country study report*. Blackburn South: Transparency International Australia.

Thompson, Michael, Verweij, Marco, & Ellis, Richard J. (2006). Why and how culture matters. In Robert E. Goodin & Charles Tilly (Eds), *The Oxford handbook of contextual political analysis* (pp. 319–40). Oxford: Oxford University Press.

Williams, Raymond. (1983). *Keywords: a vocabulary of culture and society* (rev. edn). New York: Oxford University Press.

www.ingramcontent.com/pod-product-compliance
Lightning Source LLC
Chambersburg PA
CBHW061238270326
41927CB00031B/3454